To Mary
and Anne

Contents

A TIME
TO CHOOSE
LIFE

INTRODUCTION

FOR MORE THAN TWO DECADES abortion has been a matter of intense debate in Canada and the United States. Judges have ruled, politicians have legislated, but the issue seems no closer than ever to resolution. In the view of many there is nothing new to be said on the topic. People are weary of the sit-ins, the demonstrations and the angry words. Images of coathangers and fetuses have been etched on our retinas and opinion seems irretrievably polarized. Is there any point to discussing the matter further?

I think there is. For all the journalistic ink that has been spilt, thoughtful consideration of this painful issue has been a rarity. Abortion has many dimensions: it touches women's health, human rights and freedoms, root social values and the role of law in regulating human behavior. In this book nineteen writers drawn from the fields of medicine, social work, philosophy, political science, history and law explore these dimensions in a dispassionate manner. Speaking with a fresh voice, they offer findings and reflections that will be of interest to feminists, civil libertarians, politicians, health-care workers — indeed, to anyone who cares about the future and well-being of our society.

In the first essay, the late George Grant suggests that the demand for unrestricted abortion represents the triumph of the will, in the Nietzschean sense of the will to power. Feminist leaders have demanded liberation, not from the absence of the vote or inequality in the marketplace, but against developing infants. Complete freedom, according to these leaders, requires liberation from the givenness of those individual members of their own species who happen to be in the way — located inside women's bodies.

Another philosophical perspective is presented by Samuel Ajzenstat. He raises the question whether pro-abortion feminism does not involve a repudiation of the basic tenets of liberalism. Addressing the argument of Carol Gilligan's book, *In a Different Voice*, he questions her claim that women have a maturer approach to morality than men. The springboard of his argument is her approving quotation of one woman's account of her decision to have an abortion: "Yes, this is killing, there is no way around it, but I am willing to accept that. I am willing to accept that. I am willing to go ahead with it, and it's hard . . . I don't think I can explain it. I don't think I can really verbalize the justification." In this view, one only grows spiritually through a moral decision in which one confronts the tragic inevitability of the situation one faces. Ajzenstat treats Gilligan's thesis with exquisite tact — almost with delicacy. I shall not spoil his artistry by revealing how he demolishes it. Those like Madam Justice Bertha Wilson who have recently embraced the argument for the different (and superior?) morality of women will have to take cognizance of what Samuel Ajzenstat has written.

Another contributor who engages with the pro-abortion feminist position is Janet Ajzenstat. She scrutinizes the argument propounded by Bertha Wilson that the value of the fetus depends on how much sorrow its loss causes. As she points out, this runs clean counter to the bedrock civil liberties belief that law and human rights codes must above all protect those who are *not* valued by the majority or by social groups or individuals. "Both Wilson and the pro-choice movement," she observes, "go a long way towards suggesting that only those who are loved deserve to live."

Iain T. Benson takes to task those civil libertarians who have elevated the right to liberty above the right to life. To say that you are pro-choice merely begs the question. Most citizens are not pro-choice when it comes to pornography, child abuse, racial discrimination or stopping at red lights. The superficiality of much popular argumentation in favor of abortion was revealed this past year in the frequent pronouncement that "we should not criminalize abortion because women are not criminals." Benson asks if this is logically any different from saying "we should not criminalize wife-battering because men are not criminals."

Suzanne Scorsone pays tribute to the pro-choicers' quest for human freedom, a quest shared by many pro-lifers. But the ultimate question, she says, is "Whose freedom?" In most instances the choice is between the loss of some measure of the mother's freedom for a finite period of time and the loss of the child's entire life.

Mention of the child brings us to the question of what it is that is destroyed in an abortion. Hardly anyone nowadays denies the humanity of the infant in the womb. Professor Heather Morris informs us that doctors can now treat a number of life-threatening conditions before the child's birth. It is hardly an exaggeration to say that the fetus is no less a patient than her mother. Other technologies, however, have made it easier to select the less-than-perfect, or those of unwanted sex — usually female — for destruction.

Professor Morris and Lorraine Williams also remind us of what is often overlooked: that every induced abortion entails a real, if small threat to the health of the mother. Women who undergo the operation risk perforation of the uterus, while later enduring a significantly higher incidence of ectopic pregnancy, sterility, spontaneous abortion, cervical pregnancy and premature delivery. Curiously, most of those who call themselves pro-choice are vehemently opposed to a woman being informed of these risks.

Nor do they wish women to be apprised of the risks that abortion poses to their emotional health. De Veber, Parthun, Kiss and Chisolm draw our attention to the growing evidence of the negative psychological sequelae of induced abortion. Those most vulnerable to these negative consequences are often the very women pressured into having an abortion in the first place: teenagers, those rejected by their boyfriends, those with a psychiatric history and those who abort on the grounds of the deformity of the fetus.

What are the broader social consequences of abortion? None of us is an island, and Chris Bagley, Diane Marshall and Martha

Crean suggest that unrestricted abortion makes for a more callous, uncaring and ultimately more violent society. It is not fanciful to conjecture that there may be links between militarism, degradation of the environment, child abuse, wife battering, the use of fetal tissue in cosmetics and live fetal experimentation. They all exemplify a contempt for the world of nature and of living things, including those who are smallest and most vulnerable. Has anyone expressed this contempt more memorably than the abortionist who, at the end of a morning's work, found himself surrounded by babies crying their heads off, and regretted that "I hadn't time to kill them because we were so busy . . ."?

Finally we come to politics and the law. F. L. Morton points out that since Canada's adoption of a written constitution and charter of rights, the arena for decision-making on human rights issues has shifted decisively from parliament to the courts. The influence of the people's elected representatives on many political issues has shrunk while that of judges, technocrats and left-leaning intellectuals has swelled enormously. Nor have the many abortion-related court cases enhanced public respect for our judicial system. In Henry Morgentaler's Montreal trial in the 1970s one of the jurors disqualified herself because she was offered $1,000 to vote for Morgentaler's acquittal, but no effort was made to find out if any of the other jurors had been bribed.[1] In Morgentaler's 1984 trial in Ontario, as Professor Ian Hunter shows, the questions put to prospective jurors weeded out churchgoers, housewives, young people and older professionals because they were deemed more likely to be anti-abortion. The goal was not to select an impartial jury but a favorable one.

Since January 28, 1988, Canada has been unique in having no legal regulation whatsoever of the practice of induced abortion. This situation exposes a grotesque contradiction at the heart of our legal system. On the one hand, the civil law over the past two centuries has moved in the direction of building up the rights and recognizing the personhood of the unborn child. The child in the womb can inherit property; she can sue for prenatal injuries; she can hold her mother accountable for negligence with regard to her health. On the other hand, since

1969 the criminal law has moved in the direction of eliminating the basic right without which all the hard-won civil rights are worthless: the right not to be killed. The womb is now a free fire zone for the fetus. In a pioneering essay on the Supreme Court's decision in the Daigle case in the summer of 1989, Robert D. Nadeau assesses the Court's reasons for rejecting the personhood of the unborn child. It cited the common-law rule that a child must be born alive in order to be recognized as a person. But Nadeau shows that other courts have long recognized that the child in the womb is already clothed with the full legal rights of personhood. The requirement that she be born alive in order to enjoy them was a purely procedural one stemming from the limited medical knowledge of the seventeenth century. This line of reasoning has already been accepted by the Supreme Court of Massachussetts. And the respected authority on Tort law, William Prosser, has declared, "The unborn child in the path of an automobile is as much a person in the street as the mother."

One wonders how long it will take our courts and our legislators to catch up with the more generous view of the human rights of unborn children which has been taken recently in the United States, Australia, Spain and West Germany. Whatever the answer, it is our hope that these essays will provoke new thinking on the related subjects of abortion, feminism and human rights.

The catalyst for this book was the Human Life Research Institute, a centre for the study of bioethical questions in Toronto. Without the dedicated work of the Institute's staff the book would never have seen the light of day. My special thanks are due to Anne Leavitt and Molly Fullerton.

Others who helped include Dr. Joseph Curtin, Dr. William Johnston, Dr. Colin Merry and the Reverend Edward Jackman. Donald G. Bastian of Stoddart Publishing and Kathryn Dean gave superb help at the editorial stage.

This book is dedicated to Mary Clarke and Anne Kostuik in gratitude and admiration for all they have taught me about the preciousness of human life.

I

PHILOSOPHY, FEMINISM AND POLITICS

GEORGE GRANT

THE TRIUMPH
OF THE WILL

THE DECISIONS OF THE Supreme Court concerning abortion
could be seen as comedy — if they did not involve the slaughter
of the young. Any laughter is quelled by a sense of desolation for
our country. Yet the comedy must be looked at, too, if we are to
understand our political institutions. It arises from the fact that
the majority of the judges used the language of North American
liberalism to say yes to the very core of fascist thought — the
triumph of the will. Their decisions are good illustrations of Huey
Long's wise dictum: "When fascism comes to America it will
come in the name of democracy." The court says yes to those
who claim the right to mastery over their own bodies, even if
that mastery includes the killing of other human beings.[1]

Indeed, the advocates of abortion have shown since the
Supreme Court's 1988 decision how much they are believers in
the triumph of the will when they "demand" that the government "must" immediately guarantee access and payment for all
abortions. That is, the state must pay for these processes, even
when they are not medically necessary. The triumph of the will
is realized when its advocates understand that the individual

9

will is liberated to its full power only when it can dominate the state.

The imputation of fascism to those with whom one disagrees is indeed a dangerous game. People of the left call Mrs. Thatcher a fascist when, whatever she may be, she is not that. People of the right call Castro a "fascist" when, whatever he may be, he is not that. To speak of incipient fascism in the present case requires that one discuss what fascism is. That is a useful public task, because fascism is a growing possibility in advanced industrial countries, and if one does not look clearly at such phenomena, one cannot think how to deal with them.

The English-speaking liberals quite correctly saw the European examples of fascism as despicable tyrannies. What they could not express was the difference between such totalitarian tyranny and most of the tyrannies of the past. The Marxists saw clearly the partial truth that fascism was made possible by a late state of a decaying capitalism. They had no explanation for the fact that certain fascists spoke so violently against Western capitalism. The Americans and the Russians united to defeat National Socialism in battle. As Stalin so rightly put it: "The Americans gave money, the British gave time, the Russians gave blood." But the defeat of fascism in battle has not enabled us to understand what fascism was. Its core was a belief in the triumph of the will. The result is that when the triumph of the will manifests itself politically in our societies, we just cannot know it for what it is.

What is meant by the seemingly simple word "will"? In the pre-modern world it had a certain meaning which was particularly emphasized in Christianity, because the words which were spoken in Gethsemane — "Yet not My will but Thine be done" — were paradigmatic for Christians. It meant appropriate choosing by rational souls. With the arrival of modernity, it has come to mean something different. When "will" is thought of in modern terms, it means the resolute mastery of ourselves and the world. To understand this modern illumination of the word "will," it is necessary to put aside entirely that old faculty, psychology, in which will was understood as a power of the soul, having to do with free choices. Rather, will is now considered to be the center of our aiming or seeking, the holding together of what we want. That greatest modern definer of will, Nietzsche, said that everything was "will to power." This has often been misinterpreted by traditionalists to mean that the substitution of power for happiness or pleasure was worth aiming at. But in the phrase "will to power," Nietzsche is not describing what we aim at — something outside the will. Rather, he is saying that will is power itself, not something external to power. What makes Nietzsche such a pivotal thinker in the West is that he redefined "will" to make it consonant with modern science. "Will" comes to mean in modernity that power over ourselves and everything else which is itself the very enhancement of life, or, call it if you will, "quality of life." Truth, beauty and goodness have simply become subservient to it.

How did this new conception of "will" come to be central in Western civilization? Obviously, first as science. Modern science is a particular form of science — that which issues in the conquest of human and non-human nature. This is why it is right to call Western science "technological science." Technology produces "quality of life."

This science also understands nature as being outside the idea of purpose, as being a product of necessity and chance. That is, modern science laid nature before us as raw material to be used as we dispose. How then should we dispose? In the early years of our science, Christian purposes were still operative, and later, the purposes of various kinds of secularized Christianity continued to prevail. These secularized Protestant purposes were above all expressed in the English-speaking world as the greatest happiness of the greatest number through capitalist technology. In the Marxist world these purposes were expressed as the building of the classless (and therefore egalitarian) society, through the communal ownership of the means of production. But both these ethical systems depended on something outside "will" itself. Why should I aim for the greatest happiness of the greatest number? Why should I "will" the classless society? These aims were outside will and therefore inhibited enhancement of life, by imposing on will aims from outside will itself. Therefore, the deepest movement of modern thought was to take the great step that our aim was the power of will itself. That is what is meant by "the triumph of the will."

The Triumph of the Will is, of course, the title of Leni Riefanstahl's documentary about the National Socialist Party's convention at Nuremberg — a brilliant title for a brilliant documentary. Is it not absurd, therefore, to relate the apotheosis of such an occasion to the freedom of women to have abortions as they deem it desirable? Is it not particularly absurd when the height of the Nazi occasion is essentially masculine, and women are represented in the documentary by a woman in the stance of adulation? Several points, however, need to be made about fascism (call it, perhaps more accurately, national socialism).

In the film, Hitler is seen, not as the liberator of his own will, but as the man who, through his own liberation, can make possible the liberation of each individual will in his nation. From the moment that he descends from the skies in his airplane and walks hesitantly forward, he is the ordinary German who through his own liberation apotheosizes the liberation of all Germans.

It must be remembered that national socialist doctrine despised the submergence of the individual will in the rationalized collectivism of communism, as much as it did the impotence of the individual in capitalist democracies. The doctrine was that each individual will would find its liberation in unity within the National Socialist Party. Anything that was "given" in a situation, so that it could not be changed, was seen as an unacceptable limitation on the triumph of the will. The Jewish community was strong in German-speaking lands, and the Jews were thought of as internationalists and cosmopolitans. Therefore, according to the national socialists, they stood in the way of the triumph of German will. And therefore they thought they had to get rid of these masses of human beings, this given part of Germany, who stood in the way of what they considered to be the quality of German life. Of course, when the national socialists gathered that they were being beaten in war, this terrible extermination was speeded up in the name of their will's revenge. Nothing given could stand in its way — even the givenness of other human beings.

Is it not true, however, that national socialism is a thing of the past and therefore pointless to bring into a debate about today's issues? It was a revolting regression from the modern age of reason, a finished nightmare to be put aside. This argument is sure to be made, but I am saying something very different.

When one strips away the particularities of the German situation after the intense defeat of 1918, one finds that that situation was a particular possibility for the manifestation of the triumph of the will. That doctrine expresses very closely what human beings think to be true in modernity, when they seek to express their search for meaning in a universe which is known as purposeless. This doctrine has therefore continued to be present in the English-speaking world, which has been dominant since 1945. It has expressed itself particularly in the dealings of the United States with its empire abroad. It was evident in the determination of the American leaders to have their will through airpower on the opposite side of the world, in Vietnam. It can now be seen at home in, for example, the work of medical researchers to find means of mastery over the reproduction of the species.

It is not surprising that leaders of the women's movement, seeking to overcome the injustices of a longstanding patriarchal tradition, should express themselves in the modern language of the triumph of the will. As the presentation of modernity to itself, it is in all of us at some level explicit. It is to be expected that this language should become dominant among the leaders of the women's movement, because they are so aware of what it is to live in modernity.

Of course, ever since patriarchal society began all women have had to face the fact that the enjoyment of sexuality left them with the prodigious possibility of pregnancy, while men could go forth free from that enjoyment. Perhaps this was even resented by some women in matriarchal times, in which the whole society turned on the recognition of the centrality of birth. In earlier patriarchal societies, religious control had some effect sometimes, in forcing men to assume some responsibility for pregnancy. Where land was the essential source of wealth, owner families had a great interest in forcing men to bear responsibility.

In modern technological society, most bourgeois women, and those who wish to become bourgeois, find themselves in a position where at one and the same time the emancipation of sexual desire is advocated from the earliest age, and yet where, if they are to be anything socially, they must go out to work in the world where what matters is the emancipation of greed. This is achieved under corporate capitalism through mastery over oneself and other people. How can such modern women put up with unexpected pregnancies (whether within marriage or without), which can demolish their place in the corporate market and push back their ambitions in relation to the ambitions of other people at the same level? Abortion on demand, then, appears to be a necessity under the conditions of corporate capitalism, as it presumably also appears to be under corporate communism. Indeed, women's position as potential mothers becomes particularly pressing in all advanced industrial societies, because their skilled or unskilled labor, their low or high ambitions are wanted in the marketplace. This happens at a time when it seems at last possible for them to overcome the unfairness of their sexual position.

It is no wonder, then, that the leaders of the women's movement take on the language of the triumph of the will when they are seeking to get the state to fulfill their purposes and when they are opposed by those who must be against abortion on demand for the clearest reasons. The ambiguity is that the famous feminist phrase "biology is not destiny" must also be true for all Christians, because we have been told that in Christ there is neither male nor female. At the highest reaches of human life and love, gender is simply unimportant. The question is, at what levels of life and love *is* gender important, and how should that difference manifest itself?

It is not that the leaders of the women's movement say that to be truly free, women must get rid of their gender. They do not seem to want to build an entirely androgynous society. It seems rather that, in their desire for liberation, they want not only to keep their gender, but also to use it as they will. But their ability to use their gender, and not to be controlled by it, requires their life and death control over beings other than themselves. For the "given" which their wills need to control is those individual members of their own species within their bodies. "Otherness" which must be dominated has always been that thing in terms of which the language of the triumph of the will arises. In this case, the need for liberation arises not against the absence of the vote or against inequality in the marketplace, but against developing infants. This is the terrible pain which leads certain women to the language of the triumph of the will. They feel trapped by their gender, but the means of liberating themselves from this entrapment must often include killing. The language of the triumph of the will is a means of escaping from that trap, because it frees one from the traditional restraints against killing.

What is saddest for the modern future is that belief in the triumph of the will seems to bring with it an intensity of propaganda, by which the general public is prepared for the killing which is to ensue. For a decade the national socialists had been saying that the Jews were not truly human, that they were parasites living off a healthy society. The absurdity of this lie did not prevent its dissemination and influence, and those who disseminated it believed it. Indeed, the most effective dissemination of lies is done by those who believe them. So, with the coming of mass abortion in our society, untruths have been spread by those who do not know they are untruths. Current scientific knowledge tells us that a separate human life is present from conception, with its own unique genetic pattern, with all the chromosomes and genes that make it human.[2] It is the very heart of fascism to think that what matters is not what is true, but what one holds to be true. What one holds to be true is important because it can produce that resolute will, tuned to its own triumph.

However, it must be said that where the clarity about truth which belongs to modern science has allowed us to know what the fetus is in a matter-of-fact way, more difficult implications arise when modern science is used as if it provided the whole truth about life. This has sometimes led to a belittling of human life and to the arising of the doctrine of the triumph of the will. It has been said by advocates of abortion on demand that the fetus is a few cells attached to a woman's body that can be easily clipped away. It has been said that it is simply a parasite that has attached itself to a woman's body. Lies have been told or truths neglected to prepare people to accept the mass feticide which now characterizes our society.

Post-Darwinian biology has set before us the account that all animals can be essentially understood as matter in motion, driven by the necessities of the struggle for existence. To say the least, such an account of life makes it difficult to know whether there is something about human beings that should make us hesitant to kill them. National Socialist ideology was impregnated with this thinking. In terms of such an account of life, why should we care about the life of a fetus when it conflicts with the will of a fully developed woman? And then, of course, we are led inexorably to the next stage. Why should we care about the lives of human beings outside the womb if they are only an accidental conglomeration of cells and if they stand in our way? The science which explains everything in terms of necessity and chance has been the basis of our obvious progresses, but at the same time its intellectual victory over all other kinds of thought has left Western human beings questioning whether their own lives have meaning except in terms of the triumph of the will.

After the 1988 Supreme Court decision, the victorious advocates of abortion on demand paraded with signs, on some of which was written the slogan "Abort God." They were right to do so. What they meant was "abort the idea of God because it has held human beings back from liberation — from the triumph of the will." But what is given us in the word "God" is the fact that goodness and purpose are the source and completion of all that is. Only in terms of that affirmation can we dimly understand why our lives and others' partake in a meaning which we should not hinder but enhance. It is in the name of the fact that the human fetus is a member of our species, called to partake in meaning, that in the past we have turned away from abortion, except in extreme cases. All this was affirmed not only in the teachings of Christians, but also in the Hindu Vedanta — that greatest Eastern teaching. Those who see life simply as a product of necessity and chance are inevitably more open to feticide, because they do not see the destiny of meaning to which human beings are called. This is the prodigious predicament that the intellectual triumph of modern science has cast upon us human beings.

To say all this is not to imply that North American society is yet close to fascism as a form of government. There are many influences in our society which hold us back from that. Obviously, all sane people hope that these influences will continue to prevail. What I am implying is that these influences are fragile in the face of the doctrine of the triumph of the will. Nor am I saying that North American fascism would be, in outward appearance, much like the national socialism of Europe. The trappings of romanticism in North American fascism would be quite different from the trappings of German romanticism.

It is interesting that, alone among Western countries, West Germany has a law which gives the fetus a legal right to life, with some conditions. The Constitutional Court says that this is to make plain the German historical experience and "the present spiritual-moral confrontation with the previous system of National Socialism." In 1988 West Germany forbade surrogate motherhood and the production of human embryos for research. The Germans have a great advantage over us in that they have *already* faced the political incarnation of the triumph of the will.

I am, however, saying two things: The triumph of the will as an individual view of life passes over into politics, and even into government, in advanced industrial societies when those societies see themselves as threatened or fading or even at the point of defeat. It was certainly the smashing of Germany by the Allied powers in 1918 and the ruthlessness of the defeat imposed upon them which led to fascism in Germany. The unequivocal victory of American capitalism in 1945 meant that we had no need of fascism. But if in some unpredictable future the power of American capitalism appears to fade before the power of Japan and

China, and if the economic powers in America recognize the consequences of that threat, then very different forms of government might arise within the bounds of their democratic constitution.

Secondly, the living forth of the triumph of the will among the strongest advocates of complete liberty for abortion does not imply that such advocates are in any sense a core for fascist politics. They simply give us a taste now of what politics will be like when influential groups in society think meaning is found in getting what they want most deeply, at all costs. They illustrate what pressure this puts on a legal system rooted in liberalism, whose leaders have not been educated in what that rootedness comprises. Even in its highest ranks the legal system in its unthinking liberalism simply flounders in the face of those who find meaning in the triumph of the will. This has been shown in both of the liberally appointed American and Canadian judiciaries. When society puts power into the hands of the courts, they had better be educated.[3]

Fast technological change is always accompanied by fast moral and religious change. It is good, therefore, to look clearly at what the advocates of abortion on demand portend in the way of unrestrained politics. The politics of the triumph of the will are controlled less and less by any considerations of reason, let alone by tired liberal reason which expresses itself only in terms of a contract. However important these questions about politics, the more immediate, burning question is the massive slaughter of the innocents, which goes on and on.

S U Z A N N E   S C O R S O N E

FREEDOM:
CHOICE OR LIFE?

T HE PASSION WITH which each side of the abortion issue is argued is one of the most obvious characteristics of the political reality that we confront. To be fair, those who call themselves pro-life, as well as those who call themselves pro-choice, have to deal with the fact that there are some on the other side who think they are entirely altruistic and who have thrown themselves into the fight with all the passion and unwillingness to compromise which that implies. Thus, one part of the abortion reality is the clash of two altruisms that appear to be utterly opposed.

Yet are they really so clearly opposed? I wonder. Is the argument not really about two partially opposed applications of one single principle — that of freedom. Both sides believe deeply in the freedom of the individual. The problem is, *which* individual: a mother or her child? Who is to be free, and at what cost to the other?

Historically, we in Canada have received from a number of directions — Catholic, Protestant, English, French and American — the conviction that personal liberty is essential. That conviction is one principle which now seems to be held in one form or another by virtually everyone in the country. It is also held by individuals and groups in all the mutually influential Western nations in which the abortion controversy has developed over recent decades.

It is this "one form or another" which has evolved into the conflict over abortion. Gradually, over the centuries and in various groups, individual liberty has been detached from responsibility to and for the family (whether extended or nuclear), from the local community, from the church and, at a certain level, from the state. It would never have occurred, for instance, to Luther or Knox that an individual could leave spouse or children without support merely because they prevented that individual from attaining a "self-actualizing lifestyle." Calvin would have been the last person to say that a person need not follow the teachings of his church. The American revolutionaries who rejected the authority of the king and had, if the truth be told, their doubts about churches, assumed the solidarity of the family and the local community.

There is a tendency, however, for good or ill, as people explore ideas and ideologies over the centuries, for the complex associations and interrelationships between ideas and assumptions to be broken down, questioned and, if possible, discarded. So it has been with individual personal freedom. It has retained for many the fervor which fired earlier generations and made it compelling. It has, however, also been progressively detached from the communal assumptions and convictions with which it was combined and moderated in our forbears.

Detached from responsibility for others, the ideal of freedom becomes something quite different. In its extreme form, it becomes hedonism, even nihilism. In a more moderate form, it becomes possible for some people, even people who acknowledge interpersonal ties for themselves, to rephrase the words attributed to Voltaire and say, "I disapprove of abortion, but I will defend to the death [someone else's death] your right to have one." The inculcation of the principle of freedom into all of us from our earliest youth makes it possible for people to be blind to the process of detachment which has occurred, and thus to feel the same altruistic fervor in defending the "freedom" to abort a child that their ancestors would have felt in defending free will or freedom from foreign tyranny.

The defence of the unborn child, while based on this same principle of the defence of freedom, is not detached from responsibility and care for the other. We say that the *child* must be free to live and that we will defend his or her right to live. Living is not something that anyone, of any age, can do alone, so others will have to make possible that child's freedom to live: the mother by bearing him or her (at least) and the mother or someone else by caring for him or her. This is in no way different in essence, although it is different in degree, from the care and support which make possible the freedom of any of the rest of us, dependent upon one another as we are. A total freedom, unrelated to others, is impossible for any human being; it is necessary, therefore, for us to balance our freedom with the self-gift which allows for the freedom of the other.

All of this is one reason why the battle cries of both sides are actually so similar, why they are both so compelling and why, in the minds of those who do not think the thing through, they seem to cancel each other out, resulting in a political stalemate (as in the recent history of the abortion situation). Both are talking about the deeply held value of freedom, whether it be in the form of the woman's choice or in the form of the life of the child. Both create profound emotional reverberations because they strike the same chord. Thoughtful people on both sides will, for the same reason, acknowledge the difficulties seen by the other side.

Most pro-life people see clearly the dilemma of the woman and the need for real support for her so that abortion will not seem to be a "solution." Pro-choice people are, in many cases, backing away from dismissing the unborn as amorphous "tissue." Unambiguous information and photographs demonstrating the nature of the unborn child have definitely had that effect. Pro-choicers now often talk about the importance of the "potential human life" and its value, but at the same time they insist on the "overriding value" of the "choice" and the "well-being" of the mother. Both are defending freedom and seeing its complexity; ultimately, however, nobody can have it both ways. Where the freedoms of two people conflict, one must be given precedence. Ultimately, it comes to the final question: freedom — but whose?

It seems obvious that the choice is between the loss of some measure of the mother's freedom for a few months or a number of years of a life which may be expected to last seventy-five or eighty years and the loss of the child's entire life. If we believe that all human beings are equal in value, the choice is not of the more valuable over the less valuable, but the choice of the smaller loss of freedom. There seems to be no question as to which is the smaller loss of freedom, and therefore which loss is to be chosen.

Pro-lifers who present their case in courts, before governments or over coffee with their neighbors will be most effective if they do three things. First, they have to recognize the good intentions of many (by no means all) of their opponents. It is much easier for people to move towards the view of someone who thinks well of them than towards the view of someone who thinks they are not only mistaken but personally bad.

Second, the most effective approach is to use simple, sober facts to dissolve ideologically loaded stereotypes. One obvious example is the stereotype that every candidate for abortion faces certain disaster otherwise: lifelong poverty as an undereducated, unemployed, single mother, perhaps. The underlying notion is that the person will be forever unfree. In fact, however, a child safely born and given up for adoption releases the mother for education, employment and full social integration. Indeed, these things can also be achieved if she raises the child herself, albeit with more difficulty. The loss of a small amount of freedom need last only a few months; it is never as total as it is sometimes represented. The mother is free of guilt, while the child is free to live a full, long life. This is not the quick fix to which our advertising-trained minds have become accustomed, but the diminution of freedom that it entails is nonetheless brief.

Third, it can be shown that this way of fulfilling one's altruistic principles *works* better than the pro-choice ideology does. Pro-lifers, too, believe in freedom: the freedom of the child to live is a human rights principle. They also support the freedom of the woman to act as an adult human being, capable of making choices — when she chooses whether, when, how and with whom to be sexually intimate and when she chooses how to carry out her responsibility to the tiny life she has conceived. Pro-lifers support the right of every woman to an education and opportunities in life — and they support ways of pursuing those rights which do not deny the freedom and rights of another person, the child. They strongly uphold the principle that women are full legal persons in their own right.

Given that the full legal personhood of women was acknowledged in Canada only in 1929, it is still conceivable that other classes of human beings may be unjustly denied legal recognition of their personhood. Why should the unborn person, male or female, not enjoy the rights that have already been won for the rest of us? Such legal recognition would in fact fulfill the highest principles of the pro-choice side better than their own way does. In the battle for the opinions and votes of both the general population and crucial groups like judges, politicians and (even) journalists, it is essential to make this clear.

Certainly, it is not the desire of the majority of the Canadian people to legalize abortion on demand. Even among those who do accept abortion, the majority would restrict it to hardship cases of genuine medical risk. In addition, all of the Supreme Court justices in their 1988 decision saw the need to balance the rights of the fetus against the rights of the mother, and invited Parliament to determine the precise point of that balance. Laws placing abortion under the Criminal Code do, at least, affirm the principle that these unborn babies (entities? human lives? children? persons?) are of significant value and that abortion is not a matter of indifference. Thus far, however, no law since 1969 has done anything to protect the rights of the unborn child at the level of concrete reality.

Through the many strands of our tradition, Canadians have affirmed personal responsibility and self-giving love. It appears that we all affirm the same principle, but that we no longer all mean the same thing — and because we do not, unborn children are dying.

IAIN T. BENSON

WHAT'S WRONG
WITH "CHOICE"

ON JANUARY 28, 1988, the Supreme Court of Canada struck down the abortion section of the Criminal Code in the *Morgentaler* decision. In so doing, the Court effectively brought to an end a long period during which the stated purpose of the law was continually contradicted in practice. In some areas of Canada abortions could be obtained for the asking, while in others they were rarely performed. Few people were pleased with this. Those who have been seeking change, either to do away with any laws restricting abortion or to afford greater protection for the unborn, now wait expectantly to see what the politicians will do.

Careful review of the Supreme Court decision reveals that, far from vesting Canadian women with an untrammeled right to abortion, the Court left Parliament leeway to change the law in ways that are significantly more favorable to the preservation of fetal life than the law which the court struck down. All of the majority judges, while expressly leaving open the content and extent of fetal rights, suggested that the state will, at some point, have an interest in balancing the rights of the woman and the fetus. How this should happen the court did not say. This was left up to the country's legislators.[1]

What follows is an examination of certain arguments used by proponents of the "pro-choice" position in the abortion debate. In the course of this examination, I shall challenge the use of such expressions as "freedom of choice," "potential life," "pluralism," "the life or health of the woman," "compromise," "the woman's right to 'control her own body'" and the term "coercion." I shall argue that "choice" itself should not be determinative in moral debates and that several other terms frequently relied upon by "pro-choice" advocates are unacceptable.

THE PLACE OF "CHOICE" IN MORAL DEBATE

What is meant by the phrase "pro-choice"? Those who have followed the abortion debate from its inception will remember that this phrase replaced an earlier slogan, "pro-abortion," which was dropped because it indicated approval of abortion itself. This was considered inappropriate because proponents of "freedom of choice" were beginning to argue that they were not really in favor of abortion *per se* but only desired "the right to choose." Once this term came into common usage, it was then logical to say that those who opposed abortion were "anti-choice". What is behind all this terminology?

It should be noted that choice itself is morally neutral and can be evaluated as right or wrong only in terms of the framework of rights in which it is exercised. Thus, to ask the question "Should I have the freedom of choice to fire my pistol?" can be evaluated *morally* only in terms of what you intend to shoot and in what setting.

In a similar fashion, it is sometimes said that those who are against abortion are "seeking to force *their* moral views on other people." This statement implies that moral views may be held personally but have no applicability between individuals. This, in turn, suggests that morals are purely subjective and that no person should attempt to force their views of what is "right" or "wrong" on other people.

Yet most of our criminal law is based on moral notions of what is "right" and "wrong," on the effects of one person's behavior on others in society and on the principle that such rules of right and wrong should apply regardless of the views of individual citizens. Furthermore, it is worth asking whether people who say that "no one should attempt to force their views of what is 'right' or 'wrong' on others" really function in accordance with this principle themselves. A moment's reflection would show that they do not.

Advocates of particular moral positions on a whole host of issues expect the law to restrict behavior of certain types or to force compliance with certain rules. Here, one might list legal restrictions governing sexual abuse, discrimination of various sorts, the production of pornography and requirements that the provinces fund medical procedures and social services deemed necessary. When moral advocates support such laws, they are seeking to enforce through law their notions of what should or should not be done in society.

In the pornography debate, for example, those who oppose the pornographer's freedom of choice to produce pornography do, in fact, attempt to impose their moral views on those who want the freedom of choice to produce or consume pornography. It is particularly interesting to examine the reasons why some feminists, for example, are against pornography. They take this stance for reasons that have to do with a moral evaluation and not because they value "choice" itself. The issue for them turns on the "victimization" or "degradation" of women. These terms *are clearly moral evaluations.* They turn on standards of, for example, "right" views of women, the "correct" way of portraying and treating women, etc. The conclusion is clear: no person who holds a moral position on the issue of pornography can view the abortion issue solely in terms of choice without undermining their own method of moral evaluation in the pornography debate. A person who holds a "pro-choice" view of abortion but an "anti-choice" view of pornography is unlikely to respond favorably to the suggestion that pornography is not a moral issue but is, rather, an issue of choice between a pornographer, a distributor and the purchasing public.

In all areas of moral debate, one must evaluate the rights that are at issue. In the abortion debate, this necessarily involves an evaluation of what a woman's life is about as it relates to the fetus within her. One must also discern what the fetus is and whether it has an interest to be taken into account. Since human rights are the property of those who are living individuals whose membership in the human species begins at conception, the question as to whether the fetus is deemed to have moral and legal rights is a matter of critical concern which ought not to be avoided by an unsound use of the term "choice."

One of the central questions in the abortion debate is this: "When and on what basis do we recognize the right to have rights?" In answering, it is important to remember that the onus is on those who would remove rights to indicate why the rights in question should be removed. Another fundamental issue arises from the questions "What is the morally relevant distinction between the fetus before birth and the child after birth such that we say one has a right to life and the other doesn't?" Various attempts, some of them exceedingly ingenious, have been made to devise a morally significant distinction.[2] Until a satisfactory answer to this question is found, it is my considered opinion that one must support the "presumption in favour of life".[3] That is, until it can be shown that there exists a morally relevant distinction between a fetus and an infant, one must assume that the rights of the living fetus and those of the living infant are the same.

In summary, an appeal to freedom of "choice" cannot, by itself, provide a satisfactory resolution to the abortion debate for the abortion debate concerns the most central of all "rights." The importance of discovering a better resolution cannot be understated. The right to life is, after all, the one right which is the precondition for the exercise of any other right. The appeal to "choice" in this debate, as in any other moral debate, simply will not do.

THE "PRO-CHOICE" MOVEMENT AND THE FETUS

In the abortion debate, where the "pro-life" side is continually talking about the fetus's "right to life"[4] and the fact that abortion pits the life of the fetus against the life or will of the woman, one of the techniques used by the "pro-choice" side is not to mention the fetus at all.[5] This failure to address the issue of the status of the developing fetus becomes even more striking in the recent arguments of certain groups to the effect that the fetus ought to have no rights at all until birth. This approach effectively denies any rights to the fetus despite the fact that, when a late-term case is concerned, the "fetus" is in all respects except location, identical to a newborn child.[6]

A second strategy employed by "pro-choice" advocates is to deny that the fetus has rights, because it lacks some quality necessary to the holding of rights. The most common manner in which this is done is to say that the fetus does not have standing in the matter of "life-rights" because it is not yet a person and does not have moral personhood. Another similar argument says that the fetus is not "human." Yet another, referred to by a justice of the Supreme Court of Canada, says that the fetus is merely "potential life" and therefore has a lesser interest or no interest at all, its "right" to protection accruing, somehow, at a later stage of its development.[7]

Attempts have been made to suggest that the fetus's rights should exist only from a certain point, whether it be development of the central nervous system, viability outside the womb, birth itself or some version of the trimesteral approach formerly accepted by the U.S. Supreme Court.[8] All of these arguments turn on two conceptual errors: confusion regarding "potential" of the fetus and failure to take into account the fact that the genetic individuality of the fetus remains unchanged from the moment of conception.

A good example of the way in which commentators confuse the "potentiality argument" may be seen in an article by Jane Fortin.[9] In discussing this argument, which she says "has great popular appeal," Fortin suggests that the fact that sperm and eggs have equal "potential for life" is "persuasive criticism" of the potentiality argument. On the contrary. Fortin and others have failed to recognize that it is not "the *potential* for human life" that "pro-lifers" argue for protecting, it is *the unique developing human life itself.* This developing life is *already*, from the moment of conception, unique and needs only time and nutrition to be fully developed.

Some commentators, including certain judges in the Supreme Courts of both Canada and the United States, have failed to note an ambiguity in the use of the term "potential." The error is a failure to distinguish between a thing that has the present capability for something (needing only time for it to occur naturally and necessarily) and the possible future achievement of a thing, in which case the thing itself may never become anything else. It is not true of the sperm or the egg to say that they are potentially a unique individual in the same way that it is true of the fetus to say that it is potentially a fully developed adult.

A failure to recognize this improper use of "potential" is what leads some writers into a failure to differentiate between contraception (in reference to which it is possible to speak of a particular sperm and egg as containing the constituent elements of life and therefore being "potential life" in the "possible future achievement" sense) and abortion (in reference to which we speak of that particular unique genetic entity which exists after conception — in other words "a human life," "a developing human life" or "a human life with potential" in the "present capability" sense). Fortin falls into this confusion further when she comments that the Warnock Committee's minority opinion opposed the use of human embryos for research purposes "since this would obviously deprive them *of their potential for life*."[10] An embryo that is only potential life cannot be deprived, in a way that is morally offensive, of what it only has potentially (in the "possible future achievement" sense). If the minority of the Committee objected to research on human embryos it must have been because, "having accepted the potentiality argument," they recognized that research on a human embryo would deprive that embryo of its developing life, not its "potential life." An individual human being has no potential life unless it is already alive.

The developing fetus is not "potential life"; it is life with potential (in the "present capability" sense). It is, without argument, "a developing life." All the changes after conception are changes of degree, not of kind; the fetus is merely the beginning stage of all of us at the start of the continuum of life. As unique individuals we remain, as far as our individuality is concerned, the same from conception onwards. To hold otherwise is bad science which depends on a questionable manifestation of terms like "personhood."[11] The fact that the common law tradition has said that life begins, as far as murder is concerned, only after the child has proceeded in a living form outside the mother, does not mean that it is or ought to be unworthy of consideration prior to this point. The law has historically criminalized abortion precisely because of its realization that the fetus prior to birth is in need of protection.[12]

"LIFE OR HEALTH"

It is important to recognize, that in its *Morgentaler* decision, the Supreme Court did not define either what it meant by the life and health of the pregnant woman or the content or extent of fetal rights. This is central, since the Court also said in its decision that Parliament would likely want to recognize a balancing between the rights of the fetus and the rights of the woman. This requires that there be a definition of the rights involved and this, in turn, requires a delineation of the interests of the respective "parties." Then, if the fetus is considered to be an interested party, its interest must be allowed to develop. The interest of the woman will vary from wanting to avoid degrees of emotional and physical trauma to, in some cases, avoiding death itself. The fetus's interest is in continuing its developing life.

Although the Supreme Court has recognized that the fetus has some interests and that the protection of the fetus has always been and continues to be a valid legislative objective, in the legal sense one cannot say much more than that the fetus has "some interests" because the Court expressly did not address the extent of these rights. Rather, it addressed itself to evaluating and then striking down section 251 of the Criminal Code, largely on grounds relating to the manner in which the section was operating procedurally. Parliament must, therefore, decide the extent of any limitation on the fetus's right to life taking into account, one hopes, principles that would set out clearly what circumstances will allow the termination of that life.

The term "health" contained in section 251 of the Criminal Code is not actually defined in the Code, but obviously, if abortions are going to be allowable in certain "life and health" situations, some substance must be given to these terms. The definitions of "health" that were used by therapeutic abortion committees functioning under section 251 of the Criminal Code varied considerably. Where abortions were liberally available, the "working definition" of "health" was often that of the World Health Organization: "a state of complete physical, mental, emotional and social well-being, not simply the absence of illness and disease."[13] This is a definition of almost complete elasticity and impracticality. While it may be a positive statement of objectives in the area of health, it is useless as a working definition for purposes of abortion. Daniel Callahan has commented:

> Its attractiveness as an ideal is vitiated by its practical impossibility of realization. Worse than that, it positively misleads, for health becomes a goal of such all-consuming importance that it simply begs to be thwarted in its realization. The demands which the word "complete" entail set the stage for the worst false consciousness of all: the demand that life deliver perfection.[14]

The Law Reform Commission of Canada has also voiced concern over the WHO "definition":

> Those general terms of wide public use have ethical, social and political implications and their reach extends to every

element of human happiness. The concept of "social well-being" far exceeds the meaning presently contemplated in Canadian criminal law for it includes political injustice, economic scarcity, food shortages and unfavorable physical environments. *All human misfortunes and disorders are not forms of illness from which one must be saved under the rubric of health in criminal law.* . . . [A] state of well-being, in law, ought first to be notionally sufficient to cope with the ordinary living in modern society, but does not carry a guarantee of stress-free, non-responsible life-style, because stress as well as responsibility for one's behaviour are incidents of living in society.[15]

Indeed, it is disappointing that Canada's proposed new abortion law is no clearer on this issue. While it effectively makes the decision to have an abortion a medical one, it lets the individual doctor decide what sorts of considerations are medically relevant.

In its most principled form, abortion is permissible to prevent a woman's death, on the well-recognized grounds that individuals have the right to "self-defence." If allowances are made for "life" threats or on the more morally problematic "health" ground then, at the least, the danger to life or health ought to be grave and potentially permanent and should expressly *exclude* social health reasons such as familial, social or economic well-being — all of which were used under the World Health Organization's statement of health and led to abortion on request in most parts of Canada.

Particular care should be taken to avoid the use of definitions which would allow abortions for "psychiatric" reasons where the "threat" is not related to some meaningful criterion of health. Quite apart from the lack of a meaningful definition of health, evidence exists which suggests that most of the vast medical literature available on abortion is seriously deficient in various areas. This makes it impossible to speak without doubt about *any* situations in which abortion is psychiatrically indicated. In a study prepared for the scientific council of the Canadian Psychiatric Association and published in the *Canadian Medical Association Journal*, B. K. Doane and B. G. Quigley, after reviewing approximately 250 journal articles and books on the psychiatric and related aspects of therapeutic abortion, commented:

> ... both the antagonists and the protagonists of therapeutic abortion should be aware that no scientific evidence exists to show that emotional risks vary in accordance with legislative restrictions on abortion ... [and that] despite the large number of articles and studies in the literature, there are insufficient data on which to base planning of medical and social programs for the management of undesired pregnancies.[16]

In a more recent article in the same journal, following a review of all the available literature on the incidence of complications of pregnancy in women who had been denied abortion, an editorial writer raised some important points:

> Few [medical] interventions are accepted without systematic evaluation. Drugs shown to be effective in the laboratory are evaluated in clinical trials, and surgical procedures are constantly criticized and revised. Even diagnostic tests must be shown to be safe, to cause only minor side effects and to have adequate test validity. Therapeutic abortions appear to be a major exception; they apparently have been "privileged" to bypass evaluation. *Why are they being done without clinical validation, even in the face of mounting evidence that they are not necessary for the prevention of maternal disease or the birth of unwanted children?* ... Physicians must take a more scientific approach to unwanted pregnancies and realize that abortion is not the answer to social ills. *Legislators should base their decisions on clinical reviews rather than succumb to public pressures.*[17]

One final point: given that the initial response of some provincial governments to the striking down of the Criminal Code provisions appears to involve issues related to the funding of abortions, it is essential to distinguish between the primary issue (the morality of abortion itself, the assessment of the health of the mother against the life of the fetus) and those issues which are secondary (funding and access to abortion). A failure to distinguish between these two types of questions can result in an ongoing failure to address the primary issue and a disproportionate expenditure of time and energy on secondary aspects. Many authorities suggest that abortion is not, in fact, a necessary medical procedure except in rare circumstances where the woman's life is threatened. If the medical profession cannot provide meaningful guidance as to which abortions are necessary within a substantive definition of "health," then there is no reason why such abortions should be considered therapeutic and even less reason that citizens should be required to "foot the bill" for them.

CANADA AS A PLURALISTIC COUNTRY

The statement is sometimes made that Canada is a pluralistic country and that, therefore, one must acknowledge each person's differing beliefs. As a recognition of Canada's multicultural makeup, this statement is impeccable. However, this valid recognition of cultural diversity should not be confused with *moral* pluralism. In fact, the basic notion that underlies many people's use of appeals to pluralism is not fairness to different cultural groups, but moral relativism.

Throughout the centuries, many of the greatest thinkers have discussed the importance of learning and preserving the central truths which define society. These truths are not relative or subjective but transcendent. Nobel laureate Michael Polanyi has written that

> . . . the adherents of a great tradition are largely unaware of their own premises, which lie deeply embedded in the unconscious foundations of practice . . . [I]f the citizens are dedicated to certain transcendent obligations and particularly to such general ideals as truth, justice, charity, and these are embodied in the tradition of the community to which allegiance is maintained, a great many issues between citizens,

and all to some extent, can be left — and are necessarily left — for the individual consciences to decide. The moment, however, a community ceases to be dedicated through its members to transcendent ideals, it can continue to exist undisrupted only by submission to a single centre of unlimited secular power.[18]

That many people in our society "are largely unaware of their own [moral and ethical] premises" is a fact. That it should be the function of all who believe in transcendent moral truths to try to change this state of affairs is also the case.

What I mean by "transcendent truths" can best be illustrated by a brief consideration of C. S. Lewis's brilliant work *The Abolition of Man*.[19] In this work, Lewis provides a framework within which one may argue that "fundamental truths" should be recognized and used as a basis for legislation and that this can be done without offending current notions of pluralism.

Lewis's analysis of the central tenets of world civilizations shows that, contrary to popular belief, the religions and ethical codes of the world share a core of objective truths. He terms this set of truths the *"Tao,"* or "way" (not to be confused with the religion Taoism).

> What is common to [all accounts of the *Tao*] is something we cannot neglect. It is the doctrine of objective value, the belief that certain attitudes are really true, and others really false, to the kind of thing the universe is and the kind of things we are.

He goes on to say, "Only the *Tao* provides a common human law of action which can over-arch rulers and ruled alike. A dogmatic belief in objective value is necessary to the very idea of a rule which is not tyranny or an obedience which is not slavery."[20]

Lewis further argues that an understanding of the *Tao* is fundamental to any modification:

> Those who understand the spirit of the *Tao* and who have

been led by that spirit can modify it in directions which that spirit itself demands. Only they can know what those directions are. The outsider knows nothing about the matter. His attempts at alteration, as we have seen, contradict themselves. So far from being able to harmonize discrepancies in its letter by penetration to its spirit, *he merely snatches at some one precept, on which the accidents of time and place happen to have riveted his attention, and then rides it to death — for no reason that he can give.* From within the *Tao* itself comes the only authority to modify the *Tao*.[21]

It will be clear from the discussion of the way certain people use the notion of "choice" in the abortion debate this usage is just such an impermissible "snatching" of one precept and "riding it to death — for no [acceptable] reason."

Alasdair MacIntyre, like Lewis, is concerned that once the *Tao*, which MacIntyre refers to as "some version of the Aristotelian notion of virtue," is abandoned, one is at the mercy of power divorced from principle.[22] The same concern is also expressed by one of Canada's leading philosophers, the late George Grant. Grant explores a number of the contradictions which underlie current liberal thought and points out that remnants of the *Tao* (he does not use this word for it) are used by liberals. He writes:

When contractual liberals hold within their thought remnants of secularised Christianity or Judaism, these remnants, if made conscious, must be known as unthinkable in terms of what is given in the modern. How, in modern thought, can we find positive answers to the questions: (i) what is it about human beings that makes liberty and equality their due? (ii) why is justice what we are fitted for, when it is not convenient? Why is it our good? The inability of contractual liberals (or indeed Marxists) to answer these questions is the terrifying darkness which has fallen upon modern justice.[23]

In any society concerned with justice it is imperative that all citizens be concerned, as individuals, with justice. To be knowledgeable about what is just and unjust, one must first believe there *are* "rights" and "wrongs."[24] One frequently encounters people who deny that things can be "right" or "wrong," yet who promptly complain of an injustice done to others or to them personally. It is this type of contradiction which shows just how far from the *Tao* we have come. And it is a very real question whether judges, lawyers, law professors and parliamentarians can coherently discuss the "fundamental rights and freedoms" set out in the Charter of Rights and Freedoms unless they have some workable idea of why certain things *are* "fundamental" and where "fundamentals" come from. It is now suggested by some that liberalism itself may provide neither a basis for, nor an understanding of, the very rights it deems central and tries to administer.[25]

If we believe that there are "rights" and "wrongs" which underpin our society and our laws, then any appeal to pluralism as a justification for abortion is unacceptable because there is no evidence that the core principles of world religions and ethical codes support abortion.[26] More importantly, a review of laws must be done within the context of moral evaluation and must not simply be a catalogue of "the world's increasingly liberalized abortion laws" in, for example, the Commonwealth countries.[27] It is self-evident that doing a thing does not make it morally correct. Therefore, the fact that many countries may have enacted permissive laws in an area does not serve as a moral justification for the practice.

THE IDEA OF COMPROMISE

In addition to notions of "pluralism," one occasionally hears people argue that, in a country which has such divided views on a moral issue, "compromise" is the only way to "resolve" the social debate. What is missed in such an approach is that it erroneously assumes that either both approaches are morally acceptable prior to the compromise or that what results from the compromise will be morally acceptable. Thus, where fundamental presuppositions are not shared, the attempt at resolution may be morally impossible because what one side deems moral is to the other side immoral. In such a situation, "compromise" is without moral basis and potentially dangerous. This may be easily demonstrated by examples.

If one opposes the murder of people and is told by others that due to debate and a lack of consensus on the issue, the only workable compromise is to make a law which allows the killing of small people, one could be excused for concluding that the law fails to make moral sense. Similarly, to those who view abortion as the killing of the innocent or at least arguably the killing of the innocent, allowing abortions until some arbitrary point is arrived at cannot be an acceptable "compromise." To allow wife beating on Saturdays but not on other days would be similarly unacceptable to those who think it wrong in all circumstances, and to allow some people to be slaves over the objections of those who believe there should be no slavery at all would not be a satisfactory "compromise."

A gestational approach which would allow abortion until some point is reached during the pregnancy is not a "compromise" in the abortion issue. Assuming that one decides there must be compromise on the abortion issue, an accurate compromise would be based on the question "What grounds are sufficient to allow abortion?" *not* the question "When will we restrict abortion on demand/request?" Any attempt to answer the latter by way of legislation would be based on the logical error of including the conclusion in the premise. It is not clear that there should *ever* be a period of unrestricted access to abortion. As with arguments based on notions of "choice," arguments for unrestricted access to abortion at some time fail to note that a "compromise" like this is only useful once one has established whether or not the subject is one that admits of compromise at all. A failure to recognize that there are various forms of compromise, some of which vitiate one of the positions at issue, is akin to the failure to see the limitations of "choice" in moral debates. Lawmakers must base laws on responsible and morally coherent positions.[28]

THE WOMAN'S "RIGHT TO CONTROL HER OWN BODY"

It is sometimes asserted that the fact that the fetus is inside a woman means that it cannot have any rights separate from the wishes of the woman. These arguments all turn on notions of "power" or "control." However, ignoring the fetus because another being has power over it is eerily reminiscent of arguments used to deny the personhood of women on the basis of the husband's right to control his own wife — the two being "one flesh." Even this control did not allow the right to terminate life. There is something counter-intuitive about attempts to square this kind of control over life with notions of "nurturing life."

Such arguments also amount to weighing *any* reason (or no reason at all) for destroying the fetus against what is, undeniably, a life right. The emphasis on control rather than life is more clearly seen as the fetus develops and will be most difficult to justify in late-term abortions or situations like the *Baby R* case. Where power or control is seen as the significant issue, concern for the fetus, predictably, is not expressed. This thinking underlies the approach taken by those who view abortion merely as another means of contraception.[29]

Obviously the separate assertions of the "right to terminate a pregnancy" and the "right to decide what to do with one's own body" must be evaluated in terms of the moral claims that are in conflict. Just as the statement "We should not criminalize abortion because women are not criminals" is erroneous because it contains the answer in the question, so is the bald statement, "A woman has the right to control her own body." Compare the statement "We ought not to criminalize wife battering because men are not criminals." Both statements are equally fallacious. Both can be evaluated only by determining whether the conduct in question *ought* to be criminalized and this can be done only through a moral evaluation of the issues involved.

The extent to which certain feminist arguments are selective and confused can readily be seen when these feminists want to argue as follows: All abortions are a matter of a woman's personal choice and ought not to be interfered with by the state; the decision to have or not have an abortion is the moral issue; abortions for reasons of sex-selection are wrong and ought to be restricted by law. This type of argument is illuminating because it shows that, for certain feminists, the gender issues are the only morality that they either understand or will acknowledge. They say, in effect, "Any reason, or no reason at all, is sufficient to allow you the right to choose an abortion *unless* your choice is motivated by what sex you want your baby to be."[30]

What cannot be ignored is the fact that there are *two* bodies involved in the abortion issue; one is inside the other. Those who argue that there is only one body contradict the premises of medical science, according to which physicians treat a pregnancy as two patients. We must be wary of any position that refuses to discuss the morality of its claim in the light of all the available facts.

THE STATE AND THE "COERCION" OF WOMEN'S BODIES

R. Allan Borovoy has expressed the above position with admirable clarity: "Even if it is conceded that life indeed begins at conception, it does not follow that such life should have a right of sanctuary in the body of a person who doesn't want it there. The mother is also a person whose welfare is worthy of protection. . . ."[31] Having made this point, Borovoy recites the fact that several juries refused to find Henry Morgentaler guilty of breaking the laws against abortion despite clear evidence of his guilt. He then suggests that Parliament ought not to enact a law that would force a woman to carry a pregnancy to term in all cases except where her "life and health" are at risk, because any other law would be "unworkable."

Since when does the validity of a law that seeks to protect life turn on its "workability"? While it may be very difficult to enforce all sorts of laws (e.g., laws governing incest, child abuse, discrimination, etc.), who would reasonably suggest that this difficulty casts doubt on the importance or validity of the law itself? In fact, the pragmatic is only one of the two important functions which criminal law serves: the other is *symbolic*.

Borovoy suggests that the juries' failure to convict was based on the fact that their members had been " . . . exposed to the norms of the democratic system, which accords a high priority to the autonomy of people *over their own bodies*."[32] But this statement has two erroneous implications: first, that controlling one's own body through abortion is a democratic phenomenon and, second, that such conduct is moral. Surely the juries' failure to convict reflected not so much the morality of the conduct being judged as the moral views of the jury. And in a society composed of evil or morally confused people, one would expect that juries would come to evil or confused conclusions. The moral realities remain. What happens to Borovoy's argument if we assume that juries someday *do* convict Henry Morgentaler?

According to Borovoy, this would still be wrong because the key point is that " . . . we don't have to embrace the moral merits of an abortion in order to rule out state coercion as an appropriate remedy."[33] So much, therefore, for Borovoy's argument based on the "workability" of law. All along he was really arguing that the state is never justified in "coercing" a woman to do what she does not want to do with her body whether or not the law "works" in the state.

This, however, avoids the issue of whether there are two life issues at stake. Since civil liberties are usually concerned with the "margins," why is no real attention paid to them here, particularly when life is the most basic of rights? It appears as if the usual discourse of civil libertarians, rushing to the barricades to ensure that no breach of civil liberties occurs no matter how unpopular the issue in the general public's mind, has been completely abandoned in this case.[34]

Furthermore, why does Borovoy select a "liberty" right in preference to a "life" right? As he (correctly) notes, "most anti-abortionists would readily grant the woman a right to have an abortion in order to save her life."[35] Philosophers used to recognize that rights were rank-ordered and that, for example, "life, liberty and the pursuit of happiness" were not only interrelated, but were rank-ordered with happiness depending on liberty and liberty in turn depending on life. Here, however, liberty has been yanked out of context and elevated to preeminence, with no explanation. This is puzzling when seen alongside the fact that the infringement of the woman's liberty is, after all, time-limited, whereas the termination of the fetus's life is permanent.

In fact, there are a lot of situations in which the liberty of one is not greater than the life of another. I cannot terminate the life of my crying baby at 3:00 A.M. because it interferes (significantly) with my psychological or physical health no matter how serious an interference it represents. Nor am I justified in killing and eating my baby even though it is the only thing around to eat and I would die if I did not kill and eat it. Assume that the stress caused by my children is so great that I am going to have a nervous breakdown or commit suicide. Wouldn't I be justified in killing my children, in the most humane possible way of course?

These questions cannot be adequately answered by saying that "the fetus is different from the child because it is inside the woman," "the fetus is not as fully developed as a child outside" or "birth is the time at which we start protecting human life." These statements are in the nature of conclusions, not reasons, and provide no basis on which to answer the questions "How does the location of the fetus give a person a 'right' to kill it?" or "What is relevant about birth that negates the right of a fetus to live up until the minute it is born?"

The argument from coercion in fact begs the question of whether or not the state has a right to "coerce" (that is, forbid particular conduct). We cannot decide this until we know the rights that are involved. By the nature of the process of life (with the present stage of technology), one life is located inside another and is dependent upon it. It is far from clear, however, that such a location or dependency relationship allows for the termination of a life right and it is even less clear that location or dependency confer upon a woman a "right" so to terminate. Such "privileging" of the woman's control over the life within her is strikingly like arguments used to defend wife battering on the grounds that it occurs "in the home" and "what goes on in the home should be privileged from the scrutiny of the state."

How much weight can plausibly be given to the woman's liberty when weighed against the life of the fetus? Let us suppose that a technique is developed which would allow, with minimal infringement on the woman's autonomy and insignificant risk to her health, the separation of the fetus from the woman. Let us also assume that the fetus could then be raised outside her body until it is viable. Is her liberty so great that it still trumps the life of the fetus? Liberty starts to look increasingly fraudulent when it trumps life to such an extent as this; but then, Borovoy has said that he is not concerned with the morality of abortion. If we are not concerned with the morality of abortion, why should we be concerned with coercion? Isn't our concern regarding state coercion merely another way of saying we think that autonomy/liberty *ought* (note: "ought" is a moral term) to be protected by restricting or eradicating state coercion?

Borovoy cannot give any reason morally why liberty is a greater moral good to protect than life, yet he depends on our acceptance of the moral good of autonomy and liberty in order to make an argument at all. Seen in this way, one ascertains clearly what George Grant meant by the liberals' use of "shreds of the Judeo-Christian morality" and what C. S. Lewis meant by the "snatching" of one moral principle out of context.

It is not surprising to note that Borovoy cites Judith Jarvis Thomson's argument that the fetus has no right to the use of the woman's body.[36] But it is curious that he did not make reference to, or was not aware of, the refutation of Thomson's argument offered by Baruch Brody. Brody points out that when we grant that a fetus has no right to the continued use of a woman's body,

. . . all that we [mean is] that he does not have this right merely because the continued use saves his life. But, of course, there may be other reasons why he has this right. One would be that the only way to take the use of the woman's body away from the fetus is by killing him, and that is something that neither she nor we have the right to do . . . I conclude therefore that Professor Thomson has not established the truth of her claims about abortion, primarily because she has not sufficiently attended to the distinction between our duty to save [the fetus's] life and our duty not to take it. Once one attends to that distinction, it would seem that the mother, in order to regain control over her body, has no right to abort the fetus from the point at which it becomes a human being.[37]

If Professor Thomson has not "sufficiently" attended to the distinction, Allan Borovoy has not attended to it at all, and neither, for that matter, have many who use the "control," "coercion" or "good Samaritan" arguments.

THE FETUS AND EXPERIMENTATION

If the fetus is merely "tissue," as some would have it, then why should we have any scruples about using, not to say farming, such "tissue" for the good of society? What reasons can there be (apart from a sentimental feeling or a sense of "taste") for restricting such research on the unborn? The Medical Research Council, in its recently released guidelines, states that it is unwise and unjustified to ban embryo research but that such research should not be allowed on embryos older than seventeen days. One must ask, "Why the hesitation *after seventeen days?*" Surely, if fetuses would otherwise be disposed of, they should be used "for the good of society." Yet, given that viability is somewhere between five and six months of gestation, or that we may be able to abort up until nine months, seventeen days seems rather frugal, not to say, arbitrary.[38]

Lest anyone think that they can refute such arguments by simply stating that they are of the "slippery-slope" variety, it should be pointed out that categorizing a concern is not the same thing as answering one. Several years ago, many would have considered it inconceivable that abortions could be obtained without any criminal sanctions for the full nine months of gestation. Yet that is precisely the situation in Canada today.

The argument that after some point beyond twenty-two

weeks of gestation what is being aborted is a human being that would be viable but for the violence of the methodology or the neglect of medical staff, is met with statements as to the rarity of the event or the fact that "responsible women will not wait so late to have it done," etc. No concern is expressed for the horror of what is occurring, the cheapening effect it will have on our respect for human life or the complete lack of difference there is between a viable human *in utero* and one *ex utero*. In the area of life issues, where medical technology is increasingly allowing us to do what we have never done before, the realization that technology is not its own moral guide must inform all our steps.[39]

CONCLUSION

Where human life is concerned, even where there are doubts about the nature of that human life, all who claim to be civilized and interested in human rights or civil liberties must make principled arguments to support their positions. I have attempted to show that a number of the arguments often used to justify the "pro-choice" position are unacceptable. Those vested with the responsibility of legislating for the social good must formulate laws based on correct moral approaches, not on erroneous philosophy. Those who have torn down the philosophical walls which historically protected the unborn and seek now to protect that life at some other point with walls of sentiment can have no moral basis for complaint when sentiment changes.

Given developments over past decades, it is likely that technology will sooner or later provide a way in which the whole human generational process can be accomplished "artificially" (outside the womb). Once this occurs and the issue of fetal development is separated, on one level, from issues of "control by the woman over her own body," what is and has been said about the nature of the fetus and how and why we do (or do not) respect it, will inevitably color future developments. However, if arguments based on "control" have vitiated certain of our traditional moral principles, it is hard to see on what basis any future protection can be afforded. If "control" has, as suggested, a limited time frame given the advances of technology and if it does not provide a consistent ethic of protection of life, then it is foolhardy to embrace "control" arguments until such an ethic is established (if it ever could be). Where there is doubt, we must err on the side of life and presume, if at all, in favor of it.

SAMUEL AJZENSTAT

THE LIBERAL CRISIS: FEMINISTS ON ABORTION

FOR MANY WHO FIGHT for abortion rights in the political arena, abortion does not raise fundamental philosophical issues. Probably quite rightly, they see no serious political alternative to a basically liberal order (emphasizing the equal right of all to personal autonomy and individual self-realization and the use of law for no purpose but to protect as large as possible a private space for each person's pursuit of such self-defined goals), and they are convinced that abortion rights follow directly from such goals and are as uncontroversial as the goals themselves. Those who seek legal restrictions on abortion are therefore seen merely as holdouts against the obvious, mired in a repressive and now, happily, outmoded conception of the aims of life and the uses of coercion in a political community.

Philosophical discussion of abortion over the last two decades or so shows a much different picture. For one thing, to the extent that both sides have claimed to occupy the liberal ground, the abortion issue becomes an incomparably profound probe of just what liberalism is, what its foundations are, what sort of laws it allows and what we have to do to defend it. But an even more illuminating aspect of the philosophical debate for me has been the way in which some of the most sophisticated defenders of the pro-choice position have been increasingly tempted to move away from liberalism under the pressure of what they have found themselves forced to say in order to defend the decriminalization of abortion. Currently the major pro-choice arguments among feminists are made as part of a critique of liberalism, while pro-lifers stress all the more the link between liberalism and laws limiting abortion. It is this aspect that I want to concentrate on, partly because it points us to one of the ways in which liberalism faces a serious crisis today and to the fact that the acceptance of this philosophy cannot simply be taken for granted by those who believe in it; and partly because it has helped to confirm my own conclusion, tentatively arrived at over the years, that a pro-life liberalism makes sense.

The reason for the pro-choicers' earlier pro-liberal stance is easy to see. Liberalism is devoted to the reduction to a bare minimum of the control that law or social practices can be allowed to exercise over individual choice. Since it celebrates autonomy and the taking charge of one's own life, it wishes to see associations with others, that crucial aspect of one's own life, as voluntary rather than involuntary as much as possible. Because liberalism entails the inborn suspicion that involuntary relationships rather obviously diminish personal autonomy, the institution of the family has been a problem for it from its beginnings. Thus, John Locke struggles to show that family relationships, at least among adults, are essentially voluntary associations even while he acknowledges the coercive force that parents are able to exercise through their children's hopes of inheritance.[1] Inheritance is the archetype of the problem of the family for liberalism. For liberal feminism, this ideology cashes out in the form of making it possible for women to form alliances with men and children who can provide them with strong supports of all kinds against others while building in guarantees that these alliances will remain voluntary ones.

Within this context the pro-choice position can be seen as a liberal rejection of an involuntary relation between a mother and a child in the interest of self-determination. But obviously the attempt to provide liberal credentials for the pro-choice position would become much more ambiguous if the situation had to be understood as one in which a woman could stay out of an involuntary entanglement with another person only by killing that other person. It thus became important to the earliest, simplest and still influential wave of the pro-choice movement to attempt to argue that in the relevant sense no other person was involved. At this stage, therefore, the fight between the pro-choicers and the pro-lifers came to center on the status of what the latter called the unborn child and the former called the fetus, the products of pregnancy or even fetal matter or wastage.[2] If I choose often to call it the unborn child, I do so not only to mark my own affiliation, but also because, as I will try to show, this question is no longer the real issue for serious thinkers on either side of the debate.

The early argument used to defend the definition of the unborn as a nonperson was helped along by the brash determination of the feminism of the sixties to de-sentimentalize and demystify pregnancy. Women had been trapped because they had been taught to idealize and to romanticize sex and childbirth, so they had to be re-educated into seeing these as mere bodily functions. This was the period in which one feminist writer could feel that it was good for women to believe that "having a baby is like shitting a pumpkin." But by 1971 the argument was moving to a different plane. A good indication of this is the justly celebrated article "A Defense of Abortion" by Judith Jarvis Thomson.[3] Though she says that she is "inclined to think that we shall . . . probably have to agree that the fetus has already become a human person well before birth," she also still denies "the premise that the fetus is a human being, a person from the moment of conception." Having said this, however, she gets to her real point: "It seems to me to be of great interest to ask what happens if, for the sake of argument, we allow the premise. How, precisely, are we supposed to get from there to the conclusion that abortion is morally impermissible?" Thomson thus intends to mount a defence of abortion that can survive the most radical attribution of humanity to the unborn. But by doing so she has also, perhaps inadvertently, made it at least possible for feminists to re-think their views on the status of the unborn.

What Thomson most crucially does is to shift the main question from "Is the fetus a person?" to "What does one person owe another?" More specifically, she cleverly canvasses a number of examples whose point is: Whoever I am, fetus or adult, I don't have a general right to make others do something or stop doing something simply because I will surely die otherwise. Clearly this is a much more interesting, but also much more contentious defence of abortion than the superficial claim that having an abortion is like having a wart removed. It is surely to Thomson's credit that she has helped to move the abortion issue into the ranks of the profoundest philosophical consideration of what one person is entitled to ask of another and expect to see enforced by law, even if, on this point, the pro-life party was there first. Furthermore, anyone with liberal instincts must, I think, have considerable sympathy for the claim that there are limits on what can be expected of someone even when someone else's life is at stake. To simplify one of Thomson's most celebrated examples: That I have a very rare blood type probably would not justify the taking of my blood against my will or a demand that I never go anywhere without notifying the authorities of my whereabouts in case they run out of blood of that type. Generally, simple prudence suggests such limits on what can be asked of people. Extreme selfishness may be reprehensible but probably should not be against the law. Is this enough to defend abortion rights?

Critics argued that it was not. Thomson's examples seemed to establish only that people could not generally be forced to keep others from dying. But Thomson herself seems to accept a distinction between letting people die and killing them, even saying at one point, "I am not arguing for the right to secure the death of the unborn child . . . the desire for the child's death is not one which anybody may gratify, should it turn out to be possible to detach the child alive." How, then, can an argument meant to show that we must often allow people to let other people die when they might have been saved then constitute a defence of abortion? If Thomson acknowledges some claims on behalf of the unborn, what sort of guidelines might there be to adjudicate between these claims and the claims of the pregnant woman? And who ought to have the job of applying those guidelines?

One of the most interesting aspects of subsequent discussion for me has been the way in which some pro-choicers, using hints provided by Thomson, including the acknowledgment of the status of the fetus, have attempted to work out answers to these questions in a way that would leave abortion rights philosophically intact. Clearly anyone who thinks of abortion as the killing of a human being and admits there is no right to do so but still wishes to defend an unrestricted right to abort is walking a very narrow line indeed.

This is the line that Christine Overall, a Canadian feminist philosopher at Queen's University, seems to take. Because her book *Ethics and Human Reproduction*,[4] was published in 1987 and her feminist credentials are unimpeachable[5] and because others have written in this vein recently,[6] we can take her as a fair example of a current strand in the abortion argument among feminists. Thomson is still a major presence and Overall makes crucial use of the distinction we saw Thomson making, though rather incidentally, between detaching the child and killing the child or, in Overall's language, between evacuation and destruction. Overall is at pains to argue that what is specifically being affirmed when a woman is said to have the right to an abortion is the right to have her uterus emptied. She puts this negatively as follows: "the embryo/fetus has no right to occupancy of its mother's (or anyone else's) uterus." This represents for Overall what is true in the pro-choice position. An example of the kind of argument she gives for it asks us to consider an egg fertilized *in vitro*. If, before the embryo is reimplanted, the woman who wanted it develops a disease that makes pregnancy dangerous or, having had some of these embryos frozen for possible future use, enters her forties, does that embryo have a claim on a place in her womb or, lacking that, in some other woman's? If the woman is killed in an accident, are we obliged to find another womb for that embryo? Overall says no. And for the examples given, I feel some inclination to agree.

What examples like these conjure up is the rather horrible image of political authorities, police authorities, if you like, empowered to commandeer wombs for embryos dispossessed by the technology of *in vitro* fertilization. When one adds the consideration that when this technology is used as a cure for infertility, many more eggs are fertilized than are used, the prospect is indeed bizarre. But one of the reasons this argument seems to me not entirely conclusive on the abortion issue is simply that an embryo's claim to be able to stay in a womb it already occupies might be argued to be stronger than an embryo's claim to be put back into a womb after having been removed.[7] At least this becomes more possible once one acknowledges that embryos and fetuses have any claims whatsoever. And this, Overall does.

For various technical reasons, Overall couches her arguments not in terms of what rights can be claimed but in terms of what rights cannot be claimed. Thus, just as the unborn are said not to have squatters' rights in a womb, so, on the other side, Overall argues, no one (pregnant woman, doctor, etc.) has the right to kill the embryo/fetus. And she is led further to "suspect that perhaps no one has a *right* to injure, mutilate, or cause pain to it." Though this is only a *prima facie* responsibility — that is, it can be overridden when the result would be only the least possible injury, mutilation or pain compatible with the overriding considerations — the acknowledgement of this responsibility nevertheless supports the conclusion that "the embryo/fetus therefore appears to have a different moral status than that which is possessed by a body part."

Overall gathers together a number of arguments tending to this conclusion. Most of them, which I shall not enlarge on here, are based on considerations for denying that a fertilized ovum can appropriately be treated as anyone's property. She is thus one of the latest in the lineage of those thinkers who, though feminists, can defend abortion only if they can do so in the face of their own recognition of very strong claims against the killing of the unborn. That these writers feel forced to acknowledge considerations that are not in line with their "interests" as activists is inspiring evidence both of their probity and the power of philosophical thought to lift us above the narrowest perspectives. The question is: can they be this honest and still get the answer they want?

The upshot of Overall's argument is a classic philosophical dilemma. A single act (the abortion) turns out to be both something there can be a right to do and something there is no right to do. It is the former if it is described as an emptying of the womb and the latter if it is described as the killing of a fetus. But it is normally both of these. There are essentially two ways a philosopher can get out of such a dilemma. We can limit ourselves to situations in which the two descriptions would not both apply — in effect, an emptying of the womb that would not be the killing of the fetus. Or we can try to find reasons for thinking that one of the descriptions somehow takes precedence over the other, is truer or deeper. The pro-choice solution would be to show that the emptying of the womb is what is really being done.

Overall tries both of these methods of resolving the dilemma. She does the first — separating the two descriptions — by noting the likelihood that medical technology will before long be able to remove the embryo from the womb from the moment of conception without killing it. The dilemma will then dissolve because we will be able to meet both requirements. This argument, as we saw, was present in Thomson and has surfaced in a number of other places. The usual conclusion is that it would then be a general responsibility to keep that removed embryo alive.

How should we react to this argument? In some ways it comes out supporting arguments often made by pro-lifers. For example, at least in theory, it undermines the argument for abortion rights based on the claim that many women feel less trauma in having the fetus killed than in giving it up for adoption. If Overall is right, then in the future she envisages, a woman who has an abortion will have to adjust to the fact that the child she "aborted" is being brought up by someone else. The best kind of adjustment would arguably consist in being able to take real satisfaction in the fact that her child is still alive though her womb is empty — that is, in the fact that she did not do something she did not have the right to do.

Many questions crowd in at this point. Coming down for a moment from the philosophical heights, does Overall wish to demand that all abortion counselling include the clear statements: (1) that though the woman has a right to an empty womb, she has no right to kill the fetus; (2) that the operation, at least for now, will almost certainly kill the fetus; (3) that the doctor willingly performing the abortion nevertheless feels duty-bound to try to save the life of the fetus if possible while knowing that it will of course not be possible; (4) that in spite of all this, the decision as to which of these considerations is really most important is entirely up to her?

To try to neutralize these kinds of questions, Overall clearly needs to come back to the issue of what to do before the technological millennium arrives, while emptying a womb still means killing an unborn child, the more so during the early period of pregnancy when almost all of the more than 80,000 abortions officially recorded per year in Canada alone, take place. Can she provide a principle of precedence that would reduce the need to confront women with the dilemma?

But this may be a misconstruction of her approach. For while some passages in her treatment of abortion suggest that she has or might be trying for a principle of precedence, others seem to avoid commitment to any such generalization. Passages of the former kind seem to move towards the view that being able to empty the womb overrides the fact that one does not have the right to kill the fetus. This would be suggested by her endorsement, elsewhere, of the decriminalization of abortion.[8] But a somewhat different approach surfaces, in another passage in which she seems to adapt the principle of double effect of the Catholic tradition in aid of some very unCatholic ends. This principle is one which Catholic thinkers use, contrary to what their opponents say of them, to allow procedures that save the life of the mother by taking the life of her unborn child. The principle argues, for example, that the removal of the cancerous womb of a pregnant woman or part of the fallopian tube in an ectopic pregnancy has as its intention the saving of the mother and not the death of the child. The real effect is the intended one, the death of the child merely an incidental, though unavoidable, one. It can then be argued that such operations are not abortions at all if abortion is understood as intending to eliminate the child. Overall seems to suggest that in morally acceptable abortions the intention is simply to empty the womb and not to kill the child or, since motives are hard to determine directly, that we can at least identify the sorts of situation in which this is likely to be the case.

This, if it could be made to work, would give her not so much a principle of precedence as a way of saying that since the mother did not set out to kill the child, the fact that she would not have had the right to do so need not enter into consideration. She simply acted on her right to empty the womb and set out to do only that. Any further intent would have made her act morally unacceptable.

Even some who would draw the line between permissible and impermissible abortions at about this same point, have nevertheless been critical of it.[9] The strongest objection to it appears to be that it smooths over an intractable situation in which whatever one does is wrong. And it does so by suggesting a not entirely plausible distinction between what we intend and what we know will happen as a result of our action. Furthermore, it masks the fact that we are, after all, bringing to bear a rule of precedence, one which favors the mother. If this were not so, we could use the principle just as well in cases in which it was the mother's life or the baby's, to save either one on the grounds that we really did not intend the death of the other. Double effect thus stops us from considering what might be said in support of a principle of precedence favoring the mother and from considering the possibility that when we face the situation of saving one life at the cost of another, we are out in the cold beyond the help of moral formulas.

The abortion situation is not usually that extreme. But even when Overall does not suggest that it is but continues to argue as if rational principles might be available to us, it strikes me as odd and peculiarly symptomatic that she should be able to talk about what we have and do not have a right to do as if that were purely a matter of concrete ethical relations — something to be worked out in intimate interactions — and had nothing to do with the rules and regulations of politics. It is in the vaguely apolitical nature of her discussion that we find, I believe, the deepest clue to what the abortion debate means to our society as a whole. To explore some of this we have to turn from Overall to the work of Carol Gilligan, whose book *In a Different Voice*[10] helped to start a revolution in feminism. A large part of this book is devoted to a study of attitudes to abortion among women both when they were deciding whether to have one and later after the decision had been made.

The relation I want to suggest between Overall and Gilligan is roughly as follows: Overall uses a distinction crucial to her between evacuation and destruction in order to depict the abortion situation as a dilemma, a confrontation between what a woman has the right to do and what she does not have the right to do. But while she depicts the dilemma fairly clearly, what she says about how it is to be faced or, if possible, resolved, is very murky. In Gilligan we find precisely an account of different ways of confronting dilemmas in human life and an interpretation of them that makes it much easier to understand why Overall writes as she does and seems at first to be obscure on these questions. Gilligan's work also brings us closer to understanding why the pro-choice argument, pursued more and more in her terms, precipitates a crisis for liberalism.

Gilligan's theorizing is based on surveys of how people approach moral dilemmas. She can thus claim to bring empirical data to bear on the perennial philosophical issue of what ethical maturity really is. She, like a number of moral philosophers, contrasts two very different ways of confronting such dilemmas. What has made Gilligan famous is her claim that the more mature of these two ways is more typical of women than men and so has come to be downgraded as less mature by the male-dominated disciplines. This is an important issue and needs much more critical discussion than I can give it here. It will come into what I have to say only insofar as it relates to abortion.

The approach Gilligan characterizes as less mature and largely male is to look for the "single right answer" to ethical dilemmas as if they were math problems. The point is to characterize the dilemma as one of a certain kind to which a certain general rule or formula is relevant. The rule provides the solution in all cases of this kind and is hence objective and fair. We might call this approach moral legalism, though the phrase is not Gilligan's.

What Gilligan suggests is that the more mature approach recognizes that rules are of scant help for two reasons. First, each situation is unique. Who and what the individuals involved are and have been, every particular facet of their relation and its history, their strengths, weaknesses, the intensity of their needs should color our sense of the moral demands of this situation. Morality may involve a total commitment to doing what is least hurtful in each situation, but that is not a formula that we can apply abstractly. We can only tell what is least hurtful here and now by throwing away the formula and opening ourselves up to the particularities of life. Secondly, the least hurtful act may still, and in the deepest dilemmas always will, cause considerable hurt. In this sense the moral life has a tragic dimension which the search for the one right answer does not face. Moral dilemmas are not puzzles with a solution. They are unsolvable, if a solution means finding a way not to hurt anyone. Nor do we get a solution by adopting the rule that we will always hurt ourselves rather than others. The altruistic formula is as much an abdication of mature responsibility as any other formula is. But we have to go on living. We do so by seeing as clearly as we can and doing what seems best to us, taking upon ourselves the responsibility for our perceptions and our moral responses.

There is considerable truth in Gilligan's account. The tradition of ethical theory has often incorporated this view, ever since Plato and Aristotle first argued that laws are inadequate to deal with the particularities of human reality. But when we turn to Gilligan's account of the abortion decision, we can nevertheless see reasons for misgivings. Her interviewees generally think of themselves as having considered the present and the future both of themselves and of their unborn children in a serious, responsible way, finding an abortion to be the better way in their unique circumstances. Furthermore, Gilligan argues, having to make the decision contributed to the spiritual growth of these women.

She argues that the decision to abort was an occasion of growth for the women in her sample who made their choice exactly because they did not flinch from understanding it as a decision to kill a baby. One of these women, Claire, had been counselling in an abortion clinic and, growing uneasy about her instructions to tell women who wanted to see their aborted babies, "You can't see anything now. It just looks like jelly at this point," decided to look herself, to "face up to what was going on." After that "I just couldn't kid myself anymore and say there was nothing in the uterus, just a speck. This is not true and I knew it wasn't true, but I sort of had to see it." She describes her own decision to have an abortion this way: "Yes, this is killing, there is no way around it, but I am willing to accept that. I am willing to go ahead with it, and it's hard . . . I don't think I can explain it. I don't think I can really verbalize the justification."[11] For Gilligan, then, one only grows spiritually through a moral decision in which one confronts the tragic intractability of the situation one faces.

I have considerable respect for this position and I have no desire to detract from the seriousness and even truth of what Claire is saying here or from her determination to be honest with herself. But when she says, "I have seen too many pictures of babies in trash cans and it is so easy to say, 'Well, either/or' and it just isn't like that," I can't help thinking that neither Claire nor Gilligan are facing up to what has happened in the past when human beings have set out to live by an ideology that links spiritual growth with the strength to decide to kill others. In particular, in spite of many good reasons not to invoke the Holocaust in discussions of abortion, I can't help hearing in Claire's words the echo of a pep talk given by Heinrich Himmler to death camp functionaries on October 3, 1943:

This is one of those things that are easily said. "The Jewish people is going to be annihilated," says every party member . . . Of all those who talk this way, no one has seen it happen, not one has been through it. Most of you know what it means to see a hundred corpses lie side by side, or five hundred or a thousand. To have endured this and to have remained decent . . . In our history this is an unwritten and never to be written page of glory.[12]

I quote from this speech not to close down discussion by invoking guilt by association but in order to open up discussion in the broadest terms possible. The abortion situation differs in many ways from the Holocaust, one of the most important being that abortion is usually done with a different basic intent than the killing of the unborn; another important difference is that abortion is not yet and may never be a compulsory government program. But there is at least one philosophical similarity worth pondering. In both cases, there are those who would justify the taking of human lives by appealing beyond the realm of abstract right and the rule of law (and other trappings of "bloodless," "decadent" liberalism) to the felt needs of the given, organic situation.

There are perhaps gentler ways of making this point. Gilligan's book is about ethics not politics — that is, it is an account of the complexities of human relations and not of the sorts of rules that may be necessary for a minimally decent social life. It may be said, then, that the fact that Gilligan displays little sympathy for or understanding of the importance of purely legal and political structures is not a point against her. However, it is unfortunately impossible for her to remain in the realm of pure ethics. For her position on the ethics of abortion and the imperatives of spiritual growth towards maturity seem to dictate that the legal or political system must refrain from legislating on the subject of abortion in the interests of the higher moral value of human growth towards autonomy. This means one of two things: either the values associated with ethics (e.g., human flourishing and self-realization) take precedence over the values associated with politics and the legal order (i.e., rights, the rule of law and the private-public distinction) or else these latter should come to be seen as a merely liberal account of the concerns of politics which should then be transformed into a concern for the kind of public life that leads to self-realization, etc.

From fairly early in its history, liberalism has been concerned about whether the importance it attaches to enforceable individual rights in the public realm does not tend to undermine precisely the autonomy that these rights are instituted to nurture and protect. This concern appears in a striking way in Kant's philosophy. Even though Kant's account of moral principle is very different from Gilligan's, he is nevertheless like her in stressing that the point of moral action is the achieving of that full human estate which comes when one freely chooses to act out of one's own perception of what is required. This is a major part of what he means by autonomy. But he also recognizes, as Gilligan does not explicitly seem to, an imperative to institutionalize what is required in our treatment of others in a legal, political order. Because he sees this, he is led to worry about the fate of liberalism. In a liberal regime the law requires us to respect the rights of others on pain of punishment. But the more the law demands this from us, the less we are likely to be respecting the rights of others because of our own recognition of this respect as an expression of our inner natures — that is, our autonomy. Liberalism's legal requirement of enforceable rights is in conflict with its moral requirement of personal autonomy. A liberal regime turns out to be a counterfeit, a simulation of moral autonomy in which people are doing the right thing for the wrong reason.

Because even Kant is unable to resolve this dilemma convincingly, it seems to me that the moral to be drawn is that the idea of respect for the individual produces an ineradicable tension between two quite different pulls, which we can call, even though it is an oversimplification, morals and politics, the former demanding that my freedom not be circumscribed by others, the latter necessarily circumscribing it so that my freely chosen acts do not victimize others. The fate of liberalism may well be an endless pendulum swing back and forth between too much law and too little without any clear guidelines as to how much is enough.

But on this basis a fairly good case can be made for limitations on abortion. Gilligan is quite right to say that laws limiting abortion would inhibit autonomy. But Kant is right to say that all law inhibits autonomy; so unless one wishes not to have any laws — and I don't know very many feminists or pro-choicers who do — autonomy is not a sufficient consideration. Giving us all the power of life and death over each other would undoubtedly confront many of us with the tragedy of existence and make us dredge very deeply into our own selves. But to confront us with the tragedy of existence does not, for better or worse, seem to be the function of the political or legal order, at least according to the liberal understanding of it. A liberal does not take it that political relations are meant to express the rich fullness of personal moral relations. That is one of the reasons why liberals tend to distinguish the private from the public realm, the life of thick interaction from the world of thin interaction, and argue that it is one of the jobs of a decent political order to stop us, as far as possible, from doing things we do not have the right to do. These separations are, of course, extremely hard to maintain and in practice there is a good deal of slippage. But it is not entirely useless for abstract theory to keep attempting to bring concrete reality into line. In this context, the dilemma that Gilligan is confronted with is this: the decision to abort or not, cannot function as part of a woman's mature confrontation with moral complexity and ambiguity unless she understands abortion to be the killing of a human being. But the moment she sees it that way a woman of liberal tendencies cannot be content to have it unlimited by law, for liberalism limits the extent to which the lives of others can be included within the sphere of my self-realization. If Gilligan drops her commitment to the humanity of the unborn, all her talk about women bravely looking the hard truth in the face starts to ring rather hollow. Her only alternative is to drop any commitment to the politics of liberalism.

She has not, as far as I know, quite done this, though others, some of them drawing on her work, have. Everywhere in political philosophy at the moment, from Marxism to organicist conservatism, the concept of individual human rights is under attack as a fatally false abstraction that desiccates human relations and reduces public life within the community to the shallowest possible formalities.[13] In this context the push for abortion rights can be seen as one part of a move to downgrade individuals in order to enrich the idea of relationships, of which women are said to have a special understanding. The irony is that in the first flush of feminism women objected to song lyrics like, "You're nobody 'til somebody loves you," because liberalism (and for that matter, I would argue, classical thought and the religious tradition) held that you were somebody whether any other human being loved you or not, and women wanted to share in that sense of being someone in their own right. The current tide, including that of feminism, is flowing strongly and frighteningly in the direction of saying that, after all, one *does* become a person, a somebody, only by entering a relation with someone else, so that it is entirely natural that one's fate should depend on just what that relation happens to be. I hope that thoughtful women (and men) will soon find themselves disenchanted with this trendy organicism, will discover that there is no way to justify the denial of the unborn child's humanity and will find themselves forced to acknowledge that the claims for basic protection of unborn life make a good deal of sense after all. They will then, again I hope, be led to restore a conception of maturity which includes the ability to live within the limits of laws that protect others as we would expect them to protect us.

I have done little more here than survey the work of a number of basically pro-choice feminists who have been honest enough to find themselves moving more and more in the course of time towards the acknowledgment of some kind of status within the human race for the unborn child. Their search for ways to combine this acknowledgment with a continued commitment to the pro-choice position leads them sometimes to press liberalism very hard, trying, for example, to show that it might give the right to evacuation of the womb precedence over the prohibition of killing the fetus. Or else it leads them to flirt with illiberal accounts of the relations between human beings which, I have suggested, contain some moral truth, but are disastrous as accounts of the political and legal aspects of moral life. But there are many other things I have not touched on: further dilemmas that come out of reproductive technologies, further reasons for seeing the unborn as having human status, questions touching on the peculiarities of the jurisprudence in the various Morgentaler trials and the question of what a reasonable set of restrictions on abortion might be.[14]

Perhaps the best way to end is by going back to Claire for a minute. I can imagine Claire some day saying to me, "Yes, Sam, I know I'm killing you, there's no way around it, but I'm willing to accept that." I hope that there's still someone around at that point to wonder whether I'm as willing to accept it as Claire is.

II

THE MEDICAL AND SOCIAL
CONSEQUENCES OF ABORTION

H E A T H E R   M O R R I S

THE PATIENT
BEFORE BIRTH

A GENERATION AGO, the developing baby in its intrauterine habitat was essentially an unknown being, inviolate and minimally observed by those responsible for the care of the pregnant woman. During the past two decades, intimate knowledge of the fetus and its environment has accumulated. Williams' *Obstetrics* — a widely used, standard textbook — states that "the foetus is no longer dealt with as a maternal appendage ultimately to be shed at the whim of biological forces beyond control. Instead the foetus has achieved the status of a second patient."[1] It is a strange paradox that advances in diagnosis and treatment have clearly established the fetus as a patient during an era when the developing infant is accorded diminishing legal recognition and moral respect. A physician establishes a relationship with a patient, seeks to make a diagnosis of that patient's condition of health or disease and treats him or her accordingly. The obstetrician's relationship with the fetus is not different. Genetic makeup and environmental factors affect the health and welfare of all individuals. We, in turn, influence our environment. This is equally true of the developing human still within the uterus of its mother.

In the natural order, one of the numerous eggs present in the human female ovary since the fourth month of intrauterine development will be released every month for her entire reproductive life. A new human life begins when that egg is fertilized by a sperm, one of millions deposited into the vagina during intercourse. The meeting usually takes place in the Fallopian tube. At that time the genetic makeup of the conceived individual is forever fixed. Repeated cell divisions result in the formation of a ball of cells, each cell carrying that genetic uniqueness. Even as this blastula is embedding into the wall of the uterus, chemicals produced by the conceptus (fertilized ovum) are detectable in the maternal blood. A diagnosis of pregnancy can be established before a period has been missed. Normally, the small being is housed in the appropriate intrauterine environment, but it can become delayed in its travel, developing instead in the Fallopian tube. As early as the fourth or fifth week of pregnancy age — that is, two to three weeks after conception — a gestational sac can be detected in the uterus by ultrasonography,[2] confirming that the blastula is in the normal position.

In this safe environment, receiving nourishment both from within the conceptus and from the uterus, development proceeds. The tissue which later forms the placenta differentiates, as do the various organs and systems of the human being. Limbs, heart and brain are formed; bones, bowel and bladder, eyes, ears, nose and mouth are all completed before the being is three months old. These events take place according to an orderly, predetermined sequence. Movement occurs as the nervous system develops and motivates the muscles of limbs formed in space and time. To provide the blood circulation that organs and systems need to survive, the heart begins beating. The diagnosis of a living embryo can be made by ultrasound detection of a heartbeat at six weeks, although science tells us that the pulsation starts two or three weeks earlier, twenty-one days after conception.

Within the first three months of this young life, diagnostic tools other than ultrasonography can be used to observe its

welfare. Its genetic makeup may be subject to scrutiny, particu\
larly if the parents have histories of inherited disease or if the\
mother is in the latter years of childbearing, as chromosomal
abnormality has been statistically demonstrated in mothers of
increasing age. Through the process of chorionic villus sampling, deviations from genetic normality may be detected.[3]

That part of the chorion, later the placenta, which is formed
from the conceptus and is identical in genetic makeup to the
fetus, is sampled. The cells are obtained and cultivated, and
when growing, they are examined for their chromosomal
makeup. The sex of the developing human being is determined
and a young embryo with Down's syndrome may be identified.
We may wish that this genetic detection technology were used
to make life-sustaining diagnoses, but at present it is almost
always used for the opposite purpose. Even healthy human
beings of the "unwanted" sex (usually female) may be condemned to death, thanks to this technology. At no other time
in medicine has the establishment of a diagnosis of physical
perfection or imperfection led to the pronouncement of a death
sentence by a fellow human.

In the first half of the twentieth century, prenatal care was
directed solely at maintaining the health of the pregnant
woman. Examination of the fetus was confined to measuring its
growth by assessing the size of the pregnant uterus, ascertaining
in the second half of the pregnancy the position in which the
fetus was lying and listening with a trumpet-like device, the
fetoscope, to the heart of the developing baby. Today, the
intrauterine environment of the embryo or fetus is of para-
mount concern for the obstetrician, as it is now known that the
developing human is highly susceptible to the introduction of
noxious factors into that environment. Most pregnant women
know that cigarette smoking is harmful, that it retards the
growth of the developing baby and many pregnant women who
smoke will strive to reject the habit. It is also known that
although prescription medications may be necessary, alcohol,
street drugs and over-the-counter medications taken by the
pregnant woman can adversely affect the environment in which
the fetus grows and develops. This knowledge is so widely

accepted that more than one pregnant woman has been admitted to hospital or taken into protective custody on the grounds that her behavior constitutes child abuse in providing a hostile environment for her baby's growth and development.

We know that certain viruses are particularly hostile to the fetus. Rubella, the virus that causes German measles if contracted by the pregnant woman, especially in the first three months of pregnancy, will result in a significant possibility of damage to the young intrauterine human being. The virus poses risks of heart deformity, deafness, blindness and other abnormalities. In Canada, an immunization program has been set up for children and for women before pregnancy, so that developing humans will not contract this infection.

In the fourth month, the human being passes from the so-called embryonic phase, during which time its organs and systems have been formed, to the growth and maturing period of its intrauterine life, known as the fetal phase. Early in this phase, the fetal heart can be heard in the physician's office through a simple device, the doptone. The moment of hearing the rapid pulsation of life is a time of great joy and excitement for the pregnant woman. Several weeks later, she may feel her baby kicking. An ultrasound picture of this baby, usually taken between sixteen and twenty weeks, will reveal a human being moving his limbs, sucking his thumb, swallowing and urinating. The stomach, bladder and kidneys may be visible, along with a well-formed head, face, back and limbs.[4] His size is appropriate for the stage of life that he has reached. His sex may be revealed or he may lie bashfully with his legs together. The amount of fluid around him will either indicate well-being or alert us to a medical problem. Too much fluid now or later in the pregnancy may mean that the developing human cannot swallow or that the upper bowel is blocked. The intrauterine environment may contain too much sugar if, for instance, his mother's diabetes is not well controlled. Too little fluid may mean that his kidneys are not functioning or that he cannot urinate because there is a blockage from his bladder to the "outside." If so, his bladder will be much larger than normal.

This last condition was one of the first to be treated by fetal surgery.[5] If untreated, the urine in the bladder will "back up" and the pressure will destroy the baby's kidneys. Relief of this condition may be obtained by inserting a plastic tube through a needle which penetrates the wall of the mother's abdomen, uterus and the baby's abdomen into the bladder. After the needle has been removed, the plastic tube curls up and stays in place in the uterus, thus enabling the urine to drain into the amniotic fluid around the baby where it belongs. Some babies are saved by this procedure. The greatest difficulty is that the diagnosis may be made too late and the damage may therefore be too great. If the baby is far enough along in its intrauterine development, it may be delivered, on the assumption that it will have a better chance of survival in the outside world.

Another abnormal condition that involves too much fluid in one place is hydrocephalus. In this case, there is too much fluid in the brain cavity, which can destroy brain tissue, especially the cerebral cortex.[6] If the developing baby is too immature for delivery, this fluid can be aspirated with a needle placed in position using ultrasonographic vision. The success of this treatment is limited, however, because it is difficult to establish a diagnosis soon enough.

An ever-increasing number of diagnostic procedures is available to ascertain the well-being of the developing baby. The late Professor Liley, who, appropriately, has been called the "father of fetology" recognized that the degree of destruction of Rhesus positive blood of the baby carried by a Rhesus negative mother was reflected by the breakdown product, bilirubin, in the amniotic fluid. By sampling this fluid at intervals during the pregnancy and by looking for evidence of heart failure in the baby, he was able to determine which babies needed blood transfusions in utero. He carried out the first of these blood transfusions by placing the blood into the abdomen of the fetus from whence it was absorbed.[7] Today, with more sophisticated ultrasound, this transfusion can be carried out by placing the transfusion needle directly into the vessels of the umbilical cord.[8] In other babies, blood may be taken from this cord to make diagnoses of health or life-threatening conditions, including sickle cell anemia and metabolic diseases.

Amniotic fluid sampling is carried out for many reasons, not all of them life-sustaining. At sixteen to eighteen weeks, amniocentesis may be performed to determine the genetic makeup of the baby. The cells that are shed from the baby's skin into the fluid are cultivated and chromosomes are examined. Chemicals found in the fluid may also be measured. If abnormal substances are detected, indicating a problem in the baby's metabolism, treatment may consist of removing potential poisoning substances from the mother's diet or giving her extra vitamins.[9]

Alpha feto protein is one of the chemicals that can be measured. It exists at elevated levels in babies with open neural tube defects such as spina bifida or anencephaly. Low levels indicate other conditions, such as Down's syndrome. Alpha feto protein levels are also reflected in a mother's blood and can be measured by a simple screening test — maternal serum AFP — at sixteen to eighteen weeks.

In another procedure, a special telescope called a fetoscope is placed into the uterus to observe the fetus and the color of the amniotic fluid. Abnormality in either of these may be an indication of distress.[10] Although only tiny portions of the fetus can be observed at any one time, the combined observations may be enough to establish a diagnosis, particularly one concerning abnormal skin or limb conditions. However, fetoscopy may result in accidental rupture of the membranes or premature labor. By comparison, amniocentesis and chorionic villus sampling cause unplanned miscarriages less often and the ultrasound procedure is remarkably safe for both mother and child.

Some fetal conditions, such as anencephaly, are incompatible with sustained life outside the uterus. Many other conditions, while not life threatening, indicate a degree of permanent disadvantage, physical or mental. In a world where only the perfect and the planned can expect birth in due time, a diagnosis of imperfection may lead to a death sentence. For others, happily, there is treatment and a full life. Through ultrasonography, fetal heart problems may be detected by direct observation or by discovering extra fluid in the baby, which may indicate heart failure.

A special procedure, fetal echocardiography is used to delineate the nature of the problem. Abnormal heart rhythms and rates may be treated by drugs such as digoxin. These may be administered to the mother for transmission across the placenta to the baby, or they may be injected into the fetal abdomen and absorbed into the circulation. The heart thus receives much needed medicine.

As the expectant mother enters the last trimester of pregnancy, a fetus that is structurally normal may nevertheless be threatened. Maternal high blood pressure, severe kidney disease and diabetes are among the diseases that can compromise the functioning of the placenta, as can its structural abnormalities. Such conditions can jeopardize fetal well-being. To determine the status of the fetal heart at this stage, the doctor uses a doppler device. Ultrasonographic observation of the amount of amniotic fluid, of the size of the fetus, of fetal stretching, breathing and movement, and of the state of the placenta can indicate distress of the baby in the uterus. This detailed biophysical profile gives guidance as to the timing of delivery and may be truly life-saving. Decisions may be based on observation of the amniotic fluid.[11] A specimen of amniotic fluid might reveal, for instance, that the fetal lungs are too immature for easy breathing, even though the time for delivery is at hand. A steroid medication may then be administered to the mother to aid fetal lung maturation.

In recent years, the fetus as a patient is often threatened, especially in the first half of the pregnancy. Sophisticated diagnostic procedures frequently lead not to treatment but to instigated death by abortion of the less-than-perfect.

This situation is ironical, given current developments in antenatal care, which are based on a recognition of the fetus as patient and which emphasize the effect of the intrauterine and external environments on that patient. While some medical technology is being used to extend and preserve the lives of the wanted and the well, patients who are undesirable or unhealthy are condemned to death by the use of other medical technology. Is the fetus as patient not a member of the human family? Is the welfare of the unborn child not included in the physician's pledge, "Above all, do no harm"?

HEATHER MORRIS,
LORRAINE WILLIAMS

PHYSICAL COMPLICATIONS OF ABORTION

ONE OF THE MOST comprehensive examinations of the physical consequences of induced abortion performed in hospital settings using sophisticated medical techniques was produced in 1972 by Margaret and Arthur Wynn. Presented to Britain's Lane Committee on the Working of the Abortion Act, the Wynn Report was a well-documented and sobering look at the impact of abortion on women's health and, in particular, on their future childbearing capacities.[1]

Since that time, there has been much speculation as to how these earlier findings have held up. Some have wondered if they were "scare tactics" employed to deter women from seeking abortions and whether further developments in diagnostic and treatment methods have resulted in the elimination of physical complications after abortion.

Worthy of consideration in this context is the "West Jerusalem Study," published in 1975. It presented careful research on 11,057 pregnancies, 752 of which involved mothers who had previously had induced abortions. The findings of this study confirmed those in the Wynn Report. Induced abortion has serious repercussions on both the woman and any subsequent children. They reported that

the 752 mothers . . . were more likely . . . to report bleeding in each of the first three months of the present pregnancy. They were subsequently less able to have a normal delivery and more of them needed a manual removal of the placenta or other intervention in the third stage of labor. In births following induced abortions, the relative risk of early neonatal deaths showed a 3-to-4 fold increase. There was a significant increase in the frequency of low birthweight, compared to births in which there was no history of induced abortions.

The researchers concluded by saying that "a disturbing finding in this study [was] the excess of malformations in the births following induced abortion."[2]

CURRENT FINDINGS

Medical evidence in the late 1970s and early 1980s indicates two trends: the existence of the same kinds of complications documented in the earlier reports, and the discovery of new types of complications, as patient histories continue to be compiled. In the April 1985 number of the *British Journal of Obstetrics and Gynaecology*, Frank, Kay et al. concluded:

Changes have occurred so quickly in public and professional attitudes and practices that many issues once thought to be important no longer seem so, whilst the widespread use of abortion has revealed problems and posed new questions which were not, and could not have been answered at an earlier date.[3]

In the 1982 edition of the *Cumulated Index Medicus*, there are thirty-three entries under the titles Induced Abortion, Adverse Effects; Legal Abortions, Adverse Effects; and Therapeutic Abortions, Adverse Effects. The 1984 *Index* lists thirty-six entries and the 1985 edition lists twenty-eight. Some of the papers deal with isolated cases, but most study several hundreds or thousands of patients, so that, while percentages of physical complications may be small, valid conclusions can be drawn from the overall number of cases. Many medical reports about induced abortions in the late 1980s have focused on methods to achieve easier, safer early abortions. Researchers report on the use of laminaria, a substance that facilitates cervical dilatation, and on chemical abortifacients, including intravaginal and intracervical prostaglandins and R.U. 486, a progesterone antagonist. Cameron et al in Scotland indicate that the efficiency of R.U. 486 in producing a complete abortion before the eighth week of pregnancy is 60 percent.[4] Couzinet et al in France report an 85 percent efficacy. Without the addition of prostaglandin they note that 22 percent of women experience significant nausea, 18 percent bleed heavily and 26 percent report significant pain.[5] The addition of prostaglandin increases the rate of abortion but also markedly increases side effects with vomiting in 23 percent and diarrhea in 33 percent.[6]

SERIOUSNESS COMPLICATIONS

A 1985 Joint Study of the Royal College of General Practitioners and the Royal College of Obstetricians and Gynaecologists dealt with a group of 6,015 women undergoing induced abortion. It was found that 10 percent of them suffered ill effects related to the procedure, of which one-fifth (2 percent) was considered to be major.[7]

An American study stated that "although induced abortion is a relatively safe procedure, the potential for complications is a major public health concern." This study found that, of 82,030 women who obtained abortions at less than twenty-four weeks' gestation, 342 (or 0.4 percent) had serious complications. These included 130 with fever lasting three or more days, 172 who required transfusions, 67 who required surgery and 3 who died.[8] A Vermont study of 2,458 first-trimester abortions disclosed an overall complication rate of 2.9 percent.[9]

As the authors of the Vermont study acknowledge, a short-coming of their, and presumably of all such studies is that they miss complications occurring after the patient has been discharged and for which it is possible that "some women sought treatment for serious complications at facilities other than the abortion facilities and that these complications were not reported."[10] Frank et al. underline the same point: "The underreporting of early miscarriage [after induced abortion] mentioned by several authors (Schoenbaum et al., 1982; Chung et al., 1981) cannot be eliminated . . . Early miscarriages are more likely to be reported to the family doctor than to other health service agencies."[11]

Possibly the most significant of the abortion complications are the serious effects on women's reproductive ability. The incidence of ectopic pregnancy, for example, is severely aggravated by abortion. In a Hawaiian study it was found that 3 percent of women who had had their first pregnancy terminated had contracted postabortion infections and had five times the risk of experiencing subsequent ectopic pregnancy.[12] Levin and Schoenbaum's study concurred with these findings.[13] This statistic is worth noting because even as late as 1978, 12 percent of all maternal deaths were still due to ectopic pregnancy.[14]

In a U.S. study, women who were hospitalized for ectopic pregnancy in five hospitals were interviewed concerning history of induced abortion. For comparison, women who had delivered a live-born child during this same time period were also interviewed. Relative to women who had never undergone an abortion, the risk in those who had "was increased to a modest degree," although the rate was not as high as that found in the aforementioned studies when the women had had only one previous abortion. Those women who had had two or more previous abortions, however, risked ectopic pregnancies to a degree that was "worrisome."[15]

Noting that "the association of cervical pregnancy and induced abortion . . . is well documented," Dicker et al., describe five cases of cervical pregnancy treated with hysterectomy. In all of these cases, induced abortion preceded cervical pregnancy. The clinician, they conclude, "must be aware of [the] association [of cervical pregnancy] with previous iatrogenic intervention, such as induced abortion. . . ."[16]

Workers in Copenhagen in 1986[17] were concerned about the significant risk of infection at the time of a first-trimester induced abortion. The prophylactic use of antibiotics in these circumstances reduced the risk of pelvic inflammatory disease from 11 percent to 5 percent. In patients who had a prior history of pelvic inflammatory disease antibiotics reduced the incidence of postabortal recurrence from 22 percent to 2 percent. Pelvic infection is a serious, not infrequent complication of induced abortion and a common cause of subsequent involuntary infertility.

Spontaneous abortions are one of the effects of first-trimester abortions. One New York study unequivocally demonstrated that women whose first pregnancies were terminated are 3.4 times more likely than those whose first pregnancy resulted in a live birth to have a midtrimester spontaneous abortion during their second pregnancy. (It should be noted that most of these women underwent abortions using the dilation and curettage technique.)[18]

Spontaneous abortion is often associated with cervical incompetence, which can result from dilation and curettage procedures. The Australian experience with abortion has documented the presence of complications in over 75 percent of women who had forced dilation of the cervix, either to induce abortion or to evacuate the retained products of conception.[19] Schulz and his fellow researchers report that in a study of 15,438 women who had suction curettage at about twelve weeks or less from 1975 to 1978, cervical injuries requiring suturing occurred in approximately one out of a hundred abortions.[20]

U.S. hospitals have found that cervical injury during first-trimester abortions can be reduced by the use of laminaria. They also reported that women to whom general anesthesia was administered ran half the risk of women who received local anesthesia. It was also discovered that women who had abortions performed by resident specialists in training had twice the risk of cervical injury compared with women on whom the procedure was carried out by fully trained physicians. In addition, women who were under seventeen ran twice as much risk of cervical injury as women eighteen and older.[21]

REPRODUCTIVE CONSEQUENCES

University of Glasgow researchers Pickering and Forbes have stated that "the possible risk to reproductive outcome after abortion is clearly an important issue." Basing their study on an analysis of hospital records, they concluded that women with one previous termination showed significantly increased risk of pre-term delivery. Furthermore, they said, for women aged twenty-five to thirty-four years, one induced abortion was associated with a significantly higher risk of having a small-for-gestational-age infant when compared with women with one live birth.[22] Frank and Kay's 1985 report on a long-term study of the effects of induced abortion concluded that "the results of the present study indicate a consistent increase in the relative risk of adverse outcome in the pregnancy following an abortion."[23]

THE TEENAGER AS ABORTION PATIENT

Research indicates that the most serious impact of abortion with regard to future reproductive health is among adolescents. In a study by A. Wadhera, head of the Therapeutic Abortion Unit in the Health Division of Statistics Canada, complications from abortions were found to be distributed as follows.

From 1974 to 1978, teens underwent 84,039 (30.9 percent) of 271,779 legal abortions performed in Canada, with the numbers increasing yearly. Of these, 13 percent were under sixteen years old, 38 percent were sixteen to seventeen and 49 percent were eighteen to nineteen years old. The complications were listed as: retained products of conception (69 percent); laceration of the cervix (12 percent); hemorrhage (8 percent); infection (7 percent); perforation of the uterus and other complications (4 percent). Wadhera attributes the high rate of complications (4.1 per 100) in teens to the fact that more than 25 percent of them were twelve weeks pregnant or more at the time of the abortion.[24]

Cates reports that although teens had a significantly lower rate of complications from saline induction abortion after twelve weeks' gestation than older women, they still experience the three most common complications from dilation and evacuation abortions: a fever of three or more days' duration, transfusion and unintended surgery. The authors then warn, "These complications cause concern, because cervical injury in initial unplanned pregnancies may predispose young women to adverse outcomes in future planned pregnancies." In spite of the fact that abortion puts a teenager at greater risk of having complications in future pregnancies, the concluding part of this particular study offers this advice: "What should a teenager with an unplanned pregnancy be told about the medical risks of legally induced abortion? If she elects to abort her pregnancy, she is at no higher risk than an older woman of having a serious complication, and she is at lower risk of death. Thus abortions in teenagers appear to be safer than abortions in older women."[25]

MAJOR COMPLICATIONS AND DEATH

The truly irreversible complication of abortion is the death of the mother. In the United States alone, from 1972 to 1981, inclusive, there were 175 maternal deaths caused by legal abortions, not including deaths from ectopic pregnancies. In contrast, from 1975 to 1979, there were approximately seventeen deaths from illegal abortions, although the numbers of such abortions are hard to estimate.[26]

What causes these deaths after legal abortions? Dr. David Grimes states that, from 1972 to 1979, the most frequent causes were infection, complications of anesthesia or analgesia, and hemorrhage.[27] A 1986 U.S. study identifies the major causes of death related to abortion as infection (23 percent), embolism or blood clot (23 percent), hemorrhage (20 percent) and complications of anesthesia (16 percent).[28] Other studies refer to death due to prostaglandin injection (for the purpose of inducing premature labor),[29] and amniotic fluid embolisms.[30] In reference to other drugs such as oxytocin, sparteine sulphate, ergot derivatives and quinine, all of which can induce uterine contractions, Castadot asserts that "some can create life-threatening situations."[31]

Grimes says, "Little is known about why deaths from hemorrhage occur despite safeguards. It is particularly associated with curettage abortions. Lack of postoperative monitoring was blamed as a cause of death from hemorrhagic shock."[32] He warns that freestanding abortion clinics often do not have the capacity for rapid transportation to a nearby well-equipped hospital in the case of complications: "Inordinate delays while waiting for the ambulance contributed to several deaths." Women who sustained a uterine perforation or rupture were over one thousand times more likely to die from hemorrhage than those who did not.

Mittal and Misra, in a study of uterine perforation following vacuum aspiration published in the *International Journal of Gynaecology and Obstetrics* in 1985, observed that perforation of the uterus is a rare complication of medical termination of pregnancy (MTP) if the physician is well trained and the vacuum aspiration method is used. However, it is "the most serious complication and is associated with much agony to the patient." The authors go on to say that uterine perforation is, nonetheless, a well-recognized complication of MTP, regardless of technique, and that they had found a higher incidence of perforation if MTP was performed after a recent birth or on a patient with a retroverted uterus.[33]

Even hemorrhages that are not fatal may entail severe blood loss. For instance, a report in 1984 showed that the estimate of blood loss in second-trimester dilation and evacuation was as follows. In 27 out of 215 patients, blood loss was between 301 and 500 grams. In 20 of those 215, blood loss was *greater* than 500 grams.[34]

The death rate due to legal abortion on teenagers was 1.3 per 100,000, compared with 2.9 per 100,000 for women over thirty. The cause of death from abortion in teens is most often infection, whereas in older women death more commonly results from embolic events.[35] Buehler et al., conclude that " . . . older women with advanced gestational age, and parous women [those who have borne children] are at increased risk for serious complications shortly after abortions. . . . Awareness of these findings should lead to increased attention to the counselling and management of patients who have an increased risk status."[36]

OTHER TYPES OF COMPLICATIONS

This report emphasizes the major complications from legal abortion. There are, however, increasing numbers of papers reporting other problems, such as an increase in menstrual symptoms among women who have had induced abortions.[37] More serious are indications that "an induced abortion in the absence of having a live birth shows some elevation of risk" for breast cancer.[38] As more information accumulates about the troubled outcome of subsequent pregnancies after a previous pregnancy has been aborted, abortion is coming to be recognized as one of the contributing factors to the increasing number of birth defects found in newborns over the past few years.[39]

In comparisons of complication rates in abortions performed by physician assistants with those in abortions performed by physicians in Vermont, the most frequently observed immediate complication was incomplete abortion (40 percent) in both early uterine evacuation and suction curettage procedures. The most frequently observed delayed complication in suction curettage procedures was infection, which accounted for two-thirds of these complications. Uterine hemorrhage, retained products of conception and infection were the most common delayed complications in the early uterine evacuation procedure, together accounting for almost all (96 percent) of these delayed complications.[40]

One of the most unusual "complications" is a "continued pregnancy." In 1978, Waldo Fielding did a study which demonstrated that out of every 1,400 first-term abortions, one pregnancy was not successfully terminated.[41] A more recent study puts the incidence at 2.3 failed abortions per 1,000 performed.[42] By encouraging better follow-up procedures with abortion patients, Fielding says that some success can be attained in "eradicating the unsuccessful induced abortion complication." However, most of the studies show that approximately one-third of all abortion patients do not return for follow-up visits. One supposes that these pregnancies either become acceptable or are aborted elsewhere during the second trimester.

Physical complications from abortions done in legal settings are multiple and, in many cases, severe, but it is difficult to assess the full picture, since follow-up attendance is poor for postabortion patients. In some cases, there is a tendency for medical practitioners to make the decision for the patient about whether the risks are worthwhile. For example, Harlap and Davies write,

> For the unmarried woman, the very young and the poor, the small increased risk for subsequent pregnancies is likely to be outweighed by the undesirable consequences of letting the pregnancy continue. The well-off married woman, however, who wants to postpone her first birth or to space her children, may not be willing to take the risk of death or haemorrhage to a later, wanted child.[43]

What is unknown is how many medical practitioners communicate knowledge of this risk to the abortion seeker. Castadot says, "Like any other surgical procedure, vacuum D and C and D and E present a number of risks of complications; these should be both kept in mind and shared with the patient to give substance to her informed consent."[44] It is difficult to think of any other procedure where this kind of information with regard to risks, both short-term and long-term, is not fully shared with the patient.

Conclusion

Despite the continuing development of techniques in induced

abortion procedure, physical complications stemming from it continue to be documented by researchers. Two major studies — one American and one British — found that the overall rate of major or serious complications ranged from 0.4 percent to 2 percent. This rate may be even higher, however, as the researchers note that patients experiencing postabortion complications do not necessarily return to the agency where they underwent the abortion.

This problem is likely to be accentuated in the United States, where a high proportion of abortions is carried out in abortion clinics. Such clinics offer extremely limited and, in many cases no, follow-up service. Researchers also warn that many complications linked to a previous abortion which occur around future pregnancies — particularly early miscarriages — are underreported. This may be due to the time lapse between such miscarriage and the abortion, and also to the fact that the miscarriage may be reported to the patient's personal physician but not to the health service agency where the abortion was performed.

Finally, it should be noted that physical complications of induced abortion fall into several well-defined groups. Medical practitioners have particular concern about the impact of abortion on the patient's capacity for future childbearing. Such capacity can be seriously affected by ectopic pregnancy, spontaneous abortion, premature delivery and difficulties at the time of delivery. Maternal death, while rare, is still a documented event, with fatal hemorrhage, embolism or infection as the usual causes.

L. L. DE VEBER, MARY PARTHUN,
DOROTHY CHISHOLM AND ANNE KISS

ABORTION AND
BEREAVEMENT

A GROWING BODY of literature suggests that grief and a sense of bereavement after induced abortion are more common, more intense and more prolonged than is generally suspected. While it may be that only a small percentage of women experience severe distress following abortion, it would nevertheless seem that we face a community problem of significant proportions. There are more than 80,000 induced abortions in Canada annually.[1]

In this article we review recent attempts to describe the psychological consequences of abortion for women and to determine the size of the problem. We suggest that although most reports to date are flawed, the difficulties researchers experience in addressing the effects of abortion are themselves revealing. For the most part, studies have tended, perhaps understandably, to focus on the woman's immediate circumstances and reactions. Recently, however, physicians and counsellors have begun to test the idea that reactions to the abortion experience may be deeply buried, surfacing months or years after the event, perhaps when the woman gets married, carries another child to term or seeks counselling for apparently unrelated problems such as drug abuse or marriage difficulties.[2]

We argue that a helpful understanding of abortion-related distress emerges when it is described in terms of Post Traumatic Stress Disorder, the syndrome recognized by the psychiatric profession as the long-term reaction found in veterans of the Vietnam War.[3]

HOW MANY WOMEN ARE AT RISK?

Using Danish health records, H. P. David, N. Rasmussen and E. Holst compared rates of admission to psychiatric hospitals for some 27,000 women who had had abortions, with 72,000 who had carried to term, during a three-month period after the procedure or birth.[4] Women with an admission during the fifteen months prior to the delivery or birth were excluded. In the postabortion group there were 18 admissions per 10,000 and in the postpartum group, 12 per 10,000, suggesting that post-abortion women are significantly more likely to suffer psychological problems. The sheer size of the samples in this study commands respect. A recent review of some 300 reports on the psychological after-effects of abortion found that of David et al. to be the best-conducted.[5]

The Danish results stand in sharp contrast to a British comparison of postabortion and postpartum women that found a significantly higher rate of admission to psychiatric hospitals in the postpartum sample (17 admissions per 10,000 for the postpartum women; 3 per 10,000 for the postabortion group).[6] However, whereas the Danish study used computerized health records, the British relied upon lists of admissions compiled at the researcher's request by psychiatric consultants. At least one commentator has suggested that this method admitted an unacceptably high subjective element.[7]

A Canadian comparison of postpartum and postabortive women that relied on interviews found that abortion patients exhibited "poorer psychological adjustment" than maternity patients, immediately after the procedure and at a four-week follow-up.[8] But, the overall tone of the Canadian study suggests that the authors, D. Gold, C. Berger and C. Andres, wished to assure women of the safety of abortion. They concluded, for example, that "abortion does not cause any psychological damage to the majority of women who have had an abortion."[9] Their own findings and, indeed, the very reference to a psychologically undamaged "majority" do much to suggest, however, that a number of women are psychologically damaged by the abortion experience.

Other Canadian studies bear out the idea that induced abortion has adverse psychological effects on a number of women. A Saskatchewan review of the use of health services one year before and one year after pregnancy-related events (including deliveries, spontaneous abortions, induced abortions and sterilizations) found that postabortive women were diagnosed by their physicians 40.8 percent more often than postpartum women for accidents or conditions relating to violence.[10] Women in the postabortive sample subsequently consulted physicians twice as often as the postpartum women, often for reasons related to mental health. A five-year study in Alberta comparing postabortive women with women in general showed a significantly greater use of medical and psychiatric services in the postabortive sample.[11] Twenty-five percent of women who had had induced abortions made visits to psychiatrists, in contrast to 3 percent in the comparison group.

The fact remains that induced abortion is still widely regarded as having no significant adverse psychological effects. Studies have often been carried out poorly with the result that observers have little confidence in well-conducted studies like the Danish one by David et al. The Surgeon-General of the United States argued recently that it is impossible to say from the available evidence whether abortion does or does not have an adverse effect on a woman's psychological health.[12] Poor selection of subjects, high numbers of drop-outs, inadequate controls and the failure to use reliable assessment measures are common.[13] The Canadian study by Gold, Berger and Andres, for example, was noticeably handicapped by noncompliance in the postabortion group. At the four-month interview, the postabortive sample had shrunk to 16 percent of its original size. One commentator on the Gold et al. report points out that there is no reason to suppose that the remaining postabortive subjects were representative of the original group, let alone, as the authors claimed, representative of "the majority of women who have had an abortion."[14]

More than one observer notes that studies are typically deficient in that they ignore the possibility of long-term effects.[15] Others criticize reliance upon questionnaires and single interviews, arguing that these methods may not reveal deep-seated psychological or psychiatric problems.[16] Among Canadian researchers, Ian Kent in particular is dubious about the merit of short-term studies and the use of survey techniques.[17] Another possible source of bias — one that is perhaps obvious — is that physicians may be reluctant to recognize that a "therapeutic" process can have a damaging effect.[18]

What leads observers to think that there may be deep-seated, long-term reactions to the abortion experience are a multitude of observations and group studies, all admittedly less than satisfactory in terms of strict research design, but nevertheless thought provoking. Very often these small-scale studies contain the very element that is missing in the large projects; they examine reactions over years and probe for after-effects in a variety of behavior and symptom areas. By studying fifty postabortive women in psychotherapy, Kent et al. found that although none had entered therapy because of adverse emotional reactions to abortion, they expressed deep feelings of pain and bereavement about the abortion as the treatment continued.[19] They were struck above all by the fact that the bereavement response emerged typically during the patient's recovery period, when the symptoms of the presenting problem had largely disappeared.

Administering a questionnaire on their abortion experience to seventy-two postabortive women who were not in therapy, Kent et al. found that, in contrast to the fifty women of their therapy sample, these women expressed a marked absence of affect. They concluded that the initial reaction to abortion is likely to be numbness or relief and that only therapy uncovers the true picture.

In a handbook for mental health practitioners, W. J. Warden argues that "abortion is one of those unspeakable losses that people would rather forget" and suggests that although "the surface experience after an abortion is generally one of relief . . . a woman who does not mourn the loss may experience the grief in some subsequent loss."[20] Counsellors agree: a typical immediate response is emotional numbing; distress may surface only after months or years.[21] Such a case is described by J. O. Cavenar et al.: a woman whose bizarre behavior, crying spells, inability to sleep and bulimia were, in part, a reaction to an abortion that had taken place twenty-one years before.[22] Her delayed reaction appears to have been occasioned by the fact that she was reaching the end of her childbearing years. M. Parthun and A. Kiss point out that studies conducted by abortion practitioners may be unsatisfactory because they tend to be concerned with the immediate crisis; their observations about women's reactions are necessarily short-term.[23] When distress does surface, the woman is likely to seek help from another agency entirely, making it more probable that the connection between trauma and symptoms will be obscured. In any event, Parthun and Kiss note that a woman unhappy about her abortion is not likely to be forthcoming with interviewers associated with the physicians who performed the abortion.

Another reason why short-term interviews with postabortive women may not turn up evidence of distress is offered by A. Speckhard. She argues that most women attempt to keep the fact of their abortion secret. In her sample, some 89 percent tried to hide the fact of the abortion or to minimize it.[24] The Surgeon-General of the United States, comparing survey results with official statistics, concludes that "50 percent of women who have had an abortion apparently deny having had one."[25] Others note that abortion is still viewed as a deviant act and is not freely discussed in society.[26] Some researchers put considerable emphasis on the idea that women may even hide the abortion from themselves. Clinical practitioners in particular describe denial as significant. Cavenar and other observers report that women may exhibit symptoms of distress on the anniversary of the expected delivery date or on the anniversary of the procedure.[27] Speckhard notes that women express surprise at the intensity of the grief uncovered by therapy.[28]

WHO IS VULNERABLE?

M. K. Zimmerman argues that research on the psychological effects has moved from the general question of whether abortion is psychologically damaging to identifying women at risk.[29] It might be closer to the truth to say that, although there is no consensus about the magnitude of the problem, there is considerable agreement about who is more likely to suffer adverse effects. It is worth noting that the groups considered most at risk in the professional literature are precisely those whom the public tends to view as most in need of abortion as therapy.

Women with a history of psychiatric disorders are clearly at risk. An editorial in the *British Medical Journal* points out that seriously disturbed patients, "who may appear to have *prima facie* grounds for abortion for psychiatric reasons," are likely to suffer serious psychological consequences.[30] A World Health Organization report of 1970 noted the same effect.[31] To put this in perspective, it should be said that observers have found evidence of postabortive psychotic reactions among women with no previous history of trouble.[32] J. R. Ashton found that, in a sample of sixty-four women assessed eight weeks after induced abortion, 5 percent had "enduring" psychiatric symptoms.[33] He concludes that women with a previous psychiatric or abnormal obstetrical history, those with only physical grounds for abortion (not emotional or social grounds) and those expressing ambivalence towards the abortion are especially at risk. Fifty-five percent of his group experienced at least short-term adverse reactions.

Women who undergo abortion for medical reasons seem more vulnerable to distress, perhaps because their pregnancies were planned or desired. In one sample of thirteen families who had elected induced abortion following a diagnosis of genetic defects in the fetus, twelve of the women and ten of the men were found to be suffering from depression.[34] Some observers argue that parents who have decided to abort a potentially defective child grieve in the same way as other bereaved parents.[35] Others have found markedly more grief among women who aborted for medical or genetic reasons than among postabortive women in general.[36] It has been suggested that support services for women who abort following a diagnosis of fetal malformation are inadequate.[37]

Abortion appears to be especially stressful for adolescents perhaps because it affects their fragile self-esteem. After studying twenty-two postabortive women, J. S. Wallerstein et al. found that symptoms were more dramatic and more severe among the fourteen- to seventeen-year-olds. The symptoms included "withdrawal from social relationships, preoccupation with feelings of 'ugliness,' severe crying spells upon seeing children or pregnant women, increased dependence upon parents, one suicide attempt and several acute anniversary reactions."[38] The researchers were struck by the pervasive long-range effects of the pregnancy and abortion experience in four of these very young women, including sex role oscillation, self-reproach, social regression and obsession with the need to become pregnant again. A. J. Margolis et al. found considerably more evidence of ambivalence and guilt among women under eighteen and advise greater care in recommending abortion for this age group.[39] Other researchers have found negative feelings to be most acute immediately after the abortion in very young teens. They argue that the most favorable outcome will occur when the patient freely chooses the abortion and receives support from parents and clinical personnel.[40] These results are to be contrasted with the Danish study,[41] which did not find substantial evidence of more marked distress among women under nineteen years. This study also notes that postpartum women between the ages of thirty-five and forty-nine were more likely to be admitted to psychiatric hospitals than postabortive women in the same age group.[42]

It is generally supposed that women receiving support from

family and counsellors will suffer fewer adverse consequences. According to the Danish study, separated, divorced or widowed women are most likely of all to suffer severe, adverse reactions. The rate of admissions to psychiatric hospitals for separated, divorced or widowed postabortive women was 63.8 per 10,000; the rate for the comparable group of postpartum women was 16.9. However, the Canadian study by Gold et al. found that patients who were accompanied at the time of the abortion suffered more distress than unaccompanied women.[43] The authors suggest that the experience of a stable sexual relationship may heighten ambivalence towards an abortion. E. R. Greenglass reports a similar pattern of distress among married women.[44] Others note that ambivalence heightens the likelihood of adverse reactions to abortion; women who delay seeking an abortion are at risk.[45] Still others argue that women who have been coerced into the decision experience more distress.[46]

POST TRAUMATIC STRESS SYNDROME

The observation that society still views abortion as a deviant act might suggest that we should understand the adverse psychological effects of abortion as being, at least in part, culturally induced. This, in turn, might suggest that with time, as people shed inhibitions, we will find postabortive distress occurring less often. Yet nothing in the record of the past twenty years of relatively free access to abortion enables us to say confidently that women are becoming less prone to this distress.[47] There is no reason to suppose that changing society's views on induced abortion will reduce the incidence of distress, particularly with the increased visibility of the fetus by ultrasound, fetal surgery, etc.

Numbers of women have now written first-hand accounts of their abortion experience, often many years after the event. Their stories typically convey the idea that a woman's distress can become more acute with time and suggest that, for some, the sense of grief, anger and bereavement can be crippling.[48]

Crisis pregnancy counselling agencies and family service organizations are now called upon regularly to provide postabortive counselling. Other organizations offering postabortive counselling are staffed chiefly by postabortive women. The names of these groups speak volumes: Women Exploited by Abortion; American Victims of Abortion; Victims of Choice. To ignore the voices of these women is certainly to risk censure by those health-care critics who argue that the psychological and physical complaints of women are rarely given sufficient credence or attention.

Researchers like David et al., of the Danish study, and Gold et al. emphasize what they believe to be the case: that only a minority of women are adversely affected by induced abortion. But can we ignore this suffering minority? Among the adverse effects noted in the literature are guilt, depression, grief, anxiety, sadness, shame, feelings of hopelessness, lowered self-esteem, distrust, hostility, insomnia, suicidal feelings, drug dependency and difficulties with both family and sexual relationships. It is our considered opinion that the psychological problems consequent on early pregnancy loss represent a significant community health-care problem even if only a small proportion of postabortive women are adversely affected. It must be noted that no woman comes through the abortion experience entirely unscathed.[49]

The American Psychiatric Association describes spontaneous abortion (miscarriage) as a moderate psycho-social stressor capable of causing symptoms associated with the long-term reaction known as Post Traumatic Stress Syndrome.[50] The Association lists the death of a child as a catastrophic stressor. Following the implications of this model, we see the trauma of induced abortion falling somewhere between the moderate and catastrophic categories. Vincent Rue is one researcher now pursuing the idea that for some women the distress that comes as a consequence of abortion should be understood as a syndrome that is part of Post Traumatic Stress Syndrome.[51] His guidelines — still in the process of elaboration — appear to offer a concrete and coherent explanation of the perplexing diversity of findings described in the literature on the psychological effects of abortion. We believe that they will prove important to both researchers and diagnosticians.

Rue argues that the symptoms consequent upon abortion fall into the following categories: (a) "re-experience," including recurrent and distressing nightmares, intense stress at exposure to events that symbolize the abortion experience (pregnant women, clinics, subsequent pregnancies); (b) "avoidance," including denial of feeling associated with the abortion, diminished interest in significant activities, feelings of detachment and withdrawal, the sense of a foreshortened future; (c) "associated features," including sleep disturbances, outbursts of anger, hypervigilance, difficulty in concentrating, depression, guilt and self-devaluation. The Post Abortion Syndrome is present, Rue asserts, when a woman exhibits symptoms from each category and when the duration of symptoms is more than one month or the onset is delayed until six months or more after the abortion.

In summary, a growing body of evidence strongly suggests that many women who undergo abortions will suffer from the debilitating psychological distress associated with Post Traumatic Stress Syndrome. And, as we noted at the beginning, there are more than 80,000 abortions performed annually in Canada. Even if only a small percentage of these women experiences the long-term distress associated with the syndrome, it would appear that we face a community health problem of significant proportions. To identify the true extent of post abortion psychological problems, we need to conduct a large, carefully controlled long-term study. The study should be carried out by an unbiased and competent group of researchers.

CHRIS BAGLEY

SOCIAL SERVICE AND ABORTION POLICY

TODAY IN NORTH AMERICA, Europe and many parts of the world, the existence of hundreds of thousands, perhaps millions of fetuses, is deliberately terminated each year by acts of medical policy.[1] The grounds on which this action is justified are largely those which concern the future welfare of the woman, her existing children and welfare of the expected child. Abortion is, on these grounds, a crucial issue in social and child welfare.

One of the basic questions to be considered is this: Are there cases in which future consequences for a mother and her child, if the child is born, are so bad, and foreseeable with such accuracy, that the termination of the child's existence *in utero* is justified? I shall argue that although life can be tough for, say, a single parent, such status by no means justifies this "ultimate solution" to the problem of poor children or distressed parents. Furthermore, I shall argue that utilitarian solutions to social problems based on the most "useful" outcome are in principle wrong. Among the moral absolutes which should guide human action in problems and crises is the principle that the taking of human life is a moral evil justified only in the most extreme circumstances and that social and psychological arguments for ending an unborn child's life do not constitute such "extreme circumstances." It is implicit in this argument that the developing fetus does constitute, in a very real sense, a human life, and that terminating that existence is a form of killing.

PHYSICAL AND PSYCHOLOGICAL HEALTH

I do not intend to explore in detail the vast literature that has emerged in recent years which indicates that induced abortion carries with it a vast number of serious risks to a woman's physical and psychological well-being. Two excellent studies in these areas, "Abortion and Bereavement" by L.L. de Veber et al. and "The Physical Consequences of Induced Abortion" by Heather Morris and Lorraine Williams, are included in this volume. The conclusions of this research underscore the fact that very few abortions are performed because of a physical threat associated with pregnancy. Rather, in the overwhelming majority of cases, the risks associated with abortion are far greater than those associated with childbearing. This research also shows that, despite the fact that wide access to legal abortion is often cited as the answer to a wide range of psychological problems, there exist virtually no psychiatric indications for abortion. Indeed, the abortion procedure itself can cause unnecessary suffering for many women.

In Britain, and in Canada, at least 85 percent of all legal abortions are carried out on allegedly "social and psychiatric grounds."[2] Closer examination of these "grounds" is highly informative. In a typical year, according to official British returns, 631 terminations were performed because the mother was studying; 3,451 because of the effect on other children in the family; 2,981 for economic reasons; and 733 because of housing problems. In Canada, financial hardship is the most frequently cited cause for terminating a pregnancy. Two-thirds of Canadian abortions are performed on these grounds alone. The next, most frequently cited ground is "social difficulty." Only 5 percent of terminations are carried out for medical reasons.[3]

SOCIAL CONCERNS FOR THE LIFE AND HEALTH OF CHILDREN

It is often argued that psychological and social difficulties constitute sufficient cause for a woman to terminate a pregnancy. Indeed, it may well be the case that psychological problems are often a reflection of a woman's social difficulties. In such cases, the argument runs, abortion is justified out of consideration for the well-being of the child. It is often alleged that a child born to a woman facing social, economic and emotional difficulties is likely to face extreme difficulties of his or her own later in life. This kind of appeal is also often heard in cases where it is argued that it is more humane to allow a malformed or handicapped fetus to be aborted than to force it to exist in a socially hostile world. What this kind of argument ignores are the difficulties surrounding any attempt to predict the future life of any individual.

Swedish and Czech work has demonstrated the virtual impossibilty of accurately determining the social as well as psychological outcome of children whose lives are considered for termination.[4]

The studies in themselves raise an interesting problem. Suppose that the researchers had asked their subjects: "When your mother was carrying you in her womb, she sought a legal order to have you terminated. She failed in this. Do you regret her failure? In other words, are you glad that you have life?" I suppose that the majority of the adults — almost certainly, all of them — would say that they were pleased that they had not been terminated. This is virtually the only thing we can predict with any certainty about a child before he or she is born: that if we allow the individual to be born alive, he or she will be glad of that life.

This has emerged clearly in accounts of the adjustment of

children born without limbs because of the drug thalidomide and children born with spina bifida.[5] In an era which increasingly accepts that handicapped children and adults can be integrated into many areas of life and can lead normal and much fuller lives than previously thought possible,[6] it is ironic that some physicians have argued that "there is a limit to what the community can spend on health," and in consequence children who after birth are found to be "severely malformed" should be put down.[7] It appears that in Britain about 400 children with spina bifida are being killed by medical practice each year (through starvation, or injection of lethal drugs).[8] Such killing is, of course, the logical extension of the practice of abortion when justified on grounds of a child's "future well-being." In Britain, the issue of "killing" handicapped infants by starvation or denial of medical treatment has been vigorously debated. The issue is clearly whether anyone "has the moral right to shorten or end the life of a fellow human being."[9] Child welfare authorities sometimes intervene in such cases, but their involvement in this area is clearly conservative.[10]

Case histories of babies who have been rescued from the lethal intentions of medical authorities are important and instructive. For example, in Britain in 1982, a parent reported how she resisted medical pressure to have her spina bifida infant put down. The child is now healthy and happy, although handicapped, and has an I.Q. of 145.[11] Given these successful case histories, accounts of handicapped babies being "allowed" to starve to death are particularly perturbing. The brave man kills with a sword, the coward with a kiss. Starving a baby to death rather than killing it quickly seems a particularly cowardly enterprise. In any case, the argument that a handicapped child's best welfare interests are served by being killed lacks any moral basis except in utilitarian theory, which grounds "good" acts in their social usefulness.[12]

St. John Stevas brings home the difficulty of predicting success and failure before birth by citing the case of a particular fetus: The father was syphilitic and the mother had tuberculosis.[13] Of the four children already born, the first was blind, the second died, the third was deaf and dumb and the fourth had tuberculosis. Here, surely, were clear grounds for termination. As it happened, this fetus was not terminated, and the world was given Ludwig van Beethoven!

Significantly, a Canadian researcher, the psychiatrist Philip Ney, has pointed out that as the rate of abortion has increased dramatically in Canada in the past decade, so has the rate of reported child abuse.[14] While the increase in the rate of child abuse should be treated with caution (the rate could be an artifact of reporting fashions), there may be a direct relationship between the two figures. Ney argues that when the destruction of the unborn child is socially sanctioned or indeed applauded, the value of all people, including the value of children, is diminished in the eyes of society. Even if one does not accept this argument as a reason for the rise in child abuse, it is clear that the incidence of such abuse is not diminished by wide access to legal abortion.

The virtual impossibility of predicting with any certainty the social outcome for an individual means, in my view, that the utilitarian case for abortion on social grounds (like the case on psychiatric grounds) is groundless. It may now be clear that my ethical position in this matter is derived from Kant, and not from Mill.[15] It is not enough to establish general criteria for prediction — to say, for example, that 50 percent of children allowed to live will come to the notice of the authorities by the time they are twenty-one. The only possible ethical position in this matter is what Popper calls methodological individualism. Group solutions of a genocidal nature to individual problems are in essence immoral.[16]

Individual problems need individual solutions. The most logical and the most ethical solution is not to terminate the life of a child whose mother is in social and psychological difficulty, but to help and support that mother and her child.[17] In Denmark, for example, abortion legislation was amended in 1945, requiring that any woman seeking a legal termination should be referred immediately to the State Bureaux for Mothers' Aid. These bureaus help unmarried mothers through every stage of their pregnancy, and with their adjustment afterwards. In Britain and elsewhere, some groups offer similar service on a local and voluntary basis, but there is clearly a need for a vigorous expansion of services here both by public and voluntary groups.

One obvious solution to the problem of unwanted children is adoption. In considering this solution we meet yet another of those paradoxes which surround the way society regards abortion. In Britain and North America the number of babies available for adoption has been declining. There are now many more couples seeking to adopt than there are babies available.[18] There are three clearly defined reasons for this: more couples are using contraception; more unmarried women are keeping their babies; and more women are having abortions. Just what are the prospects for a child who is not aborted but who is adopted instead? We have some remarkably good evidence on this question from a systematic follow-up study of 17,000 children born in Britain in a single week in 1958. Six hundred and forty of these children were illegitimate and, of these, 182 were adopted by people other than their own mothers. Social class levels were similar in the mothers who kept their babies and in those who allowed their children to be adopted. In overall terms, the adjustment of the adopted children at age eleven was excellent.[19] Swedish work by Bohman has produced similar conclusions.[20]

Some proponents of abortion claim, however, that certain kinds of children are unadoptable and that society cannot, and perhaps will never, accept children who have physical handicaps or who are of mixed race.[21]

The abortionist's case is in essence reactionary. It proposes final solutions to events which are defined as "problems" through the observer's prejudice. Illegitimate children are the product of immorality, "colored" children are undesirable, handicapped children are to be decried, and somehow eliminated.

Social arguments for abortion are insecurely based. The social consequences of being a human being are alleged. But such consequences can never be securely predicted for any individual. Indeed the potential of any individual can never be predicted. *The virtual impossibility of providing an accurate individual prediction of the future of any child is a fatal blow to the abortionist's case.*

The logic of the social grounds on which abortion is advocated is vacuous when submitted to close examination. Many women (especially single parents) suffer severe hardships as do children in poor families. But this calls for a critique of society's stigmatization and its neglect of poor and female-headed families, not a "logical" argument for abortion. There are obvious social remedies, including massive increases in social and financial support for families under stress and freely available methods of birth control which do not involve the destruction of the unborn child. Using abortion as an alternative to rational birth control is profoundly unsatisfactory. Tunnadine and Green, for example, argue that many women who fail to use contraception are deeply ambivalent about bearing a child; abortion does not solve their problems. The most likely outcomes of abortion are varying degrees of guilt and possible further pregnancies.[22]

THE FETUS AND INFANT LIFE

Thus far I have adduced a number of important objections to the practice of abortion. A different intuitive ground seems to me to be based on direct experience. If a mother could actually see and relate to the growing fetus in her body, she would respond, I am sure, in terms of protection not only of another human being but also in terms of bonding towards this child or fetus. I make this suggestion from personal experience as a student when, as an operating theatre attendant, I had to remove to the pathology lab or to the incinerator the products of surgical operations. Included in these products were recently aborted babies — still warm, perfectly formed infants — who, I later discovered, might well have survived if transferred immediately to a special care unit.

The evidence on the fetus as a personality is impressive. Of course, the fetus carries an individual genetic code which distinguishes him or her from the mother; the child is not simply a physiological extension of the mother but an individual within her womb with individual dispositions and tastes, including preferences for position, movement and responses to stimuli. Liley, in his fascinating account of "the fetus as a personality," makes it clear that "far from being an inert passenger in a pregnant mother, the fetus is very much in command of the pregnancy."[23] The fetus is responsive to pressure and touch, has considerable idiosyncrasy in deciding where and how to lie in the womb, is responsive to light and to sound and can "learn" from these experiences, developing consistent responses to stimuli. The child *in utero* is capable of feeling pain and, without doubt, the techniques used to terminate him or her are distressing and painful.

The research summarized by Valman and Pearson does show that the fetus has life long before birth.[24] But at what stage of development does the fetus become "human"? There is no way of knowing for sure; but we can be reasonably certain that this humanity begins very early in fetal life and certainly as soon as the phylogenetic stages of development are past, at about the eighth week of fetal life.

One of the methods of abortion still used is the injection of salt into the uterus. This poisons the fetus and, after a period of labor, the child is then (usually) born dead. Schmidt has recorded the accounts of women who experienced this kind of abortion: "The labour lasted 36 hours until the fetus came away. If I'd realised what it would involve, I would never have had it done . . . It was like a doll, with lots of hair."[25] All of these accounts suggest that late abortions involve considerable psychological distress to the mother, especially if she realises the human nature of the fetus.

Quite early in its physical development (by six or eight weeks), the fetus is recognizable as a human being and consistent patterns of response begin to develop. Advances in medical technology mean that each year younger babies can survive. Usually these are immature children who have been born spontaneously or surgically aborted. For example, in March 1971, a baby of fetal age twenty-four weeks was born prematurely, weighing one pound seven ounces. He (or "it" as the abortionists would say) was fed by milk directly pumped into the stomach and his development was monitored for two months in an incubator. This child, who is known to me personally, is now a normal, healthy nineteen-year-old.[26] French workers have kept alive for considerable periods babies aborted by surgical procedures, but this kind of experimentation is illegal in Britain.[27]

Sometimes the child on whom a surgical abortion has been performed is manifestly alive and cries and wriggles like a full-term baby. "I don't think anyone made a fuss about it when it happened. It was a fetus which made a bit of noise, that was all," commented one English obstetrician after such an incident.[28] Another obstetrician commented to a researcher:

> We do a lot of late terminations . . . I do them at seven months without hesitation . . . many of the babies I get are fully formed and are living for quite a time before they are disposed of. One morning I had four of them lined up crying their heads off. I hadn't time to kill them because we were so busy. I was loath to drop them in the incinerator because there was so much animal fat that could have been used commercially.[29]

This from a practitioner in a private abortion clinic. Fetal fat is much in demand by the cosmetics industry.

Ironically, many babies aborted prophylactically (after a history of German measles in the mother, or a doubtful amniocentesis) are found, when removed from the womb, to be normal. In 1978, one such child, aborted because the mother earlier had had German measles, was crying so lustily and healthily that the theatre staff, after observing it struggling and crying in a sink for two hours, finally transferred the child to the special care unit. The baby survived for two days, but might well have lived had immediate care been provided. In another case in England, a "dead" fetus sent to an incinerator for disposal proved to be alive, was resuscitated and is now a normal, healthy infant.[30]

In an age when babies can actually begin life outside the uterus (as in the case of "test tube babies"), it is possible that we shall reach a stage where at any stage of fetal development a child is capable of normal development outside the womb. Already, a fertilized ovum can be maintained outside a womb for a short period followed by implantation in a fresh uterus and successful growth to term.

Whether this will increase the ethical dilemmas faced by

those who advocate abortion is difficult to say, although the unethical nature of destroying fertilized ova in such experiments should be clear. What I suggest is that it is fundamentally wrong, and no different from murder or infanticide, to kill a child that is alive. If a child is capable of development at any stage of fetal life, then abortion must be immoral on the same grounds that taking any human life is wrong. Ironically, "prenatal child abuse" is now a conventional medical category and usually refers to women's use of drugs and alcohol during pregnancy. In one case a child was removed from her mother at birth on the grounds of prenatal abuse.[31] But by the same logic, does not abortion constitute "prenatal child abuse"? At present it is acceptable to kill a baby *in utero*, but not to injure it. This double standard is but one of the many ethical dilemmas that surround abortion policy. An important case in English law has indeed established that a doctor who leaves to die a perfectly normal baby delivered after an abortion is not guilty of any legal wrong-doing. The case established that the doctor could smother or drown the crying, kicking fetus with impunity.[32]

THE COGNITIVE DIMENSION

A curious phenomenon in the psychology of perception is that we do not appreciate the full significance of things until we visualize and experience them.

Social attitudes to abortion might be profoundly affected, if the average person could visualize or experience the effect of surgical abortion. There is an important cognitive element in attitudes to abortion. Unfortunately, however, seeing or understanding the nature of the developing fetus is not an automatic guarantee of the development of a humane attitude towards unborn children. He who has participated in a hundred such deaths no longer feels the natural disgust of ordinary human beings. Consider the account of a woman who volunteered to be a surrogate mother, motivated by her experience of abortion:

They had you on the table and they had the jar that the baby goes into, with the fluids and everything. And they took it over to the sink and they emptied out the fluids, and then you saw this sac that fit in the palm of your hands, and you knew the baby was in there. And they just took it right next to me, wrapped in paper towels, and threw it in the trash can . . . [33]

Desensitized doctors are responsible for the experiments reported by the *International Child Welfare Review* 1983.[34] These experiments involve live, aborted fetuses at the gestational age of twenty-two weeks or more. The fetuses (or babies) are kept alive in laboratories and are said to be extremely valuable for medical research purposes. Not since the days of Belsen have doctors had such an opportunity.

Fetuses are frequently used in both Europe and North America for cosmetic purposes.[35] Take a random example from the shelves of a Canadian drugstore: Perm Repair "for troubled hair" proudly boasts on the package that it contains "lyophilized human placenta" — in plain language, the melted down product of abortion. Is there any moral difference between this practice and the manufacture of soap from human fat in the Nazi death camps? A report from Europe issued by the European parliament in Brussels suggests that, in some European countries, cosmetic research uses live fetuses:

The use made of live and dead human fetuses has assumed such proportions that this phenomenon must be examined, bearing in mind the clandestine nature of such practices . . . Experiments are carried out on fetuses between 12 and 21 weeks old which are removed whole and live, then dissected to remove certain organs which are then frozen.[36]

Ironically, laws concerning experiments on live animals are more stringent than experiments on live fetuses aborted at a viable age and kept alive for medical experiments. An American researcher reports, for example, on the last five hours of an aborted baby, kept alive for purposes of vivisection:

Irregular gasping movements, twice a minute, occurred in the middle of the experiment but there was no proper respiration. Once the perfusion was stopped, however, the gasping respiratory effects increased to 8 to 10 per minute. The fetus died 21 minutes after leaving the circuit.[37]

Such experiments, causing acute pain and distress to the baby before it is finally killed, would be illegal in animal research.

Experiencing the death of one baby or fetus may turn your mind; experiencing the death of one hundred may degrade and desensitize. In an important sense, the solution to this awful problem lies with women themselves and their ability to empathize with their growing child in creative and humanistic ways.[38] I hope, as a result, that there will come a time when the women's movement will revolt against the male imposition of death upon their growing babies. In India this male hegemony is epitomized by the widespread use of abortion to put down children simply because they are female.[39]

The most fundamental restatement of the feminist position has been made by Germaine Greer, who argues that the feminist revolution thus far has simply made women more available sexually to men.[40] Women who unwillingly become pregnant and who are then forced "to get rid of it," are not in any sense free or in charge of their own destiny. Having to have an abortion is the grossest, most demeaning intrusion upon a woman's privacy.

A woman who is asked to bear an unwanted child should be given love, support and the optimum provision of social services. Those of us who argue that all children should be loved and wanted have a bounden duty to work for a profound improvement in all aspects of social service provision for families, and for women and children. No woman should ever be tempted to terminate her child simply because having a child will create a burden of poverty or stigma.

IAN GENTLES AND DENYSE O'LEARY

ABORTION, LAW AND
HUMAN BEHAVIOR

SINCE THE LATE 1960S there have been major changes in the laws covering induced abortion in the United States, the United Kingdom and Canada. The very restricted range of medical indications within which this procedure was formerly available have now been greatly widened or even removed.

One of the major arguments put forward by those who advocated this widening of indications for induced abortion was that it would reduce the amount of death and suffering associated with illegal abortions carried out by unqualified people. According to this view, women will have abortions regardless of what the law says, and if the procedure is made available under legally and medically favorable conditions, they will be less likely to go to illegal or unqualified practitioners — the so-called back-alley abortionists.

More than two decades have now passed since the introduction of the first changes in the laws governing induced abortion in North America and the United Kingdom. So it is reasonable to ask at this point whether these legal changes have led pregnant women away from people who are either unqualified or unsuitable to carry out induced abortions or whether abortionists are still operating outside current legislation. Alternatively, it may be asked whether the changes provided a legal cover within which the unqualified or unsuitable are now able to practise without fear of the law. Other questions that need to be answered pertain to the data used as a basis for estimates of the magnitude and consequences of illegal induced abortion prior to the 1960s and the effects of changes in the law on maternal mortality from abortion. Finally, we must ask ourselves whether any of these questions can be answered objectively.

The purposes of this study are to determine:

1. The extent of illegal abortion in the era before permissive laws were adopted.

2. The maternal death rate from legal and illegal abortions.

3. The effect of permissive abortion laws on the incidence of abortion and on the activities of unqualified, "back-alley" abortionists.

4. The deterrent effect, if any, of laws banning or restricting induced abortions.

By its very nature, illegal abortion is difficult to investigate. There is no exact way of measuring its incidence or the incidence of maternal mortality from illegal abortion. Nor is it easy to determine in any accurate way how the practice of illegal abortion is affected by the introduction of permissive legislation. On the other hand, there is a considerable amount of fragmentary evidence on these questions, available from several countries. Much of it points in the same direction. A careful sifting of this evidence enables us to arrive at conclusions which, if not definitive, are preferable to the unsubstantiated guesses on which much public discussion has been based.

An accurate understanding of the phenomenon of illegal abortion has significant implications for public policy in the areas of women's health, respect for the law, population growth or decline and the general question of how best to promote respect for human life.

ILLEGAL ABORTION

The American Experience

Supporters of legalized abortion have asserted that there were "about one million" illegal abortions annually in the United States before the introduction of more relaxed abortion laws. In the words of one author:

> Estimates made in various ways place the number of illegal abortions at somewhere between 300,000 and two million: a safe figure to talk about is about one million per year. One out of every four to five pregnancies is interrupted by resort to illegal abortion. This results in about *three to four thousand deaths annually*, mostly from among those abortions done by non-physicians or self-induced.[1]

The disparity between 300,000 and two million suggests the unreliability of these figures. What, in fact, are they based on?

They are rarely based on scientifically valid data. For example, in reports on the incidence of illegal abortion in the United States in the 1960s, the phrase "one million or more each year" recurred with almost mechanical regularity.[2] This figure was an extrapolation from data derived from a study done on 10,000 women who attended the Margaret Sanger Birth Control Clinic in the late 1920s in New York. Apart from the doubtful assumption that a group of urban women attending a birth control clinic would be representative of all American women either then or forty years later, there exist other studies which call into question these figures.[3]

A later Kinsey-initiated study, also cited in support of high estimates of illegally induced abortions, likewise dealt with a nonrepresentative group of women.[4] The Kinsey study of 5,293 white, nonprison women showed that 25 percent of all conceptions ended in induced abortion. But the Kinsey women had significantly fewer babies than the national average. They were also much more likely to be divorced, separated or single, which further reduces the likelihood that their practices were representative. As one commentator remarked, "the majority of the group was, almost necessarily, made up of persons who had some interest in and comprehended the value of, sex research."[5] Put another way, they were willing to submit to detailed questions about their sex life at a time when such self-disclosure was not the cultural norm.

In other studies there were serious sampling errors. For example, one widely quoted study added together figures for natural miscarriage and estimates of illegal abortion, and presented the combined figure as the number of illegal abortions.[6] Another estimate was extrapolated from a few local cases to produce a wildly inflated national annual average.[7]

With the public campaign for legalized abortion in the 1960s, round numbers such as "one million" induced abortions and "several thousand" maternal deaths were repeated again and again. The latter estimate was clearly too high. Official figures never exceeded a few hundred maternal deaths in a given year from illegal abortion. Given that autopsies are normally performed on women who die during their childbearing years, it is difficult to accept that several thousand abortion-related deaths could have been concealed from the authorities. Dr. Bernard Nathanson, a leading figure in the campaign for permissive abortion laws in the late 1960s, shows why this skepticism is well grounded.

How many deaths were we talking about when abortion was illegal? In the N.A.R.A.L. [National Abortion Rights Action League] we generally emphasized the drama of the individual case, not the mass statistics, but when we spoke of the latter it was always "5,000 to 10,000 deaths a year." I confess that I knew the figures were totally false and I suppose the others did too if they stopped to think of it, but in the "morality" of our revolution, it was a useful figure, widely accepted, so why go out of our way to correct it with honest statistics?[8]

Both Nathanson and the First International Conference on Abortion in Washington, D.C., in 1967 estimated the annual maternal death rate from illegal abortion at 500.[9] However, this estimate, which is three to twelve times greater than official figures, is also probably too high. The increasing use of antibiotics produced steadily declining official figures from the 1950s onward, while the actual maternal mortality rate was more likely to be 25 percent than 300 to 1200 percent higher than official figures. (See Figures 1 and 2.) This would yield an estimate of about sixty maternal deaths from illegal abortion by 1972, the year before abortion was completely legalized.

One might reasonably suggest that if the actual maternal death rate was only a fraction of the estimates made in the media at the time, then the illegal abortion rate was lower as well. On the other hand, induced abortions probably increased during the 1960s, along with changing attitudes to human sexuality. The number of pregnancies perceived as unwanted appears to have increased as well.

But in light of the evidence reviewed, it is unlikely that the rate of illegal abortion matched today's rate of legal abortion. In 1980 the number of abortions in the United States reached 1,553,890, a figure substantially higher than all but the most exaggerated estimates of the previous number of illegal abortions.[10]

The British Experience

As in the United States, very high estimates of illegally induced abortions circulated in the mid-1960s when permissive abortion laws were being advocated. Both Glanville Williams and Bernard Dickens quote David Glass, who said that there were possibly 100,000 illegally induced abortions each year in England and Wales around 1940, but as Dickens notes, Glass did not provide any evidence for his conclusions. Williams also cites Eustace Chesser as suggesting as many as 250,000 per year.[11]

However, significant criticism was leveled at these figures at the time, for example by the Council of the Royal College of Obstetricians and Gynaecologists.[12]

C. B. Goodhart, writing in *Population Studies*, also rejected these estimates. His conclusion was that there were between 15,000 and 20,000 induced criminal abortions each year before 1968.[13] In arriving at these figures, he relied mainly on official mortality statistics, which, while not complete, are an accurate guide to the magnitude of the problem. There are some problems with determining maternal mortality caused by induced abortions, since such deaths may be misclassified as being due to natural causes. But autopsies are customarily carried out after deaths of healthy young women, which would make large-scale concealment of the true cause of death difficult. There were an average of fewer than thirty maternal deaths reported annually in Britain during the 1960s from illegally induced abortions (see Figure 1); there can have been no more than forty actual deaths, which would be consistent with figures of 13,000 to 15,700 induced criminal abortions per year.[14] The alternative, he points out, would be to suppose that criminal abortionists were so skilled at that time that they could perform 100,000 to 250,000 abortions while causing no more than forty maternal deaths.

Goodhart used another estimate of some interest: hospital admission figures for women suffering complications after induced abortions. He gives an estimate of not more than 15,000 to 20,000 per year, based on hospital admission figures of 69,400 for all types of abortions or threatened abortions, in 10,880 cases of which the child was actually saved.[15]

According to a National Opinion Survey carried out in July, 1966, 4 percent of British women said they had had an illegal abortion during their lifetime (of whom fully 59 percent maintained that they had induced the abortion themselves). This figure is remarkably low, but as Goodhart points out, there are serious problems with the methodology of the survey, which may make the actual figure even lower.[16]

In a sample of married women in the United Kingdom, Lewis-Faning compared the pregnancies of 933 women who had used contraception but then stopped (presumably because they wished to conceive), with 992 who reported contraceptive failure (leading the researchers to assume that the child was unwanted).[17] Taking together both spontaneous and induced abortions, 9.5 percent of the planned and 18 percent of the unplanned pregnancies did not end in a live birth. Induced abortion was admitted by 0.4 percent of the former group of mothers and 4 percent of the latter. Lewis-Faning believed that

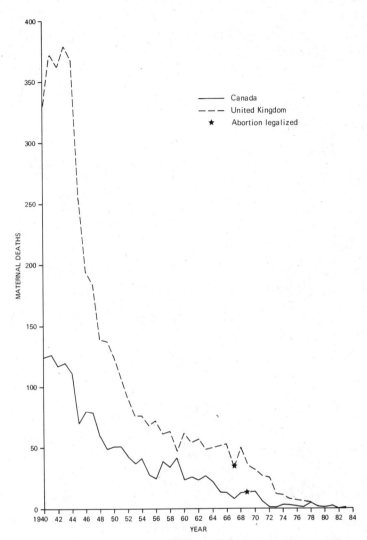

Figure 1

Maternal Deaths Resulting from Illegal Abortion, 1940-1979: Canada, the United Kingdom and the United States

SOURCES: Statistics Canada (Dominion Bureau of Statistics before 1970), *Causes of Death, Canada,* cat. no. 84-203 (Ottawa: various years); *The Registrar General's Statistical Review for England and Wales,* Tables: Medical (London: Her Majesty's Stationery Office, various years); U.S. Department of Health, Education and Welfare, *Vital Statistics of the United States* (Rockville, Maryland: various years).

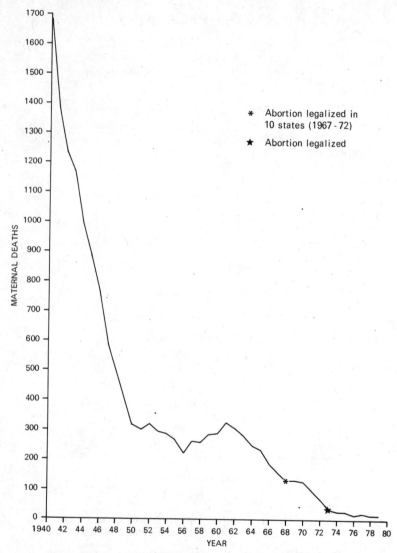

Figure 2

Maternal Deaths Resulting from Abortion, 1940-1979: United States

SOURCE: U.S. Department of Health, Education and Welfare, *Vital Statistics of the United States* (Rockville, Maryland: various years).

in the latter group of presumably unwanted children, 8.7 percent had been intentionally aborted, since it would be difficult to attribute the much higher miscarriage rate to natural causes. But this still yields a much lower rate of abortion for presumably unwanted children than high estimates of illegal abortion in Britain (100,000 to 250,000 per year) would have led us to expect.

Generally the statistics do not support high estimates for rates of criminal abortion from the 1940s to the 1960s. However, there can be no doubt that higher and higher abortion rates prevail today — in the wake of legalization in 1967. In 1983 there were 127,375 abortions recorded for women resident in England and Wales. By 1988 the figure had reached 183,798.[18]

To sum up: four sources — official statistics on maternal mortality from illegal abortion, hospital admission figures for complications from illegal abortions, a study of public opinion and a study of the abortion rate of unplanned pregnancies — point to an illegal abortion rate before 1967 in Britain much lower than the widely quoted estimates of 50,000, 100,000 or 250,000 per year. After 1967, when a permissive law was adopted, the annual number of legal abortions rose steadily to reach a figure greater than all but the most inflated estimate of the previous illegal abortion rate.

The Canadian Experience

Canada's experience before the law was changed was similar to that of Britain and the United States. From about 1959 to 1969, when there was growing demand for permissive abortion laws, very high estimates of the number of criminal abortions were circulated. For instance, abortion advocate Eleanor Pelrine took Dr. Overstreet's U.S. estimates and divided by ten because of Canada's smaller population. "On this basis," she wrote, "there would be 100,000 illegal abortions in Canada each year, and a probable three to four hundred deaths. Zealous campaigners for repeal of our abortion laws have put the annual Canadian death total at nearer two thousand.[19]

Even assuming the accuracy of the American figures that Pelrine used (and there is reason to question these very high figures) dividing by ten is a questionable way to calculate a Canadian phenomenon in relation to the United States as there are significant social differences between the two countries. Divorce and homicide rates, for example, are both significantly higher in the United States than in Canada. It is not unlikely that the U.S. illegal abortion rate was similarly higher.

Canadian maternal mortality rate figures are available: according to the highly respected report of the Badgley Commission, the number of mothers who were reported to have perished in self-induced or criminal abortions during each year between 1958 and 1969 averaged 12.3.[20] We may suppose that, as in Britain, some additional maternal deaths from abortions were misclassified or concealed, but when due allowance has been made, there is still no way of reconciling the discrepancy between the estimates of three hundred to two thousand per year cited by Pelrine and the officially documented average of 12.3. (See Figure 1.)

Badgley also estimated that in 1975 there were 46,096 Canadian women living who had *at some time* had an illegal abortion.[21] While he acknowledged that this figure may have been on the low side, it is nevertheless many times lower than an *annual* estimate of 100,000. Badgley also estimated that 55,061 tried to induce an abortion themselves at some point during their lifetime.[22] The combined total of women who had experienced illegally induced abortions — 101,157 — represents only 2 percent of the female population of childbearing age. Furthermore, since self-induced abortions are often carried out using ineffective folk methods, it is probable that a significant percentage of this latter group either were not actually pregnant or miscarried naturally, so that the total presented cannot be equated with successfully induced abortions. Badgley's findings regarding the numbers of illegal abortions in Canada are the best we are ever likely to get. If all Canadian women alive in 1976 had had roughly 100,000 illegal and self-induced abortions *during their lifetimes*, then the *annual* rate of such abortions can hardly have been higher than 10,000 during the years before the law was changed in 1969. By contrast, the number of legally induced abortions reached a peak of 80,435 in 1987.[23]

As we have seen, the estimates of illegal abortions made in the 1960s were exaggerated in all three countries discussed. The social respectability which abortion has gained during the intervening period of permissive laws has, however, produced a high abortion rate that shows no signs of decreasing.

MATERNAL DEATHS FROM ABORTION

In contrast to the shadowy world of illegal abortion, the statistical domain of maternal mortality has long been bathed in the glare of governmental attention. For many decades we have had a reasonably accurate idea of how many women perished each year from all types of abortion — spontaneous, legally induced and illegally induced. However, a certain coyness of terminology, together with quirks and changes in classification make it occasionally difficult to isolate illegal abortion deaths from other types of maternal mortality, so we must also allow for the probability that mortality from illegal abortion is underestimated in official figures. Fortunately, a British Columbia study of abortion mortality over the fourteen years immediately before legalization (1955-68) provides some reassurance on this score. While official statistics recorded forty-one maternal abortion deaths in the province, W. D. S. Thomas established from doctors' reports a figure of forty-four. For four of the years under study, the official figure was lower than the doctors' reports, but for four other years it was *higher*. Combining the maximum annual figures from both sources yields a total of forty-nine deaths over fourteen years, which is 19.5 percent higher than the doctors' official total. The fact that the official statistics were higher as often as they were lower suggests random error rather than any systematic attempt to conceal abortion deaths.[24] It is difficult to hide a body, and doctors and coroners would normally be loath to perjure themselves by falsifying a death certificate. Government figures appear thus to be not all that far from the truth and at least give us a handle on the magnitude of the phenomenon.

In addition, independently collected figures from Canada,

the United Kingdom and the United States show strikingly similar trends in all three countries over a forty-year period — a discovery that buttresses one's confidence that the official statisticians came close to getting the numbers right. In graphic form (see Figures 2 and 3) the numbers indicate an unmistakable decrease in maternal mortality from abortion from the 1940s through the late 1970s. If we allow for the rising female population of childbearing age in all three countries, the decline in the mortality rate is even steeper than the decline in numbers. Yet it would be wrong to infer that the numbers or the rate of induced abortion have also gone down over the past forty-five years. As we have seen, the reverse is true.

If abortions have increased, why has maternal mortality gone down so sharply? The answer is to be found in the improvements in medical care which have produced tumbling maternal mortality rates from almost every cause. More specifically, the discovery of sulphanimides and antibiotics in the 1940s, and their steadily increasing use in the 1950s, sharply reduced mortality from infection. Most deaths from abortion — legally or illegally induced — were the result of infection (sepsis). It is thus quite unlikely that renewed legal restrictions on abortion would produce significant increases in maternal mortality.

WOMEN DENIED ABORTION

If it is true, as alleged, that the law itself has little effect on whether or not women have abortions, one would expect almost all those who are denied a legal abortion to resort to an illegal procedure. The results of several studies compel us to reject this inference.

Let us begin with Sweden and Czechoslovakia. In both countries, prior to the introduction of abortion on request, there were abortion boards which refused some applications. A major Swedish study found that 65.3 percent of the 196 women who were turned down completed the pregnancy.[25] In another study 249 Swedish women denied abortion were followed up. At first, seventy-four (30 percent) had planned to secure an illegal abortion, but in the event only twenty-eight (11 percent) went through with it. When a criminal abortion was obtained, it was often the male partner or parents of the woman who initiated it. The vast majority of the women — 213 (86 percent) — gave birth to their child.[26]

In the Czech study, of the 555 rejected applicants who were followed up, a minimum of 316, or 56.9 percent, are known to have completed the pregnancy. In the first Swedish study and the Czech study, normal conditions for the development of the child were found to exist in the great majority of the families, although some of the children were slightly more maladapted than the children who were wanted by their mothers. As the Czech investigators concluded, the differences between "wanted" and "unwanted" children "were not dramatic."[27]

In Canada 203 pregnant women living in maternity homes or served by child welfare agencies were interviewed by the Badgley Commission. More than one out of four (27.4 percent) said they had considered having an induced abortion but had abandoned the idea because of a lack of accessible facilities or because their applications to hospital therapeutic abortion committees had been held up.[28] This finding provides indirect evidence which points in the same direction as the Swedish and Czech studies: namely, that women who find it difficult to obtain a legal abortion rarely turn to an illegal one. In this connection we may reflect on the experience of two women who made headlines in the summer of 1989 through their struggles to overthrow court injunctions that would have prevented them from having an abortion. Both were successful and both had abortions, though Barbara Dodd later announced that she regretted what she had done, and wrote Chantal Daigle urging her to let her baby live. It is likely that, had the injunction been upheld, Dodd would have gone through with her pregnancy.

In a study pulling together findings from Sweden, the U.S.A. and New Zealand, it was concluded that of a total of 6,298 women refused a legal abortion between the 1940s and the 1960s, 13.2 percent sought an illegal one. Interestingly, a majority, ranging from 58 to 80 percent, were satisfied to have borne their baby.[29] The fact that all the studies agree that a

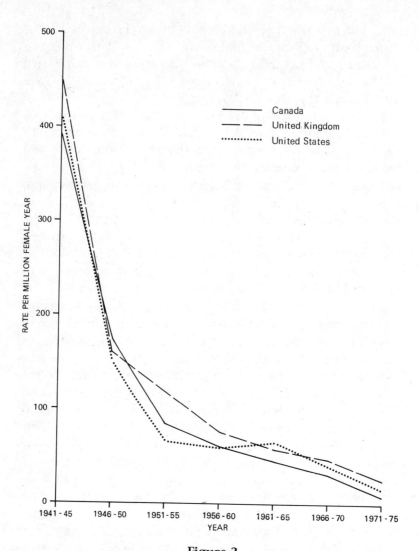

Figure 3

Maternal Deaths Resulting from Abortion, 1940-1983:
Canada and the United Kingdom

SOURCE: Statistics Canada (before 1970: Dominion Bureau of Statistics), *Causes of Death, Canada*, catalogue no. 84-203 (Ottawa: various years); *Registrar General's Statistical Review for England and Wales for the Year 1950*, Text, Medical (London: H.M.S.O., 1954), p. 52; *Ibid.*, various years, 1951-1983.

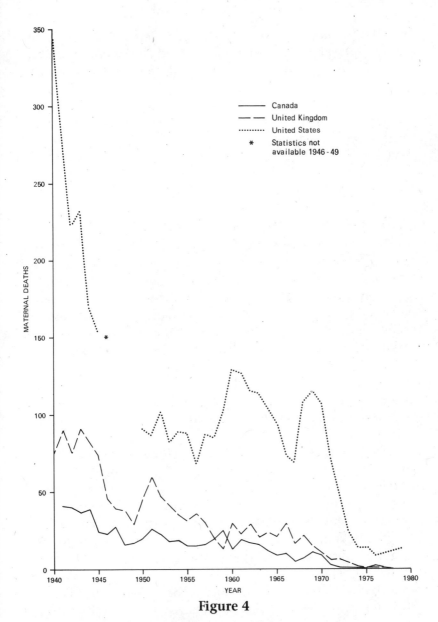

Figure 4

Maternal Mortality Rate from Abortion, 1941-1975:
Canada, United Kingdom, U.S.A.

SOURCE: Michael Alderson, *International Mortality Statistics* (New York: Facts on File, 1981).

significant proportion of women were deterred by the legal constraints placed on them suggests that the true induced abortion rate is substantially lower under a restrictive law than under a permissive one.

Findings of this sort should be kept in mind by those who try to predict accurately the effects of restrictive, as opposed to permissive, legislation.

THE CRIMINAL ABORTIONIST

In the United States

One of the commonly expressed reasons for promoting permissive abortion laws is a desire to reduce maternal deaths and morbidity from the activities of unskilled and unqualified operators. Evaluation of the success of permissive laws in this regard is complicated by the fact that maternal deaths from almost all causes relating to pregnancy have declined steeply during the last four and a half decades.[30] There is evidence that this decline, which began well before restrictive laws became permissive, would have continued regardless of changes in abortion legislation. The more and more prevalent use of antibiotics and improved medical care of complications were leading factors in the decline.

Examination of this question in the United States is difficult. As a result of the U.S. Supreme Court's invalidating state abortion laws in 1973 and a large number of subsequent local control regulations in 1983, there is now no mandatory reporting of abortions and their sequelae in many states. The abortionist might not know of later complications, since the patient suffering from these often goes to the emergency room of a hospital or to another doctor.

Actual investigative newspaper reports have also indicated that among the legal abortions that have taken place since 1973, a good number have been as dangerous as the illegal procedures of the 1960s, for instance, a Chicago *Sun-Times* investigation of four abortion clinics accounting for one out of every three abortions in the Chicago area found that some doctors "aborted" nonpregnant women and subjected their patients to high-pressure tactics and false information. Inexperienced or unqualified practitioners, including medical residents working outside their normal hours and a physician who had lost his licence, worked in unsanitary conditions, with haphazard procedures, leading to morbidity. One doctor operated after drinking champagne at a clinic party. Furthermore, rapid assembly-line procedures were used without waiting for anesthetics to take effect and there was shoddy record keeping, falsification of vital signs, failure to order pathology reports and ignoring, scrambling or losing of results of lab tests. The licensing authorities were unaware that, since 1973, twelve mothers had died in clinic abortions. Reporter Zekman concluded, "In 1973 the Supreme Court legalized abortion. As it turns out, what they legalized in some clinics in Chicago is the highly profitable and very dangerous backroom abortion."[31] Eventually, in 1989, the state of Illinois passed a law aimed at regulating some of the worst practices of abortion clinics and hospitals.[32]

The problem is not confined to Chicago. Similar incidents have occurred in other American cities, a few of which are described in a report that we have published elsewhere.[33] What has come to light shows that the phenomenon of "dangerous backroom abortion" continues to exist throughout the United States. The problem of substandard abortion procedures is not confined to clinics and "back-room" abortionists. In 1988, California state health officials ordered Inglewood Women's Hospital in Los Angeles to close because its high volume of abortions was endangering the health of its patients. Women patients were neglected under what one official described as "battlefield conditions." They were rushed through a single operating room where the blood of previous patients still stained the tables and floors. Just before the closure order was issued, a women allegedly bled to death after her uterus was perforated during an abortion.[34]

While no statistics exist, a recent development in malpractice insurance provides a hint of the magnitude of the problem of substandard care. In 1983 the Professional Insurance Management Company, one of the major malpractice insurance brokers in Florida, began requiring that all doctors doing abortions, whether or not they are obstetrician-gynecologists, must pay premiums of $41,000 per annum. Thus, a general practitioner who started to do abortions went from a low-risk Code I classification, paying $6,000 per annum, up to the highest-risk classification of Code VII, with a nearly sevenfold leap in premiums.[35] If the malpractice insurance ratings are based on the companies' knowledge of the true state of abortion practice in Florida, it would be difficult to conclude that legalization has dealt effectively with the "dangerous" abortionist.[36]

In Britain

When the Abortion Act came into force in 1967, legalizing abortion for a broad variety of indications, there was a small increase in maternal deaths associated with abortions, but thereafter, the long decline associated with improved gynecological care has continued.[37]

It would be difficult to isolate any influence that the Abortion Act had on maternal deaths (except the sharp initial increase). Did it have any influence on clandestine or unqualified abortionists? Apparently not. What happened is something quite different from what seems to have taken place in the U.S. In every year from 1967 until 1975, the numbers of women treated in British hospitals for complications after illegal abortion was higher than in 1966, the year before the permissive law was enacted. But the number of police actions and convictions dropped off very steeply.[38] The two sets of figures seem to bear out the concerns of the Royal College of Obstetricians and Gynaecologists in 1966 that "legislation of abortion alters the climate of opinion among the public and even the Courts of Law. The result is that criminal abortion becomes less abhorrent, and those guilty of the offence receive punishments so light as not to discourage others in their activities."[39]

Eight years after the passage of the Abortion Act in Britain, a paper in the *British Journal of Criminology* which studied figures from the National Hospital In-Patient Inquiry concluded that "there is no evidence of a significant decline in illegal abortions since the Abortion Act."[40]

It is possible that there have been changes since these statistics became available. But as we have already seen, a decline in police prosecutions, which are a direct source of evidence, does not necessarily mean a decline in the practice of illegal abortion. Moreover, the Lane Committee on the Working of the Abortion Act reported in 1974 that illegal abortionists were making greater use of antibiotics.[41] Given this fact, decreasing hospital admissions caused by postabortion infections would not necessarily signal a decline either. In conclusion, we cannot establish from the evidence reviewed that a decline in illegal abortion took place during the first decade after the Abortion Act in Britain, though mortality from all forms of abortion continued its decline.

In Canada

As we indicated earlier, Canada did not have severe problems with illegal abortion before the 1969 amendments to section 251 of the Criminal Code which legalized abortion if the life or health of the mother was in danger. The difficulty with determining the effect of the amendments on illegal abortion is that there is much uncertainty about what precisely they were intended to legalize. There is evidence that abortions were already being done in Canadian hospitals prior to 1969. Thus, many interested parties, including a number of physicians and lawyers, sought the amendments not as a new liberty but to legalize what was already being done.[42] Others saw them as a means of combating backstreet abortion. Yet others viewed them as breaking new ground in social betterment. For instance, Grace MacInnis, MP, for Vancouver-Kingsway, made this comment before a Standing Committee of the House appointed in 1967 to inquire into the need for a new law.

> I think it is time that we began to work toward *quality* population in this country. We are beginning to hear about the need for improving population, and certainly to have children born into a country as a result of rape or incest is not going to be too helpful . . . Also . . . if conditions like those of thalidomide babies or congenital diseases are known ahead

of time, I do not think it is a good thing for Canada to allow these beings to come into the world . . . women ought to have far more control over what happens to them when monstrosities are born . . . [43]

Clearly the aims were divergent and in some cases quite ambitious. When the amendment was finally passed after much controversy in 1969, it allowed abortions to be performed if a majority of members of a therapeutic abortion committee (which must exclude the abortionist) agreed that "the continuation of the pregnancy of [such] female person would or would be likely to endanger her life or health. . . . " But the government of the day rejected all attempts made during the debate in Parliament to clarify legislatively the meaning of the term "health."

In doing this, it acted against the recommendations of the Committee appointed to consider the issue. The Committee acknowledged that there was "a great deal of concern" over the health definition and the Committee's preferred reading was that an abortion be granted if continuation of pregnancy "will endanger the life or seriously and directly impair the health of the mother" because it "intended health to mean physical and mental health and not the wider definition given to it by the World Health Organization."[44]

The World Health Organization defines health as "a state of complete physical, mental, emotional, and social well-being and not merely the absence of disease or infirmity."[45] In British Columbia, this was the definition of health used at most of the hospitals performing abortions.[46] This same definition was likely used at many hospitals in other provinces.

Yet the federal government has still not, after twenty years, clarified its position on this question. In 1984, Arthur Pennington, the lawyer for the federal government at the Toronto trial of Henry Morgentaler on a charge of illegally procuring abortions, stated that "an obvious purpose [of Section 251] is the protection of the developing human life in the womb. Section 251 does not create in any way the right to have an abortion, nor does it create the right to perform an abortion for a doctor." Ontario Crown Prosecutor Bonnie Wein made the argument more pointedly before the provincial Court of Appeal a year later when she affirmed that the law's purpose was "to protect the state's interest in unborn life."[47]

These comments, while intended to clarify the government's intentions, actually complicated the problem. The federal government of Canada never attempted to prevent hospitals from carrying out abortions according to the WHO definition of health, yet clearly such a policy does not operate to protect the fetus.[48] In Pennington's words, "Parliament has called for an independent and accountable medical certification that the woman [seeking the abortion] meets the medical standard."[49] But in the present state of legal confusion, it is hard to know what *is* the medical standard.

Another complication arose when the provincial government of Quebec licensed some local community service centers to do out-patient abortions in the 1980s. Since these centers did not have therapeutic abortion committees, their operations were illegal under the terms of section 251. Their legality was never challenged in court, however, and when section 251 was ruled unconstitutional by the Supreme Court of Canada on January 28, 1988, their existence at once became legal.

Since 1988, Canada has been the only country in the world where abortion is completely unregulated by law. In the years since the Supreme Court handed down its decision in the Morgentaler case, a few more clinics have been established in major centres (Toronto, Vancouver and Winnipeg), while provincial governments in other parts of the country — notably in the Atlantic provinces — have resisted the establishment of freestanding abortion clinics. This reluctance is understandable. While there is, so far, little information on the operation of Canadian clinics, American experience has shown that freestanding abortion clinics may all too easily duplicate the conditions that the legislators of twenty years ago were trying to eliminate.

It is already known that some complications are unavoidable even under the rigid conditions of a hospital setting.[50] A freestanding clinic, with its more limited facilities, could scarcely fare better. Morgentaler's clinic in Montreal came under professional attack in the 1970s because Morgentaler's attitude was declared by the Disciplinary Committee of the Professional Corporation of the Physicians of Quebec[51] to be "primarily directed to protecting his fees." In 1976, his licence to practise was suspended for one year.

The committee established that Morgentaler conducted no valid interview with the patient before an abortion; that there was an almost complete lack of case history; that pregnancy or blood tests were not taken or pathological examinations performed and that there was no follow-up care. Morgentaler himself has stated that his postabortion care consists of keeping the patient "under observation for an average of thirty minutes, and having her leave when ambulatory."[52]

It has also been established that Morgentaler re-used polyethylene "vacurettes" on patients even though the manufacturer warns against this practice, since it could result in the transmission of diseases such as viral hepatitis, tetanus, venereal disease, gaseous gangrene, and Herpes II.[53] An instance of the dramas that are sometimes played out behind the walls of the Morgentaler clinic in Toronto was supplied by the testimony of a Honduran woman who was ambivalent about her decision and had the misfortune to change her mind as the operation was beginning. According to her report, the abortionist gave no painkiller before the abortion and he did not respond to her pleas to stop the abortion. When she began screaming an assistant shut her mouth and another forced a sanitary napkin into it.[54] Yet Morgentaler is considered by many to be a "model" abortionist. Would a proliferation of freestanding abortion clinics in Canada eventually duplicate the American experience outlined above? Not all freestanding clinics violate health or ethical standards, but American experience has shown that legalization does not eliminate unqualified and unethical operators: on the contrary, it may make it more difficult for the authorities to deal with them.

Incidents of the kind culled from the American press have apparently been much rarer and more sporadic in Canada. They do exist, however. In Toronto in 1980, for example, Dr. Dwight

Foster was convicted of criminally aborting a seventeen-year-old girl at her home. The unborn child had already reached six months' gestation, and the physician's botched efforts necessitated a complete hysterectomy for the girl.[55]

In summary, until 1988, the practice of confining abortions mainly to public hospitals minimized the problem of the unqualified operator. For the two years since the Supreme Court's decision, Canada has been unique in having no law regulating abortion. At the time of writing, legislation is before Parliament which would allow abortion until the moment of birth if a physician certifies that the continuation of the pregnancy is likely to threaten the woman's life or health. Since no definition of "health" has been offered, the practical consequences of this legislation will be unrestricted abortion. Except where they are blocked by provincial governments, private abortion clinics will become common. Besides legitimate concern about the medical and ethical standards of privately run clinics, there is also cause for apprehension about the moral and social tensions that these clinics will bring nakedly into focus.

RESTRICTIVE LAWS: SCANDINAVIA, EASTERN EUROPE AND NEW ZEALAND

Most advocates of restrictive abortion laws have, as their primary goal, the protection of the unborn. But one must also consider the effect restrictive laws have on mothers. We have seen that permissive laws have raised the overall abortion rate. If restrictive laws were enacted, would they lower it, either slightly or considerably? If they did so, would it be because of an increased use of contraceptives or because of an increased birth rate? If the abortion rate did not go down, would it be because mothers continued to obtain abortions through the usual medical channels regardless of a change in the law or because they resorted to unqualified or clandestine abortions, or self-induction? What is the influence of social attitudes to pregnancy, child bearing and the unborn child? It is beyond the scope of this essay to deal with these questions at length, but the experience of some countries may suggest some provisional answers.

In general, claims that women who seek abortions under permissive laws would be equally likely to try to obtain them under restrictive ones are not supported by evidence from several studies. We noted earlier a survey by Carlos Del Campo of women who had been denied abortion by medical boards in Sweden and New Zealand, or whose abortions were not funded by the government in the United States. Overall, only 13.2 percent of the women studied sought abortion elsewhere. The rates varied widely from 46.6 percent in New Zealand in 1977 to 10 percent in Sweden in 1959, but the proportion was usually between a tenth and a fifth. The laws in the countries under study differed greatly from one another and some have changed since.[56]

Interestingly, the adoption of a pro-natalist policy by the Province of Quebec in the late 1980s may also have caused a reduction in the abortion rate in that province. Women in Quebec are now offered generous incentives to bear children. Between 1987 and 1988 the Quebec birth rate rose 2.4 percent from 12.7 to 13.0 per thousand. More dramatically between 1986 and 1987 the number of abortions in Quebec clinics shrank by 37 percent, from 3,498 to 2,202. This occurred at a time when the abortion rate nationally rose by 0.2 percent.[57]

The current trend in the Western world has been to go from restrictive to permissive laws, but in Eastern Europe, where permissive laws were in force since the 1950s, there has been a trend the other way. What has been the experience there with contraception, births and clandestine abortion?

Tomas Frejka, writing in *Population and Development Review*, suggests that the Eastern European experience shows that laws which permit abortion on broad grounds or on request lead to an increase in induced abortion because some mothers abort when they would otherwise have carried to term and others fail to use contraceptives.[58]

In each country that placed restrictions on abortion (including Romania, which prohibited it altogether) an increased number of births followed. Pronatalist social policy must also have been a factor in increasing births. Frejka states that in subsequent years the fertility level may have remained higher than it would otherwise have been.

Abortions declined at varying rates as a result of new policies, ranging from only a temporary decline in Czechoslovakia and Bulgaria to an ongoing decline in Hungary (whose decline had started earlier, encouraged apparently by increased contraceptive use). There was a slight rise in the numbers of abortions listed as "spontaneous" in some countries, such as Bulgaria, Czechoslovakia and Hungary, and it is safe to assume that some of these were illegal or unregistered induced abortions.[59]

Romania registered a significant increase in maternal deaths following induced criminal abortion. That country was unusual in other ways as well, having previously recorded a rate of 7.0 induced abortions per woman per lifetime under the permissive law prior to 1966.[60] Moreover, the government discouraged contraception as well as abortion. While the hoped-for result — a dramatic turnaround in the birth rate — was achieved, it was only at the price of sharply increasing the maternal death rate.[61] In response to the callousness with which this pronatalist policy was implemented, the new government of Romania repealed the anti-abortion law at the end of 1989. It is noteworthy that the Romanian experience was not duplicated in countries where contraception was permitted or encouraged.

The Eastern European experience suggests that restrictions on abortion result in an immediate sharp increase in the birth rate, which thereafter tends to decline almost to its former level. Restrictions may also encourage contraceptive use if contraception is made available.

Among non-Communist countries, New Zealand was the first to attempt to change from permissive to restrictive legislation. Until the same year, New Zealand had a law similar to Canada's, allowing for abortion if there was danger to the life or health of the mother. However, in that year a Royal Commission on Contraception, Sterilization and Abortion found that an "abortion on request" service was operating at the Auckland Medical Aid Centre, contrary to the intent of the law. In the same year, there was one abortion nationally for every eleven live births.

The following year the rate rose to one abortion for every nine live births. In 1978 the new Contraception, Sterilization and Abortion Bill became law, with its stipulation that the danger to the mother's life or health must be "serious." The immediate result was a steep plunge in the abortion rate to one for every fourteen live births in 1978 and 1979. However, after intense pressure from the medical profession, the law was again widened, with the consequence that by 1981-82 the abortion rate had risen to an all-time high of one for every 7.5 live births.[62]

During the period when the restrictive law was in force there was no evidence of widespread resort to unqualified practitioners, though a small, undetermined number of mothers went to Australia where permissive laws exist in most states. The rapidly rising abortion rate in New Zealand is attributable to approximately the same phenomenon that occurred in many Canadian hospitals after 1969. In both countries, abortion consultants interpreted the law in an increasingly broad way and the regulatory committees were reluctant to intervene.[63]

The New Zealand and Canadian experiences suggest that if a Western country in the common law tradition wishes to enact restrictive laws, a major problem of enforcement will be posed by resistance within the medical establishment itself. Physicians may establish and defend a different and unforeseen set of definitions and qualifications which they alone are empowered to monitor.

CONCLUSION

From what we have discovered in this study, we may conclude that:

1. The incidence of illegal abortion in the United States, Britain and Canada was much lower before 1970 than is frequently alleged.

2. Maternal deaths from abortion declined steadily from 1940 or earlier. The legalization of abortion in the late 1960s had little effect upon a trend that had already been established for over a quarter of a century. It was not legalization but improved

treatment of infection that virtually eliminated abortion deaths in the half-century after 1940.

3. Permissive laws do not simply "replace" illegal abortions with legal ones. They produce instead a significant increase in the numbers of induced abortions. The brutalizing and exploitive activities of "back-alley" abortionists also stubbornly persist.

4. Restrictive laws do not necessarily lead to a large-scale, illegal resort to unqualified or unethical practitioners. Indeed, in the overwhelming majority of cases, women denied legal abortions go on to bear their children and most report that they are satisfied to have done so. The amount of illegal abortion in a given country appears to be the product of numerous factors, including the availability of means of preventing pregnancy, the attitude of the medical profession and whether or not social and cultural policy is generous towards those who bear children.

DIANE MARSHALL
AND MARTHA CREAN

THE HUMAN FACE OF A
WOMAN'S AGONY

Most PEOPLE COME TO issues of public justice with concerns born of personal experience. One of us came face to face
with the issue of abortion when she was sixteen. Her close friend,
Lynn, died following an abortion performed by a backstreet
butcher in Vancouver. The abortionist was never prosecuted.

Yet, there is something almost as haunting in the current
specter of women celebrating their "right" and "freedom" to
destroy the life they carry. We cannot help seeing it as a fright-
ening commentary on our increasingly life-denying culture.

Human beings are rapidly destroying the earth's atmosphere,
forests, animals and plant species, polluting lakes, rivers and
oceans, contaminating the gene pool through low-level radia-
tion and producing weapons that defy the imagination in their
capacity for global destruction. And recently, in the name of
"women's rights," thousands of Canadian women rejoiced at
the Supreme Court's decision to rid their country of a law that
sought to give balance and set a limit to the choice to terminate
a pregnancy.

1987 was the International Year of the Homeless in an age

where countless people, the world over, are refugees, victims of war and famine. Even in Canada, the street people of the large cities, unable to establish roots or to find affordable housing are increasing in numbers and despair. But let us not forget that, in equally increasing numbers, the unborn face a similar plight. Cast out of their mothers' wombs, there is no place for them in the families, neighborhoods, cities and nations of the modern world. In order to understand why this is so, one must confront the "human face" of those who agonize over the decision to bear a child.

Abortion confronts us all with basic questions regarding the human community. Most fundamentally, in our view, the issue of abortion demands that we consider the following: how do we create a *society* where a new generation, our children, are welcomed, wanted and adequately cared for and how do we build a *culture* that values family life — not at the expense of any member or gender — but where *all* persons are free to pursue their human calling in an atmosphere of mutual faithfulness, love, intimacy and nurture? These fundamental questions have provoked us to take a serious look at specific social policy issues that affect our lives as citizens.

There is no question in our minds that the male-female partnership is under attack in our society and that this is most evident in the abdication of men from the role and responsibility of fatherhood. A *Globe and Mail* survey on abortion, published in June 1985, shows that a higher pecentage of men favor abortion than women. Is there not a connection between this and the Playboy empire's funding of abortion lobby groups? Is there not a connection between this and the view of sex as recreation and children as nuisances, which characterizes a significant population of men who are not interested in family life? Films like *The Color Purple* and *Out of Africa*, not to mention James Bond movies, *Rambo* and *Die Hard II*, clearly illustrate that the macho cult of power and dominance makes no room for tenderness and the nurturing of new life. As citizens, we should take a serious look at the fact that the social group most supportive of abortion is middle-class, white males. For, in the face of the large scale abdication of men from the parenting role, strong measures are needed to show concrete support for women and children.

It seems obvious to us that babies should have the right to be born and that women should have the right to decide if, when and with whom they will have sexual intercourse.[1] All women should be free of sexual coercion or exploitation in conceiving a child. In saying this, however, we do not ignore the tragic, historical reality that men have too frequently behaved as though women's bodies were their possessions. The repercussions of this are evident today, as they were in the past, in serious social problems: pornography, child sexual abuse and incest, rape, wife battering and wife rape. Violence against women — including domestic violence — is a very serious social reality at all levels of our society.

For many women, abortion is a way of coping with the reality of living in a highly individualistic society which does not encourage men to make room for pregnant women or children. The emptying of a woman's womb thereby becomes a way of "restructuring a woman" rather than "restructuring society." For many women, abortion is an anguishing personal remedy for what is in fact a communal and social problem; it is an extreme example of how individualism prevails when a sense of community and partnership break down. For pregnant women who are not affirmed as women, who do not know how to affirm themselves as women and who are frequently victimized, it is difficult to affirm the life of the unborn child they carry.

Men are very much involved, whether directly or indirectly, in most women's decisions about abortion. James Burtchaell's book, *Rachel Weeping*, analyzes the results of two published surveys of women who had abortions and concludes that the dominant factor in these women's decisions was their estrangement from their male partners and, in some cases, from their parents.[2] It appears that the views of a pregnant woman's circle of family and friends have a great impact on her own views about bearing a child.

Consider the cases of pregnant, single women who, rather than receiving support from their families and male partners, face rejection from both if they choose to bear their children; of pregnant women for whom abortion seems the only alternative to a life of poverty given their lack of education and marketable skills; of pregnant women who face the prospect of losing their jobs because of the view of many employers that bearing a child indicates a lack of professional commitment; of women who face social and religious discrimination if they decide to bear an "illegitimate" child; and of women who risk losing their husbands if they increase the economic burden by having "unwanted" children. In all such cases, the choice to have an abortion can hardly be understood as "free" or "voluntary."

When the care of children is not regarded as a social priority and a mutual responsibility for both men and women, it is far too easy for men to abdicate the responsibilities of fatherhood, which go far beyond mere economic provision and include emotional support and nurture. This abdication isolates modern women in the task of child-rearing. The result is the "privatization" of pregnancy (and hence abortion) as a "women's issue." Seen in this light, widespread access to abortion is not a solution to the alienation of women from the dominant influences in their lives. Rather, it allows men in particular and society in general an easy way out of having to integrate the concerns of women into social and economic policy.

Nowhere is this more evident than in the experience of single mothers today in Canada. Fully 82 percent of all single-parent families are headed by women. Most of these families live in poverty. For the women who head these families, the prospect of having another child usually means being doomed to a welfare ghetto. The appallingly meager sums provided by welfare or mothers' allowance barely provide adequate housing and nutrition for their children.

Yet, the majority of women who are single parents did not choose to be. The majority of single-parent families are families where a father/husband/partner has left the family in the wake of a relationship breakdown. While it is the case that today there is more social acceptance for single mothers than there has been in the past, the economic hardships experienced by these women cannot but haunt others. A fear of the consequences of being abandoned by their partners lurks in the minds of many mothers. For, if abandoned, the odds are that mothers will find themselves in the profoundly lonely position of raising their children alone — without an outside source of emotional, physical and economic support. Indeed, it is this fear of marginalization, isolation and rejection that drives many women to seek abortions when tangible promises of support are not forthcoming.

Communities have a great deal to offer if only they would take the plight of sole-support, mother-led families seriously. If all that could be done was in fact done to keep single mothers in the mainstream of life, in school and in work, single mothers could be protected from isolation in the ghetto of single-parent families.

The insensitivity of our society to the needs of women is evident not only when women feel forced into having abortions for social and economic reasons. It is equally evident in the world of the hospital where abortions are routinely performed. Nurses who refuse to assist with an abortion for reasons of conscience routinely face coercion and discrimination in their place of employment. Some hospitals have application forms, which must be signed before an applicant for a nursing position can be interviewed, stating that, "I agree that my personal or religious beliefs in respect to certain hospital procedures will not prevent me from carrying out my assigned duties." Thus, nurses, who are overwhelmingly female, are unequal participants in hospital decision making.

Nurses for Life, an organization seeking to have the conscience rights of nurses protected by law, views abortion as an act of institutionalized noncaring. Peggy Madill, spokesperson for the organization explains: "Pregnancy is not a disease and abortion is not a cure." She describes abortion as a symptom of the socioeconomic undervaluing of women and children and explains the actions of nurses who refuse to assist in abortions this way: "When we refuse to care for someone undergoing an abortion, it's not the person we refuse to care for. It's the act of abortion we object to."[3]

Indeed, on an international level, Canada is conspicuous in its refusal to take in to account what institutionalized abortion is doing to nurses. Britain, New Zealand, Italy, France and forty-four U.S. states are among jurisdictions that have enacted conscience clauses for medical workers. In general, these provisions allow nurses who express an objection to assisting in abortions on religious or moral grounds to be exempted from doing so. Recognizing that many hospitals use the job application or interview to screen out otherwise qualified applicants, the Texas legislature prohibits discrimination at the hiring stage as well.

In light of the above considerations, we strongly urge women and men to work towards realizing the following recommendations:

INFRASTRUCTURE

Housing. There is a desperate need for better housing, especially in large cities. The housing that does exist is inadequate and often ghettoized. The provision of more adequate and cooperative housing, which promotes a sense of community, should be regarded as a serious social policy priority.

Transportation. There is a need for lower public transportation rates for the working poor and for single mothers and their children so that they are not confined to their own neighborhood, where they may feel isolated.

Welfare. The present system of social welfare does not encourage pregnant women to carry their pregnancies to term or to nurture their children when born. Welfare and mothers' allowance payments should be increased *especially* for pregnant and neo-natal mothers. On a current welfare budget, it is impossible to eat the healthy diet needed to nurture a developing child. It is even harder on such a budget to feed a child anything other than starches when it is born. Making hot, nutritionally balanced meals available in schools and day-care centers may be one approach. But nutrition is far from the only problem for someone trying to live on a welfare allowance. Many low-income families cannot even afford a telephone. Isolation tends to create a climate of depression and may lead to child abuse. What is desperately needed is a guaranteed minimum income.

Childcare. Broad-based day care is essential for teenage mothers, for mothers re-entering the educational stream through re-training programs and for working mothers. Childcare must be regarded as a collective and not simply an individual responsiblity. There is no way our vast numbers of single-parent families can satisfy the needs of their children without the benefit of day-care and after-school programs.

EDUCATION, CULTURE AND ATTITUDES

Education. There is a need for human sexuality courses and better pregnancy prevention instruction in schools and community organizations.

- Sex education should emphasize the *emotional* dimensions of the sexual relationship instead of focussing exclusively on the biological aspects.
- Beginning at the elementary school level, children of both sexes should be given instruction in the joys and responsibilities of parenting.
- At the junior high-school level, students should be taught about the realities of abortion.
- Students should be taught how to resolve conflicts and deal with anger so that wife and child battering become less frequent and families learn to live peacefully.

Culture. Cultural deprivation is a serious problem for low-income people. Children who have creative talents are unable to develop them when their mothers lack the means to pay for materials and lessons. Free sports activities are available to children who are athletic, but few, if any, cultural activities are provided for artistic children. Poor people usually live in crowded and squalid conditions. Again, if sole-support mothers were able to live with more dignity, they would be able to provide their children with a more nurturing and stimulating environment.

Attitudes. The payment of child support allowances must be enforced as part and parcel of society's solidarity with mothers and children who have experienced family breakdown. The current delinquency rate among those required to pay child support is an appalling 75 percent. Communities, the media and the government should play a role in making sure that fathers support their children.

Ongoing, concerted efforts are needed to reduce violence against women in our society. Some areas in which society should be expected to play a role are:

- Domestic violence. Police should be expected to lay charges of assault and not leave this up to the victim.
- Women's shelters. The public should lobby for increased funding.
- Pornography and the exploitation of women in the media through such things as sexist advertising. People should take a stand against these things.
- Programs to counteract the growing phenomenon of incest, child abuse and rape.
- The workplace. The public should contribute to ongoing efforts to reduce sexual harassment here.
- Encouraging our schools, religious communities and recreational centers to teach models of partnership and cooperation between the sexes. All such educational programs should show how the family contributes to the well-being of the child and to the well-being of society as a whole, and should affirm the notion that the task of being a parent is addressed to both men and women. Procreation, and hence contraception, are not solely "women's issues." Sexuality is not a commodity. In an age where sex has become one of the idols of consumerism, the gift of sharing one's sexuality within a caring, committed relationship needs to be affirmed.

THE WORKPLACE

Men and women in business and industry can alleviate the pressures that may make a pregnant woman feel the only recourse she has is to have an abortion by assuring just labor laws and practices.

Addressing financial need. Those in decision-making positions in business and industry can ensure that the workplace better supports family life by making sure that their companies provide good maternity benefits. In addition, companies should be encouraged to explore and implement alternative work arrangements for their employees such as job-sharing, part-time work and work performed at home.

Fathers, too, need the freedom to limit their employment responsibilities for the sake of their families. They need to be able to say no to overtime, to office parties, to taking work home and to excessive travel. Fathers, as much as mothers, ought to be encouraged to play a significant role in parenting. Both should be able to leave work to take a child to the dentist or to stay home with a sick child. By freeing up fathers for more parenting responsibilities, the workplace can ease the burden and isolation of mothers.

Conscience rights for workers. Health workers should not be forced to assist with abortions if they object to them on moral or religious grounds. The right to refuse to participate in abortions should be legally guaranteed.

GLOBAL ISSUES

Militarism. A central fact for all of us is that we live under the threat of nuclear destruction.

It should be stressed, once again, that the issue of abortion in Western civilization is not a matter of the "health of the mother" but a matter of the "health of society." The widespread practice of abortion has become, for an *individual*, a symbol of the fact that society's womb is not nurturing life but rather promoting homelessness. The two of us have known very few women who have really wanted an abortion. For most women, abortion is a way of coping with the fact that they feel they are not in a position which will allow them to nurture life. The choice to have an abortion is a choice most often born out of desperation. We cannot forget that the act of bringing forth a new human being into the world is an act of tremendous faith and courage. In a world where we all live under the threat of nuclear annihilation, it is extremely difficult to have faith that the next generation will live with the comfort and joys we wish it to enjoy. Women need peace in order to nurture life confidently. The current militarism and international touting of the will to power are a threat to a woman's ability to affirm life.

Environmental protection. Evidence shows that in areas where hazardous wastes are dumped the incidence of birth defects goes up. The detection of birth defects in unborn children puts pressure upon women to terminate their pregnancies. More research is needed to determine ways to change the attitudes and practices of industry in the creation and disposal of hazardous waste.

It is important that a new generation of young people come to understand that there is hope in the bearing and rearing of children and that this is not just "women's work." Cooperation in child care and family life should be encouraged as part of a new model of the family and taught to boys and girls from the earliest years. Without this emphasis on full partnership between men and women in all areas of political, social, economic and domestic life, we do not believe that a society can be built which genuinely celebrates a woman's ability to give birth and which welcomes and nurtures each new human being.

III

PARLIAMENT, THE COURTS AND THE UNBORN CHILD

IAN GENTLES

THE UNBORN CHILD
IN CIVIL AND
CRIMINAL LAW

THERE EXISTS TODAY a grotesque contradiction at the heart of our legal system as it touches the unborn child. On the one hand, the unborn child enjoys the right to inherit property; she can sue for injuries inflicted while in the womb; and she has the right to be protected from abuse or neglect by her mother.[1] On the other hand, she no longer enjoys that right which is the indispensable precondition of the exercise of all her other rights — the right not to be killed. How has this contradiction come about? Is there any way it can be resolved?

To begin answering these questions I shall briefly review the status of the unborn child in the legal traditions of Western civilization. It is an interesting fact that from the earliest times, protection of the unborn has never been a merely Judeo-Christian idiosyncrasy. Many centuries before Christ, the Sumerians, the Assyrians and the Hittites protected prenatal human life in their legal codes.[2] The oath framed for physicians in the fourth century B.C. by the Greek doctor Hippocrates included the well-known pledge: "I will neither give a deadly drug to anyone if asked for it, nor will I make a suggestion to this effect. Similarly, I will not give to a woman an abortive remedy. In purity and holiness I will guard my life and my art."[3] Authorities on the English common law, from Bracton in the thirteenth century through Coke in the seventeenth century to Blackstone in the eighteenth, all treated abortion as a crime.[4] Blackstone summed up the law's position in the second half of the eighteenth century in the following words:

> Life is the immediate gift of God, a right inherent by nature in every individual; and it begins in contemplation of law as soon as an infant is able to stir in the mother's womb. For if a woman is quick with the child, and by a potion or otherwise killeth it in her womb; or if anyone beat her, whereby the child dieth in her body and she is delivered of a dead child, this, though not murder, was by the ancient law homicide or manslaughter. But the modern law doth not look upon this offence in quite so atrocious a light, but merely as a heinous misdemeanour.[5]

There is a vivid illustration of the law's concern for the unborn child in the Salem witch trials. In the summer of 1692 six people were found guilty of witchcraft and promptly sentenced to death. On August 19 of that year all but one — a certain Elizabeth Proctor — were hanged. Taking refuge in a custom honored by the common law, goodwife Proctor pleaded pregnancy and her execution was accordingly stayed until such time as her child should have been born. This was done on the ground, as the historian of these events has put it, "that the child she was carrying was an innocent person." Happily, even after her child was born, the sentence against Elizabeth Proctor was allowed to lapse and she lived out her natural life.[6]

With their primitive medical knowledge, the jurists of the premodern period did not believe that it was possible to speak of an abortion before the time of quickening (i.e., the time when the mother feels the child move in her womb). Since human life did not evidently come into existence before quickening, there could not be a law against destroying it before that time. This anomaly was abruptly eliminated in 1803 when, thanks to advancing medical knowledge, a law was passed in Britain making abortion a felony at any time during pregnancy.[7] This law was inherited by Canada and remained unaltered until 1969. In that year it was amended to make an abortion permissible in cases when a three-member hospital committee deemed that continuation of the pregnancy would endanger the life or health of the mother. Four years later, the United States Supreme Court swept away all criminal legislation against abortion in that country in the historic decision *Roe v. Wade* (January 22, 1973). Fifteen years after that, the Canadian Supreme Court ruled the 1969 law unconstitutional (January 28, 1988). Since then, Canada has been in the unique position of having no legal regulation of abortion whatsoever.

The trend throughout the world in the past two decades towards eliminating legal hindrances against abortion is in striking contrast to the growing recognition of the civil rights of the unborn child. As recently as the end of the last century, Chief Justice Holmes in the United States declared that the unborn child had no rights in a court of law, since he was merely a part of his mother and not, legally speaking, a person.

This statement disregarded the fact that the unborn child's right to inherit had already been established in English common law as early as 1798, at which time it was declared that, whenever it would be for his benefit, the child in the womb was to be "considered as born."[8] The first Canadian case to overturn the prevalent view expressed by Holmes was *In Re Charlton Estate* (1919). A certain Charlton had left a sum of money to be divided among "all the living children" of his brother. A child who was born three and a half months after Charlton died subsequently sued for a share of the estate, asserting that he was living at the time of his uncle's death. The Manitoba Court of King's Bench upheld the suit on the ground that a gift to "all living children" included the child who was in his mother's womb (*"en ventre sa mère"*) at the time.[9] The same principle was upheld in another case the following year. A certain Mrs. Giddings successfully sued the Canadian Northern Railway for negligence in the death of her husband, a locomotive fireman. In addition to the damages she won for herself, the court also awarded her child $6,000, even though he was unborn at the time of his father's death. The fact that he was unborn was judged to be "immaterial so long as the action is for the benefit of the child."[10] These two cases influenced many other decisions, with the result that the unborn child's right to inherit and own property is now clearly recognized.

The much more difficult question of the unborn child's right to compensation for injuries suffered in the womb has also been decisively settled in this century in the child's favor. The Supreme Court of Canada seems to have set the standard for the rest of the English-speaking world by its momentous decision in the case of *Montreal Tramways* v. *Léveillé* (1933).[11] The court recognized that "the great weight of judicial opinion in the common-law courts denies the right of a child when born to maintain an action for prenatal injuries." Nevertheless, it boldly reversed judicial precedent by declaring that a child who suffers injury while in its mother's womb as the result of a wrongful act or default of another has the right, after birth, to maintain an action for damages for its prenatal injury. Judge Lamont justified the rejection of precedent in this case on the basis of the following principles:

If a child after birth has no right of action for prenatal injuries, we have a wrong inflicted for which there is no remedy . . . If a right of action be denied to the child it will be compelled, without any fault on its part, to go through life carrying the seal of another's fault and bearing a very heavy burden of infirmity and inconvenience without any compensation therefor.

The principle laid down by Judge Lamont was confirmed in 1972 in *Duval et al.* v. *Séguin et al.*[12] The child of Thérèse Duval was permanently handicapped, both physically and mentally, as a direct result of a car accident which occurred while she was *en ventre sa mère*. In deciding in favor of the child, the judge quoted Lord Atkin's dictum: "The rule that you are to love your neighbour becomes, in law, you must not injure your neighbour." Although the unborn child was to be regarded as the "neighbor" of the negligent driver, the judge declined to state whether the child was a person in law, or at which stage she became a person.

In the case of *Watt* v. *Rama* in the Supreme Court of Victoria, Australia, the same year, there was no such reluctance to recognize the unborn child as a legal person.[13] The plaintiff, Sylvia Watt, had suffered brain damage and epilepsy as a result of a car accident involving her mother when the mother was two months pregnant. The defence argued that a two-month fetus was merely part of her mother and therefore not entitled to legal protection. The judge rejected the plea, observing that there was no essential difference between a newborn child and a child not yet born:

> As its property, real or personal, is protected, so should its physical substance be similarly protected by deeming it to be a person in being and imposing a duty of care on any other person not to commit any act of carelessness which as a reasonable man he should anticipate would injure the physical substance of the unborn child.

The judge concluded by affirming that, for the purpose of protecting her interests, Sylvia Watt was deemed to be a person at the time of the collision — two months after conception — and was thus entitled to compensation for the injuries she had suffered at that time. Interestingly, the *Land Titles Act* of Ontario implicitly takes a similar position by referring repeatedly to the property rights of the "person yet unborn."[14]

The progress of the civil law in recognizing the personhood of the unborn child is trenchantly summarized by William L. Prosser, the dean of American Tort law. Before 1946, he points out, most American authorities were agreed that the child could not sue for prenatal injuries. However, the situation was transformed so rapidly in the next quarter of a century that "it is now apparently literally true that there is no authority left still supporting the older rule." Furthermore, "all writers who have discussed the problem have joined in condemning the old rule, in maintaining that the *unborn child in the path of an authomobile is as much a person in the street as the mother*, and in urging that recovery should be allowed upon proper proof." [15]

One problem has not yet been resolved: whether a child has to be born alive in order for a suit to be entered on her behalf. Prosser believes that the trend is in the direction of holding that a child does not have to be born alive.[16] This would seem to be a logical conclusion, since it is hard to see why one should be less liable for destroying a child's life than for merely causing her to be injured. Indeed, since the 1960s a large number of cases in American courts have ruled not only that the unborn child is a person, but that an action for the wrongful death of an unborn child is maintainable even when she is stillborn.[17]

In North America, then, it is clear that no one has the right to kill the unborn child, or injure her, or deprive her of her property. No one, that is, except her mother. And, since the decisions in *Roe* v. *Wade* and *R.* v. *Morgentaler et. al*, the mother has, in North America, the almost unrestricted right to take the child's life. Moreover, given the abortion-on-demand situation that prevailed in most Canadian cities even before the Canadian Supreme Court decision of January 28, 1988, the mother has, in fact, had this right since 1969.

This has created a profound conflict between the civil and the criminal law. Take the hypothetical example of a woman who is pregnant with her first child at the time of her husband's death. In his will he has divided his estate between his wife and all his living children. The law has established that the child in the womb can rightfully inherit a share of her father's estate. Canadian criminal law, as interpreted by the courts, now permits the woman to destroy her child at will, right up to the moment before she is born. Legally speaking, therefore, the woman is at liberty to have an abortion in order to keep all of her husband's estate to herself.

There is another instance where the interests of the unborn child may clash with those of the mother or father. Since 1963, thanks to the work of the New Zealand fetologist Dr. Albert Liley, it has been possible to make life-saving transfusions of blood to fetuses that have developed acute anemia in the womb. In one such instance where a blood transfusion had been diagnosed as medically necessary to save the unborn child's life, the mother refused the transfusion for religious reasons. Nonetheless, the New Jersey Supreme court ordered the transfusion to be administered, stating:

> We are satisfied that the unborn child is entitled to the law's protection and that an appropriate order should be made to insure such transfusions to the mother in the event that they are necessary in the opinion of the physician in charge at the time.[18]

In 1981 the first reported successful out-of-the-womb surgery was carried out on a five-month-old unborn baby. Performed in San Francisco, the critical thirty-minute operation has pointed the way to the correction of a whole series of birth defects in the future.[19] The irony of this particular medical breakthrough is that during the half-hour she spends outside the womb during the operation, the child enjoys the status of a legal person, with her life fully protected. Once back in the womb, however, she resumes the status of a nonperson in the eyes of criminal law, having, in effect, re-entered a free-fire zone where she can be killed with impunity.

The highly publicized cases of Barbara Dodd and Chantal Daigle in 1989 drew attention to earlier instances in which courts issued injunctions preventing or delaying abortions. The contradiction between the unborn child's status under the civil law and her status under the criminal law results in contradictory behavior in the courts. The Quebec Court of Appeal applied principles derived from civil law when it upheld an injunction that would have prohibited Chantal Daigle from aborting her unborn child. The court interpreted the right to life guaranteed in the Quebec Civil Code as including the child in the womb. In overthrowing this decision, the Supreme Court ruled that the Quebec Civil Code could in no way restrict a woman's right to an abortion. In effect, this decision reaffirmed the grotesque contradiction between the civil and the criminal law. Yet one wonders how long the Canadian Supreme Court can continue to quash lower-court decisions that favor the unborn child.

To compound the confusion, two cases, one Canadian and one British, have recognized the personhood of the unborn child in criminal suits. The British judge ruled that a Belfast child wounded by a bullet fired into her mother's abdomen was a legal person, with the right to sue for damages for criminal injury, and awarded her $8,800.[20] In the Canadian case, which involved a charge of criminal negligence, a British Columbia judge ruled that a fetus in the process of birth is a person under the Criminal Code. The baby in question was stillborn, allegedly because of the criminal negligence of the midwife in attendance.[21]

So far, we can see that the unborn child's rights have been unequivocally established with reference to everyone but her mother. It could, perhaps, be argued that there is nothing inconsistent or irrational in allowing the child's mother to kill her through abortion while at the same time denying to everyone else the right to injure her or deprive her of property. The mother, after all, is the only one who has to surrender her body to the nine months of possible discomfort, embarrassment or even physical hazard that a pregnancy can entail. Her relationship with her unborn child is clearly unique and qualitatively different from anyone else's. Given that her body is being occupied by a fetus who may not be welcome in her eyes, should the mother not at least have the right to dispose of it as she pleases?

Those who use this argument, which is condensed in the popular phrase "a woman's right to control her own body," have had to face an unexpected and awkward challenge. Since about 1970, in Canada and elsewhere, there has been much concern about child abuse, together with a determination to reduce its prevalence. In addition, there is now a much sharper awareness of how crucial are the nine months before birth in shaping the individual's whole future physical and psychological well-being. Many proponents of child welfare, therefore, urge that protection against abuse should extend into the prenatal period and that mothers should be accountable for the welfare of their unborn children. Furthermore, they should, like anyone else, be liable for prosecution if they are guilty, through negligence or abuse, of causing injury to their unborn child.

The Supreme Court of British Columbia accepted this reasoning in 1982, in the case of a heroin-addicted mother whose newborn baby suffered violent symptoms of withdrawal and possible long-term damage to her health. After about seven weeks, the baby was taken off the drug. At four months of age she was still withdrawing from addiction. According to the attending physician: " . . . the infant goes through the same withdrawal syndrome as an adult and experiences extreme spasms in the stomach, excruciating pain and vomiting." Moreover, the baby's nutrition required very careful attention, since drug-addicted babies need twice the calories of a normal child for brain and organ growth.

In light of this harrowing description of the consequences of the mother's heroin addicition, the court ruled that the fetus whose mother is drug-addicted is "a child in need of protection," and that such a child "is born *having been abused.*" There was, therefore, no need to wait until the mother abused the child after birth before requiring that she submit to involuntary supervision.[22]

The British Columbia decision finds support in David M. Steinberg's *Family Law in Family Courts*, where it is stated that a child in the womb may be considered a child in order to secure protection from abuse by her mother.[23]

So a mother may not neglect or abuse her unborn child. But she may still legally kill her. Aware of the pressing need to eliminate this contradiction, the director of the Canadian Law Reform Commission has advocated that the unborn child's rights already established by judicial decision should be enshrined in a statute. According to Edward Keyserlingk, "there should be no contest at all between a mother's desire to smoke or consume drugs excessively and the unborn's right to be legally protected against the serious risk of resulting disability." The provision of adequate nutrition, adequate prenatal checkups, the avoidance of excessive smoking, drinking or drug-taking should be made into a legal obligation involving potential liability for parents, doctors and others. "The Law must conclude more coherently and explicitly than it has to date that the unborn has its own juridical [legal] personality and rights."[24] Yet he goes on to say that the unborn's rights would end when the mother decides to have an abortion.

Does this make sense? Would *you* be happy to enjoy the right to "adequate prenatal checkups" while you were, at the same time, denied the right not to be killed through abortion? The stark absurdity of this position grows out of the irreducible reality that all the rights the unborn child has won in the course of this century depend, as their indispensable precondition, on the right to live. Since I possess the right to inherit, to own property and not to be injured, neglected or abused before I am born, it logically follows that I must also possess the right to life, since without it none of my other rights can be exercised.[25]

It is hard to conceive how long the terrible contradiction at the heart of our legal system can endure. Either we shall have to eliminate the civil rights that have been so painfully won for the unborn child (this is what our Supreme Court seems bent on doing), or we shall have to recognize her most fundamental right, the right not to be killed, even by her parents. We cannot have it both ways. Moreover, whatever we do, a morality will have been imposed. To think that a neutral, pluralistic and value-free policy should remove abortion from the law is to be misled. To accept the argument from pluralism is to turn a blind eye to the silent victim of every abortion — the child in the womb. It would be hardly less logical to advocate removing murder from the Criminal Code on the ground that, in a pluralistic society, we do not have any right to impose our moral views on those who wish to murder.

The argument from pluralism also ignores the fact that societies that do eliminate abortion from their legal codes do not thereby succeed in giving people a free choice in the matter. Instead an "abortion mentality" takes over, and overwhelming pressure is exerted on women to resort to abortion as the way out of any distressful or inconvenient prenancy. This pressure is exerted by husbands, boyfriends, parents, peers, social workers, doctors and governments. Goverments find abortion an easy way of avoiding hard social problems like the shortage of reasonably priced family housing.

There is yet another defect in the argument from pluralism. It is said that, since there is disagreement about whether the fetus is a human being, we should allow those who believe that abortion is morally permissable to act on their beliefs. Some people certainly *wish* that there were disagreement about the humanity of the fetus. Virtually all medical authorities, however, agree that the life of the human individual begins at conception.[26] But even if there were disagreement, would it not be both prudent and humane to give the fetus the benefit of the doubt, to accept its humanity and therefore its right to live? What would we say if people were arguing that blacks instead of fetuses were not human, and that people should have the right to kill them? This, after all, is the position that some people took in the United States of America just over a century ago. Even if we were not completely sure just what "humanity" entailed, would we not argue that blacks should have the benefit of the doubt and be included within the human family, with apropriate legal protection? Is not the best rule of thumb to frame our definition of who is human broadly enough to avoid excluding particular classes of people who may happen to be out of public favor at a given moment?

At this point some people will raise a pragmatic argument. It is all very well to talk of protecting the unborn child, they say, but women have always had abortions and they always will. No law can stop them. The only question is whether they should have abortions that are legal and safe or be condemned to seek back-alley "butchers," criminal abortionists who endanger their life and health.

This argument has a particle of truth to it, but only a particle.[27] There are some women in every society and in every age who will seek abortions no matter what the law says. But the number is far smaller than is usually alleged by advocates of legalized abortion.[28] There is little doubt that a strong law protecting the unborn child, especially if it is combined with life-promoting social policies and access to contraception, will reduce the incidence of abortion. This conclusion is borne out by studies, conducted in several countries, of women who were refused legal abortions. In every study it was found that only a small proportion of the women resorted to criminal abortions, although many of them had threatened to do so. Even more surprising, it was discovered that most of the women later said they were satisfied to have borne their children.[29]

It remains the case that even those laws which are frequently broken retain an educative function. They express the commonly accepted standards of behavior of a society, and many people consciously model their behavior according to what the law informs them is acceptable. The fact that a law is frequently broken is, by itself, no reason for doing away with that law. The laws against child abuse, theft, tax evasion and assault are broken far more often than the laws against abortion ever were. Yet they are still useful, both because they express our public moral standards, and because they undoubtedly prevent an even greater incidence of the offences they prohibit.

If I have reasoned correctly, the most enlightened social policy would be to legislate solid protection of the unborn child so as to bring the criminal law into harmony with the civil law. Such protection means that abortion would be permissible only when continuation of the pregnancy would result in the death of the mother. To adhere to this position is merely to recognize that the protection of innocent human life is the most basic duty of a civilized community. Our community will be neither healthy nor civilized so long as we fail in that duty.

IAN HUNTER

TRIAL BY JURY:
R. v. MORGENTALER

IN 1983, DRS. MORGENTALER, Smoling and Scott were charged with conspiracy to procure the miscarriage of female persons contrary to sections 423(1)(d) and 251 of the Canadian Criminal Code. After a lengthy trial, they were acquitted by the jury on November 8, 1984.[1]

What follows is a discussion of the process by which the jury was selected. A subsidiary issue concerns the address to the jury by defence counsel Morris Manning.

The jury selection process resulted in 132 prospective jurors being screened in order to obtain a jury of twelve. As will be seen, the trial judge erred in law by allowing counsel to ask specific questions on a generalized challenge for cause. The nature of these questions precluded a jury chosen "at random" from the panel and resulted in a jury predisposed to acquittal. This predisposition was then reinforced by an address in which the defence counsel invited the jurors to disregard their oath, the trial judge's instructions and the clear language of the Criminal Code.

Pursuant to section 605(1)(d) of the Criminal Code, the Crown appealed the acquittal, but it did not raise the method of jury selection as a ground of appeal, which is not surprising, since the Crown had acquiesced in the questioning of prospective jurors. Furthermore, an application by several pro-life groups to intervene solely on the issue of the jury selection procedure was refused by the Chief Justice of Ontario, William Howland.[2] The procedure followed at trial has therefore never been subject to appellate judicial scrutiny, but the Ontario Court of Appeal did comment critically on the address to the jury by the defence counsel.[3]

SELECTION

The criminal jury was created neither by royal fiat nor by administrative decree nor by parliamentary legislation: like Topsy, it just grew.[4] It grew from experience. Were it not that it worked, one might wonder at the notion of twelve men and women chosen at random — "men and women unaccustomed to severe intellectual exercise or protracted thought" as one Law Commission report tactfully put it[5] — being entrusted with the awful task of determining the guilt or innocence of a fellow human being. Implausible as it seems, the system works; jurors are sworn to render a true verdict according to the evidence, and their sagacity in doing so is one of the rare topics on which experienced judges, Crown attorneys and defence counsel agree. One reason why the system works is that we have not hitherto allowed members of a jury panel to be questioned about their beliefs, habits or opinions. The reason for this rule was succinctly stated by J.A. Seaton in *R. v. Makow*:

> In selecting jurors, we do not guarantee that they will have any particular attributes. We take 12 people from the street, with their virtues and their blemishes. We do it with the justifiable expectation that the blemishes of one will be more than compensated for by the virtues of the others. By our present methods we obtain a jury of 12 independent, conscientious people of varying intelligence and capacity. Will we get better jurors if they are cross-examined to ensure that they

have no views on the subject and have not heard about the matter? I think not.[6]

Section 567(1) of the Criminal Code restricts challenges for cause in Canada to six grounds:
1. the name of the juror does not appear on the panel;
2. a juror is not indifferent between the Queen and the accused;
3. a juror has been convicted of an offence for which he was sentenced to death or a term of imprisonment exceeding twelve months;
4. a juror is an alien;
5. a juror is physically unable to perform the duties of a juror; or
6. a juror does not speak an official language of Canada.

The specificity with which the six grounds are enumerated logically precludes argument that these are merely illustrative grounds or that challenges for cause may be asserted on other unspecified grounds. However, to put the matter beyond dispute, section 567(2) states: "No challenge for cause shall be allowed on a ground not mentioned in subsection (1)."

In *R. v. Morgentaler*, the trial judge, Associate Chief Justice William Parker, asked prospective jurors three questions under a generalized challenge for cause:

1. Do you have any religious, moral or other beliefs relating to abortion such that you would convict or acquit regardless of the law or the evidence?

Answer yes or no.

2. Have you, because of religious or moral beliefs or because of what you have read or seen in the media, formed any opinion as to the guilt or innocence of the accused?

Answer yes or no.

3. Despite any beliefs or opinions, would you be able to set aside those beliefs or opinions and reach a verdict of guilty

or not guilty solely on the evidence and the law you receive in this courtroom?

Answer yes or no.

Each question is flawed. The effect of question 1 is to single out prospective jurors who have religious beliefs. All Roman Catholics, and most Protestants, are members of denominations which have formulated a position on abortion. Roman Catholicism condemns abortion unequivocally. So do some Protestant denominations. All Christian denominations regard abortion as, at minimum, morally questionable behavior. Consequently, all Christians who take their religious beliefs seriously and who feel compelled truthfully to answer a Supreme Court judge's interrogatory, would be compelled to acknowledge religious or moral beliefs on abortion.

Question 1 goes on to inquire whether such belief would compel conviction or acquittal regardless of the evidence. There is no religious or moral belief which would compel acquittal regardless of the evidence; however, there may be religious or moral beliefs which compel conviction regardless of the evidence (e.g., if the person regarded abortion as tantamount to murder whatever the circumstances). Beneath its disingenuous appearance of neutrality, question 1 forces those with religious beliefs to search their consciences to ascertain the impact of beliefs upon action. The question appears to assume that one's religious beliefs ought not to influence one's conduct (thereby reversing the Biblical admonition: " . . . by their fruits ye shall know them"). If religious convictions might influence conduct, the juror is to declare himself, thereby resulting in certain exclusion by peremptory challenge in the unlikely event that the challenge for cause failed.

Question 2 is rather more confused. To the extent that it inquires into prejudgment based on "religious or moral beliefs," it is open to the same objection as question 1; insofar as it inquired into prejudgment based on "what you have seen or read in the media," it is improper. In *R. v. Hubbert*, the Ontario Court of Appeal unequivocally addressed this issue:

In this era of rapid dissemination of news by the various media, it would be naïve to think that in the case of a crime involving considerable notoriety, it would be possible to select 12 jurors who had not heard anything about the case. Prior information about a case, and even the holding of a tentative opinion about it, does not make partial a juror sworn to render a true verdict according to the evidence.[7]

Question 3 is superfluous. All jurors, on taking the oath, agree to reach a verdict solely on the evidence and the law. To direct such a question to prospective jurors, following two questions which inquire specifically about religious or moral beliefs on abortion, could only have the effect of intimidating them, predisposing them to the secular view of abortion which would be forcefully urged upon them throughout the trial by defence counsel.

After these three questions were put by the trial judge, some prospective jurors were asked follow-up questions by defence counsel Morris Manning: for example, whether they had children, what jobs they held and if they had engaged in any discussion of the case outside court.[8] Mr. Manning generally began his questioning of female prospective jurors by inquiring, "Is that Miss, Mrs. or Ms."? As a result of the questions asked, more than 90 percent of prospective jurors were excluded from this jury. On that basis alone the trial was improper for it was neither a jury chosen at random nor a jury representative of the community.

None of the trial judge's questions were relevant to any stated ground in section 567 of the Code except, arguably, (b) "indifferent between the Queen and the accused." But when is a juror "indifferent"?

In 1973 Chief Justice, Lord Widgery formulated the following direction to the English bar:

A jury consists of 12 individuals chosen at random from the appropriate panel. A juror should be excused if he is personally concerned in the facts of the particular case, or closely connected with a party to the proceedings or with a prospective witness. He may also be excused at the discretion of the judge on grounds of personal hardship or conscientious objection to jury service. It is contrary to established practice for jurors to be excused on more general grounds such as race, religion, or political beliefs or occupation.[9]

The recent case of *R. v. Pennington* illustrates the stringency with which this direction is applied in England.[10] Pennington, a striking miner, was convicted of vandalizing the car of a British Coal Board official. After trial it was discovered that one of the jurors was a miner who had supported the Coal Board by remaining at work throughout the strike. Pennington appealed. In dismissing the appeal, Justice Skinner held:

> It is no ground for disqualification of a juror that a juror might have personal reasons for some bias towards prosecution or defence. Even if it had been a ground of disqualification, that in itself is no ground for setting aside the verdict of a jury, provided that the juror's name was on the jury panel. That reasoning is the stronger where there is no disqualification but merely a suspicion of bias, as is the case here.[11]

In Ontario, the Court of Appeal has equated "indifference" with "impartiality."[12] Prior to trial, "indifference" requires that a juror be neutral as between the Crown and the defence. It does not require that a juror be neutral as to the offence. No juror would be excluded from a murder, rape or robbery trial because he or she believed that murder, rape or robbery was morally wrong. By proscribing conduct, by making it illegal, the Criminal Code has conclusively pronounced on the wrongfulness of the conduct. The Criminal Code speaks for all, juror and non-juror alike. It is not only the right but it is the duty of a good citizen to disapprobate crime. Jurors *should* regard with abhorrence the offence with which the accused is charged. But they should be open-minded as to whether the accused did what he is charged with doing and they should be neutral as between the Crown and the defence in the presentation of the evidence.

What is meant by indifference, in essence, is impartiality

between the adversaries, not indifference as to the offence. It is submitted, with respect, that Associate Chief Justice Parker confused the meaning of indifference. His three questions do not test impartiality between the parties. Rather they weed out jurors who have religious or moral beliefs and whose beliefs confirm the judgment of the Parliament of Canada, as expressed by the Criminal Code, that abortion is wrong.

Mr. Manning retained the services of Jury Services Inc. of Washington, D.C., to assist in selecting the Morgentaler jury. After the trial, the two consultants (a lawyer and a sociologist) acknowledged that their purpose had been to exclude religious persons from the jury. In an interview, the consultants stated:

Religion was very important. It was probably the key factor. It was not so much what religion but how active you were in your particular church. . . . There is a direct correlation between church attendance and the likelihood that someone holds anti-abortion sentiments. Generally speaking, here in this country, the more frequently someone attends church services the more likely they are to be anti-abortionists. It's a terribly important factor.[13]

This admission makes a mockery of the Ontario Court of Appeal's decision in *R. v. Hubbert*:

Challenge for cause is not for the purpose of finding out what kind of juror the person is likely to be — his personality, beliefs, prejudices, likes or dislikes. . . .

The challenge must never be used by counsel as a means of indoctrinating the jury panel in the proposed defence or otherwise attempting to influence the result of the eventual trial.[14]

The stated purpose of the questioning of jurors here, according to the consultants, was to exclude "regular churchgoers, housewives, young people and older professionals."[15] The motive was not to select an impartial jury but to choose a favorable one. As formulated, the judge's questions also constituted a none-too-subtle indoctrination of the jury into a secular view of abortion. It is difficult to imagine a more flagrant violation of the Court of Appeal's statement in *R. v. Hubbert.*

MANNING'S JURY ADDRESS

In his jury address, Morris Manning repeatedly urged jurors to find that the Criminal Code prohibition on abortion was "bad law," that it was harmful and unfair to Canadian women and that they should refuse to give effect to it. He contended that it was the right of a jury, notwithstanding the direction of the trial judge on the applicable law, to decide that the law should not be enforced. According to the Court of Appeal this was the "principal theme" of his jury address.

Such an address undermines the very basis of trial by jury. In an article written after the trial, Mr. Manning lauded the jury system and purported to defend it from critics.[16] Yet one can scarcely conceive an attack more insidious, or more likely to lead to the abolition of trial by jury, than to invite jurors to ignore their oath and the trial judge's instructions on the law and to refuse to follow or apply a law which they consider to be bad.

No objection to this address was made by Crown counsel at trial. However, Associate Chief Justice Parker, in his instructions, sought to undo the damage done by Mr. Manning's address. The Court of Appeal considered it "unrealistic" to conclude that Parker had been able to undo the damage. So unequivocally did the Court of Appeal condemn Manning's address that one wonders (had defence counsel been less experienced or respected than Mr. Manning) whether such an address might have been considered unprofessional conduct.

Per curiam the Court of Appeal stated:

> One cannot defend a criminal case by putting the law on trial and asking a jury to condemn a decision of Parliament in enacting or continuing a law because the jury thinks that it is, at the moment, bad law. . . .

In our view, defence counsel was wrong in urging the jury that they had the right to decide whether to apply the law the trial judge instructed them was applicable. The defence submission was a direct attack on the role and authority of the trial judge and a serious misstatement to the jury as to its duty and right in carrying out its oath. . . .

The submission of defence counsel was a forceful plea to the jury to nullify a law passed by Parliament. The jury was told to exercise a right that the jury did not have, to determine not to apply that law in the face of the instructions given by the trial judge.[17]

CONCLUSION

Few issues have so divided and polarized Canadians as abortion. The Morgentaler trial was subject to intense scrutiny by both sides and took place against a background of inflamed rhetoric, accusation and counter-accusation, picketing and demonstration. Had Dr. Morgentaler and his co-accused been acquitted by a representative jury, chosen at random and subject to proper instruction on their responsibilities and limitations, the acquittal could have been a significant milestone. If that had happened, fair-minded Canadians, whatever their persuasion about the morality of abortion, would have accepted the verdict. In the event, however, the decision has inflamed rather than diminished passions on both sides and it has brought the system of trial by jury into disrepute.

F. L. MORTON

THE MEANING OF
MORGENTALER:
A POLITICAL ANALYSIS

THE SUPREME COURT OF Canada's decision in *Morgentaler et al v. The Queen* is its most celebrated Charter of Rights decision to date.[1] It epitomizes the political character of the Court in its role as the ultimate interpreter of the Charter. Since its enactment in April 1982, the Charter has changed the practice of politics in Canada: it has altered the relationship between legislators and judges by conferring new limitations on the former and new power on the latter, and it has created new options for interest groups, especially those who "lose" in the more traditional arenas of electoral, legislative and administrative politics. The Charter has created a new political elite — a select group of Charter experts who influence how the Charter is interpreted by judges, reported by the press and understood by Canadians. In short, the Charter is changing the way Canada is governed. The Morgentaler case embodies many of these changes, and the following remarks elaborate eight of the more important changes.

Law Reform Through Lawsuit

The Morgentaler decision dramatizes just how much the Charter has changed Canadian politics. Just over twenty years ago, the federal government enacted major reforms to the abortion law (Section 251 of the Criminal Code) after a long and controversial process, which took almost three years from start to finish (1966-1969). Having studied that reform process quite carefully, I have not found a single reference to any proposal to use a court challenge to try to influence the process of abortion law reform. Interest group use of litigation to do an "end run" around "responsible government" was viewed as an idiosyncrasy of American politics, "un-Canadian" and generally illegitimate. From start to finish, the 1969 reform was entirely a government-parliamentary matter.

Within six years, this situation had already begin to change. Encouraged in large part by the American Supreme Court's 1973 abortion decision, *Roe v. Wade*,[2] Henry Morgentaler, an obscure Montreal doctor, set out on a one-man crusade of civil disobedience to challenge Canada's abortion law. Morgentaler was acquitted at trial by a jury in 1974, but then convicted by the Quebec Court of Appeal. On appeal to the Supreme Court of Canada, Morgentaler drew upon the 1960 Bill of Rights to argue that Canada's abortion law violated the individual liberty and right to privacy of Canadian women, which was essentially the same argument that had been accepted by the American Supreme Court in *Roe v. Wade* one year earlier. During oral argument, the Supreme Court of Canada rejected it outright. After a brief recess, the Court announced that the Bill of Rights argument was without any merit and told the Crown that it need not even rebut the argument. In its written opinion nine months later, only one judge — Chief Justice Laskin — bothered to acknowledge the Bill of Rights argument, and even he rejected it. On March 27, 1975, Henry Morgentaler went to prison.

Eleven years later, Henry Morgentaler was back in the same Supreme Court challenging the same abortion law — only this time his arguments were based on the Charter of Rights and

Freedoms, and this time he won. The Supreme Court declared Canada's abortion law constitutionally invalid. What had been unthinkable in the sixties and impossible in the seventies, became a reality in the eighties.

THE EMERGENCE OF FEMINISM IN CANADIAN POLITICS

The Morgentaler decision cannot be explained by the Charter alone. Equally important were developments outside of the courtroom and the Charter. The Morgentaler decision reflects the emergence of feminism as a major force in Canadian politics. There was almost no feminist input into the 1969 abortion law reform,[3] and in 1975 there was a feminist presence but no influence. Several pro-choice groups were allowed to intervene in the Supreme Court's hearing of the Morgentaler appeal, but their Bill of Rights arguments were not even addressed by a majority of the Court.

This situation had changed dramatically by the time Morgentaler returned to the Supreme Court in 1986. Feminists, stung by their lack of success under the 1960 Bill of Rights, worked successfully to influence the drafting of the 1982 Charter of Rights and Freedoms and then helped to mobilize public support for its adoption.[4] Feminists subsequently organized LEAF — the Legal Education and Action Fund — a nationwide organization to identify and litigate women's issues under the Charter. In 1982 the first woman was appointed to the Supreme Court of Canada — Madam Justice Bertha Wilson — who went on to write the feminist perspective on abortion into her concurring opinion in the Morgentaler decision. Subsequently two more women — Madam Justice Claire Heureux-Dubé (1987) and Madam Justice Beverly McLachlin (1989) — have been appointed to the Court. In twenty years, the proportion of women in Canadian law schools had gone from less than 10 percent to almost half.

These changes within the legal world reflected similar changes in the larger political landscape of the eighties. Feminists converted some of their legal defeats of the seventies into political victories. They persuaded Parliament to amend the Indian Act to end the disabilities previously attached to Indian women by that legislation.[5] Parliament was also persuaded to amend the Unemployment Insurance Act to cover all pregnancy-related unemployment.[6] While political elites still resist many feminist policy proposals, they are now careful not to offend feminist sensibilities, for fear of bad public relations and a political backlash.

Judges — even Supreme Court justices — are not immune to these shifts in public opinion, so the growth of feminist influence in political, educational and social elites was a necessary precondition for the Morgentaler decision. The Charter provided Morgentaler with a new weapon, but its successful use was contingent upon a more receptive legal and political context.

THE CHARTER AS A CATALYST FOR NEW LEFT-RIGHT CLEAVAGE

Historically there has been a strong tendency in Canadian politics for policy controversies to be defined in terms of jurisdictional disputes between the two levels of governments. Policy debate often turns on the issue of which government has the authority to enact such and such a law, rather than on the merits of the law itself. Constitutional litigation and judicial involvement have tended to emphasize further the jurisdictional dimension. Even when important civil liberties such as freedom of the press were at stake, the issue tended to be posed as "Which level of government has the authority to regulate newspaper criticism of government policy?" rather than "Does this law violate the tradition of freedom of speech and press essential to Canadian democracy?"[7]

The Charter changes this in an obvious way. Individuals and interest groups who believe that government policy violates one of their fundamental rights or freedoms can go directly to the courts and make their case. Less obvious but equally important is the effect that this new procedure may have on the broader conduct of Canadian politics. The Morgentaler case demonstrates how Charter decisions can force governments at both levels to act legislatively, action that in turn has political-electoral consequences.

Recent developments in American politics also suggest how judicial decisions on civil liberties issues can have significant political ramifications. The so-called social issues — abortion, "court-ordered busing," affirmative action, school prayer, rights of criminals, capital punishment, the Equal Rights Amendment (ERA), homosexual rights — have reshaped American politics in the eighties. They have divided — indeed, redefined — liberals and conservaties. All of these issues have been affected, directly or indirectly, by Supreme Court decisions, a fact that was apparent in Republican party platforms during the elections of 1980 and 1984. The Republicans called for the appointment of federal judges who believed in "the decentralization of the federal government and efforts to return decision-making power to states and local elected officials . . . [and] . . . who respect the traditional family values and the sanctity of innocent human life."[8] The judicial appointments issue has been an important part of the Republican's successful strategy to carve away socially conservative voter blocks — such as white Southerners and blue-collar ethnic Catholics — from the traditional Democratic party coalition.

While not all these issues are applicable to Canada, many are. And most are or could be touched by Charter litigation and Supreme Court decisions. Parliament's struggle to enact a new abortion law has certainly revealed cleavages that cut across party lines, and suggests that abortion could serve as a catalyst for a new left-right cleavage in federal elections. Prime Minister Mulroney's ill-fated proposal in May 1988 for a free vote on three alternative abortion "options" was an attempt to put abortion reform above partisan politics. The Liberals' and NDP's refusal to cooperate indicates the opposition's belief that there is political advantage to be gained by forcing the Conservatives to formulate their own abortion law. The subsequent failure of the government's abortion bill in July, 1988 revealed sharp divisions within the Tory and Liberal caucuses. Only the NDP took a united stand favouring the total decriminalization of abortion. The potential electoral impact of the abortion issue was negated, however, when the federal election in November 1988 evolved into an emotional referendum on the Free Trade Agreement with the United States, completely preempting all other issues.

In November 1989, the Mulroney government introduced a new abortion bill, (Bill C 43) but the old divisions remain. Under the government's much celebrated "compromise" bill, abortion at any stage of a pregnancy remains a crime, but becomes legal if it is approved by one doctor to protect the physical or psychological health of the mother. Bluntly stated, this bill says that abortion is wrong in principle but easily available in practice. The principle has infuriated pro-choice partisans in and out of Parliament, while the practice is equally unacceptable to pro-lifers.

At the time of writing (April 1990), the bill has passed first and second readings and committee hearings are being held prior to third reading. Indications are that pro-life Tories and Liberals will try to amend the bill to make access to abortion more difficult if not impossible. The New Democrats remain committed to the total decriminalization of abortion. If the pro-life coalition can succeed in enacting a more restrictive abortion law, the NDP — especially under the new leadership of Audrey McLaughlin — can be counted on to try to exploit the abortion issue. For some voters, the next federal election could become a referendum on the Tory abortion law, an issue that would cut across old regional or ethnic political allegiances.

THE POLITICS OF RIGHTS

The Morgentaler decision also signaled a new dimension in Canadian politics — the "politics of rights," which "describes the forms of political activity made possible by the presence of [constitutional] rights."[9] The Charter has created a new forum —

courts; a new set of decision makers — judges; and a new resource — not votes or money (at least, not more than half a million dollars or so) but simply the "right argument." Interest groups who "lose" in the more traditional arenas of electoral, legislative and administrative politics can now turn to the courts for a second kick at the can.

Charter enthusiasts draw a sharp distinction between the realm of rights and the realm of politics. Where politics, they claim, are in the realm of self-interest, driven by will and ruled by compromise, rights are part of the realm of justice, governed by reason and discerned by impartial judges. The beauty of the Charter, according to this view, is that it lifts questions of right out of the grimy give-and-take of party politics and into a sphere where independent judges, exercising "reason not will," can define and defend rights against the excesses of majority-rule democracy.

While this rights-interest dichotomy has merit in theory, in practice it simply breaks down. Any interest group with enough money to hire a lawyer can have their interest claim transformed into the rhetoric of rights. This is especially true under the so-called living tree approach to Charter interpretation, which exhorts judges to give a "large and liberal" interpretation to Charter rights and not be overly constrained by the "original understanding" of the rights in question (as disclosed by either the text or the legislative history). Under the "benign" shade of the "living tree," every political group — from the National Citizens' Coalition to the Canadian Union of Public Employees, from Henry Morgentaler to Jim Keegstra — can claim that its objectives are in fact protected by some "penumbra" of the Constitution.

The Morgentaler case — especially when seen in tandem with the Borowski pro-life challenge to the same abortion law — represents the "politics of rights" writ large. Neither Morgentaler nor Borowski represent the lonely individual who, wronged by the system, humbly comes to the Supreme Court asking for redress. For both men the use of the courts was a calculated political choice. It was a choice based on repeated rejections by political parties and public opinion polls. Both were represented by some of Canada's best and most expensive legal talent — Morris Manning and Morris Schumiatcher. Their legal expenses — over a quarter of a million dollars each — were picked up by the pro-choice and pro-life interest groups whose causes they champion.

Equally telling is that both Morgentaler and Borowski based their Charter challenges to the abortion law on the same section of the Charter. Morgentaler claims that section 7 guarantees a "right to privacy" for women that includes the liberty to choose abortion. Borowski claims that the same section protects the "right to life" of the unborn. The layman might reasonably ask, How can the same section of the Charter guarantee both a right to life and a right to abortion? The answer, of course, is that section 7 guarantees neither, at least not explicitly. Both Morgentaler and Borowski claim that these rights are "implied" by the broad contours of "life, liberty, and security of the person . . . [and] the principles of fundamental justice." Enter the "living tree" doctrine, which encourages judges to "find" such implied rights. Indeed, the Morgentaler and Borowski claims represent the "living tree" with a vengeance, since the legislative history behind the framing of section 7 makes it clear that it was studiously neutral on the abortion issue. Lord Sankey's hallowed dictum[10] has been invoked repeatedly by counsel for both sides, as they urge the judges not only to find "implied rights" but to ignore the legislative history behind section 7 as well.

This is the new Canadian version of the "politics of rights." The various rights enumerated in the Charter become "political resources of unknown value in the hands of those who want to alter the course of public policy."[11] Individuals and interest groups can appeal to the vague but powerful ideals enshrined in the Charter of Rights to legitimate their own policy interests. They can recast their policy goals in the rhetoric of rights, and then take them to the courts to be "enforced." Whether they succeed depends largely on how the judges exercise their considerable discretion to interpret the Charter.

JUDICIAL DISCRETION

Charter enthusiasts characterize the Charter as the extension of the Anglo-Canadian "rule of law" tradition: that no man is above the law; that the rulers must live by the same laws as the ruled. From this sanguine perspective, the Charter provides a set of explicit constitutional rules and a mechanism for ensuring that even the lawmakers must obey the Constitution. Charter skeptics respond that the Charter does not enforce itself; that it speaks through the mouths of judges. The "rule of law" cannot escape human agency, and is thus always subject to abuse by its ultimate guardians. Skeptics tend to take seriously an American chief justice's off-hand comment that "the constitution means what the judges say it means." This remark emphasizes the element of judicial discretion, the ability of judges to choose between competing meanings. It also suggests that different judges may find different rights. If this is true, rather than advancing the rule of law, the charter may actually undermine it.

The Morgentaler case supports the skeptics' view of the Charter. In response to the question "Does section 251 of the Criminal Code violate the Charter?" the seven justices gave four different opinions. Only one justice — Madam Justice Wilson — said that there was a constitutional right to abortion, and even she acknowledged a legitimate state interest in protecting the life of the fetus/unborn child at some point in the second trimester of pregnancy.

The two dissenters, McIntyre and LaForest, looked behind the text of the Charter to the original understanding of its meaning. They found that the history of the debates surrounding the framing of the Charter in 1980-81 showed that it was intentionally neutral on the abortion issue. They reasoned that judges have no authority to create rights (for either the fetus or the mother) that do not already exist in the text of the Charter. When the Charter is silent on an issue, they concluded, so too must be the judges.

The other four judges who ruled against the abortion law did so because they believed that it violated the procedural fairness required by section 7, not because there is any independent right to abortion. These four further disagreed among themselves on just how serious even the procedural violations were. Two, Dickson and Lamer, said that the requirements of the current law — such as approval by a therapeutic abortion committee (TAC) — were inherently unfair and would have to be scrapped. The other two judges — Beetz and Estey — defined the procedural problems more narrowly and thus as remediable. While certain requirements — such as the TAC approval — created unfair delays and burdens, a revised version of the TAC might be acceptable. Specifically, Beetz and Estey ruled that in principle there was no constitutional problem with the requirement of the current law that abortions be permitted only when the continuation of a pregnancy "would threaten the life or health of the mother"; nor was there a difficulty with the requirement of an independent and impartial third party to be the judge of this issue — the purpose of a TAC.

This division of the Court reflected in Table 1 was not caused by a technical disagreement over a narrow point of law. Rather it reflected a growing division in the Court between two different theories of Charter review, two different conceptions of the proper rule of the judge. One wing of the Court, exemplified by Madam Justice Wilson, adopted a broad and activist approach to interpreting the Charter. As evidenced by her opinion in Morgentaler, Madam Justice Wilson is inclined to read in new and even unintended meaning to the broadly worded principles of the Charter, and is not at all reluctant to strike down parliamentary enactments that fail to meet her vision of the Charter. The other wing of the court is best exemplified by Justice McIntyre's self-restrained and more deferential approach to Charter interpretation. The Charter, McIntyre has written, is not "an empty vessel to be filled with whatever meaning we might wish."[12] The McIntyre approach attempts to minimize judicial discretion by limiting Charter rights to their "original meaning" and as a result is usually more deferential to Parliament's decisions.

These two different approaches to interpreting the Charter lead to very different results. A pilot study of twenty-five Charter

Table 1

*Comments of Supreme Court
Judges on Abortion Law*

	JUDGES			
	Wilson	Dickson Lamer	Beetz	LaForest Estey McIntyre
1. Provincial options: Funding	No opinions from any judge on funding issue.			
2. Federal options: Criminal Code (1st trimester)	No limitations. Absolute right to abortion.	Abortion may be limited to therapeutic reasons. Current law unacceptable in principle.	Abortion may be limited to therapeutic reasons. Details of current law must be revised.	Current law acceptable.
3. Federal options: Criminal Code (2nd & 3rd trimester)		Regulation permitted to protect the life of the fetus.		
Judgements in Morgentaler case.	Current law violates substantive rights of section 7 of the Charter.	Current law violates procedural rights of section 7 of Charter.		Current law does not violate Charter.

decisions revealed that the judges had very different "voting records" on Charter cases. Predictably, Madam Justice Wilson had the highest percentage of votes supporting individuals' Charter claims — 82 percent, while Justice McIntrye had one of the lowest — 32 percent.[13]

The contrast between McIntyre and Wilson becomes still more stark when one accounts for the number and "directionality" of their dissenting and concurring opinions. The decision to write a concurring or dissenting opinion indicates a judge's dissatisfaction or disagreement with the majority opinion. Repeated use of concurring and dissenting opinions indicates that a judge is outside the mainstream of the court. Significantly, Justices Wilson and McIntyre "lead" the court in these categories. Not only do they depart from the majority most frequently, but they do so in opposite directions. In each of her thirteen dissents, Wilson supported the individual's Charter claim, while McIntyre supported the Crown in ten of his eleven dissents. Twenty-eight of Wilson's thirty-two dissenting and concurring opinions, including her opinion on the 1986 Morgentaler case, supported a broader interpretation of the Charter than the majority. In sixteen of his twenty-three concurrences and dissents, McIntyre supported a narrower interpretation of the Charter.

These data confirm what most Charter experts already suspected: in many Charter cases, the judicial philosophy of a judge is more likely to determine the outcome than the text of the Charter. Different judges "find" different rights. As the political implications of this fact are recognized by affected political actors and interest groups, there will be growing pressure to appoint the "right kind of judge" to Canadian appeal courts.

THE POLITICIZATION OF JUDICIAL APPOINTMENTS

To most Canadians, the "Bork Affair" in the United States in 1987-88, was politically repugnant.[14] It was perceived as a not-so-covert attempt to control the meaning of American constitutional law by controlling the appointment of Supreme Court judges. Such attempts at "court packing" seem to strike at the foundations of judicial independence and thus the tradition of "rule of law" in general. Like it or not, however, decisions like

Morgentaler make Canadian versions of the Bork Affair much more likely.

"Where power rests, there influence will be brought to bear."[15] So wrote V. O. Key, a leading American political scientist, explaining the lobbying behavior of interest groups in the American political system. There is no reason to assume that Key's axiom does not apply equally to Canadian democracy. In the wake of *Morgentaler*, Angela Costigan, counsel for Choose Life Canada, a national pro-life lobby group, criticized the decision as "the expression of personal opinion by the judges," and indicated that in future they would try to influence the appointment of judges who share their position. Norma Scarborough, president of the Canadian Abortion Rights Action League (CARAL), responded by declaring that while her group had never tried to influence judicial appointments in the past, it would, if necessary, in the future. "We are going to protect our position as much as possible," she declared.[16]

Two months later Justice William Estey announced his intention to resign from the Supreme Court and the search for Estey's replacement immediately attracted the attention of abortion activists. The *Globe and Mail* reported that "activists in the abortion debate and representatives of ethnic communities are lobbying hard. . . . Many members of the ruling PC Party's right wing . . . are putting pressure on PM Mulroney to appoint a conservative judge." Member of Parliament James Jepson, one of the most outspoken pro-life Tory backbenchers, explained the importance of the new Supreme Court appointment: "We now have a chance to put men and women on the bench with a more conservative point of view." While emphasizing that he had never lobbied for a judicial appointment before, Jepson continued:

But this one seems to have caught the people's attention. Unfortunately, with the Charter that Trudeau left us, we legislators do not have final power. It rests with the courts. . . . You have seen the battling in the United States for the [most recent] Supreme Court nominee. Well, it doesn't take a rocket scientist to see we have the same situation here now.[17]

In the end, the pro-life lobbying had no apparent effect on the government's appointment of Toronto lawyer John Sopinka to fill Justice Estey's seat on the Court. But Jepson's comments are a political first in Canada and are not likely to disappear as political élites become more sophisticated in their understanding of the politics of rights engendered by the Charter.

Nor should this be viewed as a wholly negative development. Attention to the politics and judicial philosophies of potential judges is consistent with democratic norms of legitimacy. To take just one example, when Bertha Wilson was appointed to the Supreme Court in 1982, no one noticed that five years earlier she had chaired a policy committee of the United Church that strongly endorsed liberal reform of the abortion law. It seems unlikely that this type of information would go unnoticed today.

For better or for worse, the relationship between courts and politics is a two-way street. The more judges influence the political process, the more political actors will try to influence the selection of judges.

RULE OF LAW OR RULE OF EXPERTS?

The Charter is often praised as extending the "rule of law" and thus as enhancing Canadian democracy. Yet as the Morgentaler case illustrates, the Charter also contributes to the growth of the rule of experts — technocrats — and thereby further erodes the influence of Parliament and provincial legislatures.

Imagine an average Canadian visiting Ottawa on October 10, 1986. Our citizen/tourist first visits Parliament Hill for question period. There are many empty seats and few reporters. As he listens to the spirited give and take across the center aisle, he can readily understand what is being said; and equally quickly realizes that it is not very important. As he continues down Wellington Street, he arrives at the Supreme Court, just in time for the first day of oral argument in the Morgentaler case. The swarm of media on the front steps (so that's where they all are!) alerts him that something important must be going on inside.

A reporter tells him that the court is deciding the validity of Canada's abortion law. Eagerly he enters the building and takes a seat (if he can find one), anticipating an articulate and enlightening debate on the divisive abortion issue. After listening to several hours of abstract and dreary legal monologues, he gives up and leaves. There has been much talk about section 7, security of the person, principles of fundamental justice and substantive interpretation, but the abortion issue seems to have disappeared. While something important is indeed being decided, it is being done in a foreign language, incomprehensible to our citizen/tourist.

Fifteen months later, on January 28, 1988, the Supreme Court announces its decision in the Morgentaler case. The decision is 199 pages long and consists of four different opinions. The sheer length of the decision precludes most people from even trying to read it. Of the valiant few who might try, most would be quickly defeated by the highly technical character of the legal writing. The language of the law is foreign to most Canadians — and the language of the Charter — the "chatter" of rights — is unintelligible even to many lawyers.

If Canadians cannot read or understand the Supreme Court's Charter decisions, how do we know what the court has decided? The answer, of course, is that the media tell us. But does this solve the problem or only compound it? The Morgentaler case suggests the latter. While the media certainly told us who won and who lost, they failed badly to explain the reasons why, and thus did little to elucidate the policy options left open to Parliament.[18]

This is hardly surprising. The media have an obvious bias for exaggerating the confrontational aspect of any news story. Television — the most common source of political information — tends to be "highly abbreviated, sensationalized and oriented to conflict and personalities."[19] The evening news on January 28, 1988, was on the same level as locker-room interviews with the winning and losing teams after the Superbowl. No substance, no information, just conflict — the thrill of victory, the agony of defeat.

Even when the media want to communicate the substance of

Charter decisions, they tend to suffer the same disabilities as the rest of us: length of judgments, lack of time and highly technical language. Typically, the media try to short-cut these difficulties through interviews with "Charter experts," who are expected to cut through the legalese of the judges and give the public a plain-language version of the decision. In the wake of the Morgentaler case, the airwaves were flooded with such interviews.

Who are these Charter experts? Can they be relied upon to give us accurate "translations" of the Supreme Court's Charter decisions? Charter experts are drawn exclusively from the ranks of lawyers, and especially from the faculties of Canadian law schools. They must not only practise Charter law but also write and publish scholarly articles about the Charter. These experts therefore have a strong academic bent, so their influence extends beyond mere "hired gun" advocacy. Through their law review articles, commentaries and media interviews, they also define the very terms of Charter discourse. This kind of indirect influence — which ultimately influences how judges interpret the Charter — is politically more significant than their advocacy role.

Relative to the legal profession generally, Charter experts are also disproportionately young. Like most academics, they also tend to be left of center politically.[20] Most are not only Charter experts but Charter enthusiasts as well. They see the Charter as a valuable instrument for achieving social and political reform — usually of the left-liberal variety, such as striking down restrictive abortion laws. The line between their profession and their politics is often a fine one.

Can these Charter experts be relied upon to give us accurate "translations" of the Supreme Court's Charter decisions? Suffice it to say that to the extent that they are themselves partisan, they can use their professional authority to advance their political agendas — of which there was some evidence in the days following the Morgentaler case.[21] The media relied heavily on interviews with women lawyers and law professors, almost all of whom were also active feminists. Consciously or not, some clearly put their politics ahead of their profession. There was a decided tendency to overstate the scope of the Court's decison;

to quote Madam Justice Wilson at length; to minimize the narrow, procedural basis of the other four majority judges; and to ignore the two dissenting judges altogether. There were also instances of extending the meaning of *Morgentaler* to include public funding of abortions, an issue that clearly was not addressed or answered by the Supreme Court's decision. This kind of selective misrepresentation misleads the public into believing that the Court has decided issues that it really hasn't. The media's use of Charter experts can thus make them accomplices, unwitting or otherwise, in promoting the political agendas of those experts.

PARLIAMENT AND THE SUPREME COURT: ADVERSARIES OR PARTNERS?

The Charter is widely perceived as creating an adversarial relationship between Parliament and the Supreme Court. It places new limitations on legislative power and authorizes judges to define those limits. The Morgentaler decision at first appears to embody this conflict. Certainly the headline of the *Globe and Mail* on January 29, 1988 — "Abortion Law Scrapped; Women Get Free Choice" — suggests this.

The reality, however, is much different. *Morgentaler* is not *Roe v. Wade*, and the Canadian Supreme Court cannot be accused of legislating a national abortion policy the way its American counterpart can. Only one Canadian judge — Madam Justice Wilson — presumed to tell Parliament that it cannot prohibit "lifestyle" abortions. The four other judges in the majority staked out a much narrower ground. In effect, they told Parliament that it could legislate as it saw fit with respect to abortion, but that if it chose to use criminal sanctions, certain procedural safeguards would have to be respected. In this regard, the Morgentaler decision may come to be seen as an act of judicial statesmanship. It has forced Canadian lawmakers to deal with the abortion issue — something they had consciously avoided — but without telling them how. Unlike *Roe v. Wade*, the Morgentaler decision has not preempted the political process but has actually stimulated it.

While the Charter creates an obviously adversarial dimension to legislative-judicial relations, in a less obvious sense, it also provides support for legislative authority. Precisely because the Supreme Court can invalidate legislation for violating the Charter, so it can legitimate Parliament's policy choices by upholding them. Judicial review under the Charter provides a substitution for the right to disobey an unjust law, a peaceful alternative to civil disobedience or armed revolt. To be credible, the Court must have the power to nullify laws, and on occasions exercise it, but by the same measure, when the Court unholds a law, it sends out a political message that the law has passed the constitutional litmus test. This symbolic constitutional "stamp of approval" serves to reconcile opponents of the law, or at least de-legitimate further opposition to it, for in the eyes of the majority, the opponents have had their second chance.[22]

Whatever Parliament decides in terms of a new abortion law, it will obviously not satisfy all parties.[23] It is equally certain that these dissatisfied groups will renew their attack on the abortion law in the courts. A restrictive law will be challenged by feminists as a violation of the liberty of women. A permissive law will be challenged by pro-lifers as a violation of the rights of the unborn and/or the father. It is not unthinkable that the government may even try to preempt such challenges by referring their new abortion law to the Supreme Court. Given that the proposed law at least amends the procedural problems identified by the Beetz-Estey opinion, it is most likely that the Supreme Court will uphold it. Such a decision would send out the message that the new law is constitutional, thus enhancing its legitimacy.

While the Morgentaler saga disclosed an adversarial relationship between courts and legislatures, future developments are likely to reveal a complementary relationship, in which the Court strengthens Parliament's authority by upholding its new abortion law and by conferring a new — and probably needed — legitimacy.

R O B E R T   D .   N A D E A U

THE ANATOMY
OF EVASION: A CRITIQUE
OF *DAIGLE*

LEAVING ASIDE FOR the moment the relative merits of the pro-choice and pro-life positions, it is obvious that the pro-choice concern is about the denial of a right of privacy that is still novel and insecurely grounded in our law and moral custom. The pro-life concern, by contrast, is about the taking of innocent human life, a concern that is foundational to the existence of this or any other civilization.[1]

With the ink barely dry on the federal government's abortion bill,[2] the Supreme Court of Canada stunned many legal observers and academics when it declared in its Reasons for Judgment in the *Daigle* case[3] that a fetus is not a "human being" for purposes of the Quebec Charter of Human Rights and Freedoms and, therefore, does not have the right to life.

Not that legal observers did not fully expect the Court to do "the sensible thing" and reach the same result some day, in an "appropriate" case, if a new abortion law were ever passed and challenged again. But very few expected the Court to go as far as it did, as quickly as it did, in the *Daigle* case. After all, the case was essentially a private dispute between two parties (notwithstanding the broad array of intervenors).[4]

What's more, the Supreme Court had already refused to rule on the question of fetal rights in the absence of legislation earlier the same year in *Borowski*[5] as there was, in the Court's view, "no longer a live controversy or concrete dispute as the substratum of Mr. Borowski's appeal has disappeared."[6] Section 251 of the Criminal Code had been struck down in its entirety by the Court in January 1988 and there was no legislation that could be tested against the Charter: the issue was now moot.

In *Daigle*, there was no longer a live controversy either, or a live baby, when the Court convened to hear the appeal. Chantal had already had the abortion. The substratum of her appeal had by then "disappeared" too: the issue was now dead. Still, the Court broke its own rules and pressed ahead with the hearing.

COURT OVERREACHES

But there's more here than a court changing rules in the middle of the game. Most legal observers and academics fully anticipated a narrow decision setting aside the injunction on some technical question of jurisdiction or division of powers. No one really expected *Daigle* to be the Court's "big case" on the question of fetal rights.

After all, the Court did not hear the application for leave to appeal until August 1. The hearing was fixed for August 8. Lawyers had one day to file all affidavits and one week to prepare their case. What's more, all intervenors (with the exception of the federal government) were restricted to ten minutes of oral argument.[7] Meanwhile, Chantal Daigle was in her twenty-second week of pregnancy, or so the Court thought. Time was running out.

This was hardly the environment in which to consider and debate the complex and weighty questions of fetal life and fetal protection. Peter Russell, professor of political science at the University of Toronto, expressed these concerns in the press only days before the hearing: "It is very difficult to accommodate her timetable and still do justice to the issues . . . You do not want to produce it in a hothouse, emergency atmosphere. This opinion will be with us for centuries."[8] Dalhousie law professor Wayne MacKay, commenting on the advanced state of the pregnancy and Chantal's vague reasons for wanting the abortion, added: "I am not sure they want this to be their big case on the rights of the fetus."[9] Maybe not. But from all appearances, that is exactly what it was.[10]

SUPREME COURT DENIES FETAL RIGHTS

The thesis of this short essay is that the Court's decision in *Daigle* was gratuitous, ill-considered and overreaching. It lacked imagination or any of the hallmarks of thoughtful judicial reasoning one would expect from a decision of such momentous social significance. Its blind imitation of the past and its uncritical acceptance of outmoded legal fictions give it an air of rationalization and posturing in the face of a predetermined outcome.

With full knowledge of the fatal implications of its decision, the Court denied an entire class of humankind any form of legal or constitutional protection, as nearly as I can make out, for no other reason but the developmental immaturity of the unborn child. The Court did not put it quite that way, of course, but it comes to the same: "A fetus is treated as a person only where it is necessary to do so in order to protect its interests *after it is born*."[11] Why a fetus is treated this way by the law, apart from the fact that it is, the Justices didn't bother to explain. Rarely has the Court gone so far to avoid the obvious or offered so little explanation for a decision that requires so much.

THE ISSUE

The basic issue in *Daigle* was whether the substantive rights existed upon which the injunction could be founded.[12] By this, the Court meant whether, as a matter of law, there were fetal rights or paternal rights that could support the injunction. The respondent (Jean-Guy Tremblay) and the pro-life intervenors argued there were; the appellant (Chantal Daigle) and the pro-choice intervenors argued the other way. The Court sided with the appellants.

Recognizing that if the right to life in the Quebec Charter were extended to the unborn the case for abortion would collapse, the Court reasoned that the words "human being" in the Charter, whatever they may signify in ordinary life, *were not* intended to include the unborn child and, therefore, presumably, *could not* include the unborn child.[13] If the Quebec Legislature had intended to include the fetus within the meaning of "human being," said the Court, it would have said so. Therefore, neither the assertion of fetal rights on behalf of the unborn child, nor the father's interest in protection of the fetus, could support the injunction.

THE QUEBEC CHARTER OF RIGHTS AND FREEDOMS

To appreciate the lengths to which the Court had to go to avoid the plain meaning of words, it is necessary to read the relevant provisions of the Quebec legislation first hand:

> Whereas every human being possesses intrinsic rights and freedoms designed to ensure his *protection and development*;

> Whereas all human beings are equal in worth and dignity, and are entitled to equal protection of the law . . .

> Therefore, Her Majesty, with the advice and consent of the National Assembly of Quebec, enacts as follows:

1. Every *human being* has a right to life, and to personal security, inviolability and freedom. He also possesses juridical personality.

2. Every *human being* whose life is in peril has a right to assistance. Every *person* must come to the aid of anyone whose life is in peril . . . [14]

While several indicators of legislative intent could be marshalled from the textual arrangements and language itself, perhaps the clearest is the obvious textual differences in language found between sections 1 and 2. In section 1, every "human being" has a right to life, and in section 2, "every human being whose life is in peril has a right to assistance." But only a "person" must come to the aid of "anyone" whose life is in peril.

Obviously, an unborn child could not come to the aid of anyone in peril. If intent can be inferred at all from language, or if language has any meaning, the legislature intended to draw a clear and unmistakable distinction in section 2 between a "human being" whose life is in peril and a "person" who must come to his aid. The words "human being" are obviously intended to be read more broadly than "person," and the necessary inference, on a plain reading of the text, is that the legislature intended the words "human being" to include an unborn child. This reading becomes all the more compelling when the other relevant sections of the Quebec Charter and the Civil Code are considered.

The Court, of course, rejected this construction. It began by raising a presumption against the legal or constitutional personality of unborn children and made it irrebuttable by excluding all relevant considerations: "The *Charter* is framed in very general terms. It makes no reference to fetus or fetal rights, nor does it include any definition of the term 'human being.'"[15] Indeed, all attempts to bring meaning to the words were ruled out of order:

> . . . the argument must be viewed in the context of the legislation in question. The Court is not required to enter the philosophical and theological debates about whether a fetus is a person, but rather, to answer the legal question of whether the Quebec Legislature has accorded the fetus personhood. Metaphysical arguments may be relevant but they are not the primary focus of enquiry. Nor are scientific arguments about the biological status of a fetus determinative in our enquiry. The task of properly classifying a fetus in law and in science are different pursuits . . . In short, this Court's task is a legal one. Decisions based upon broad social, political, moral and economic choices are more appropriately left to the legislature.[16]

If metaphysical arguments are or may be "relevant," why were they not considered? And if scientific arguments are not "determinative," they must by implication at least be relevant. Why were these ignored? The only plausible explanation is that the Court could not bring itself to meet the arguments openly in a public contest for fear the law could not withstand such severe scrutiny.[17] On that point, the Court got it right.

Having now swept aside all relevant considerations, all possible avenues for displacing the presumption raised by the Court against the legal personality of unborn children, all the Court had left to worry about was the language of the Charter (which on its face pointed strongly in favor of fetal rights).

As might be expected, here again the Court made short shrift of the textual arguments, this time by asserting that "(a) linguistic analysis cannot settle the difficult and controversial question of whether a fetus was intended by the National Assembly of Quebec to be a person under section 1."[18] In the Court's view:

> The Quebec *Charter*, considered as a whole, does not display

any clear intention on the part of its framers to consider the status of a fetus. This is most evident in the fact that the *Charter* lacks definition of "human being" or "person" . . . One can ask why the Quebec Legislature, if it had intended to accord a fetus the right to life, would have left the protection of this right in such an uncertain state.[19]

One can imagine how frightful, how chilling, these words would have sounded in the ears of Henrietta Edwards, Emily Murphy and untold thousands of other Canadian, British and American women who as recently as sixty years ago were similarly disenfranchised, stripped of their humanity and dignity and excluded from participation in all public and professional life, for no other reason but their common law "disabilities" and "legal incapacities" as nonpersons. *Daigle* was not the first time the Supreme Court turned its back on incontrovertible claims and denied an entire class of humankind the status and privileges of personhood. In 1928, the Supreme Court refused to recognize the personhood of women, in language and tone not unlike that in *Daigle*.[20]

THE *PERSON'S* CASE

The case had to do with an application by Henrietta Edwards, Emily Murphy and other Canadian feminists for the right to be nominated to the Senate. The legal issue, on a reference to the Supreme Court, was whether the word "person" in the *British North America Act* (admittedly a constitutional document) could be said to include women. The Supreme Court ruled unanimously that it did not. Chief Justice Anglin, joined by three other Justices, explicitly rejected as *irrelevant* the social and political implications of the decision (as did the justices in the *Daigle* case). What mattered, in the Court's view, was the common law disability of women and the long line of cases which had refused to include women within the meaning of "persons" in the absence of clear legislative intent. That was all that mattered.

Snell and Vaughn, in their seminal history of the Court, described the decision this way:

> The restricted views by the five Justices, the narrowness of the definitions involved, and the unexpressed but apparent insistence of the justices that change be instituted through legislatures rather than courts, stand out in the reasoning of the justices. This is particularly true when the opinions are contrasted with the opinion of the Judicial Committee, which reversed the Court's judgment.[21]

And reverse it did. The following year, the Judicial Committee of the Privy Council decided it was time to put an end to all this nonsense, to pull the mask off the law and to quit the law's blind imitation of the past.[22] Their Lordships, in a judgment delivered by Lord Sankey, in what was to become the celebrated *Person's* case, held that the word "person" *did* include women:

> The exclusion of women from all public offices is a relic of days more barbarous than ours, but it must be remembered that the necessity of the time often forced on man customs which in later years were not necessary . . .[23]

The Justices acknowledged the ambiguity of the word and pointed out that in its original meaning it would undoubtedly embrace members of either sex. Then Lord Sankey uttered those unforgettable, revolutionary words to a hushed and crowded chamber:

> The word "person" may include members of both sexes, and to those who ask why the word should include females, the obvious answer is why not? In these circumstances the burden is upon those who deny that the word includes women to make out their case.[24]

The words "human being" may likewise include members of both sexes, born or unborn.[25] And to those who ask why the words should include the unborn, the obvious answer is *why not?* The burden in these circumstances, surely, as in *Edwards,* is upon those who deny that the words include unborn children to make out their case — and to make out their case with something more substantial or convincing than the blind imitation of the past.

The Supreme Court in *Daigle* forgot, or so it seems, that it was dealing with human rights legislation, not a penal or taxing statute. The Court has itself conferred a quasi-constitutional status on human rights legislation as fundamental law.[26] Human rights legislation, quite apart from this fundamental status, is remedial legislation designed to grant or protect such "rights" or to undo such "wrongs" as the legislation was presumably intended to address and has traditionally received a large and liberal, even expansive, construction.[27]

Surely the rule of liberal construction of human rights was not meant to be thwarted by a rule of illiberal selectivity in the designation of the classes of "persons" or "human beings" entitled to assert those rights. The presumption must be that every living human being is included unless a specific intent to *exclude* particular individuals or classes can be shown. There was nothing in the Quebec Charter or the Civil Code to support the conclusion that the legislature intended to exclude unborn children from the protection of the law. If anything, the clear inferences were all the other way.

Sachs and Wilson, two leading British feminists, summarized the effect of the *Person's* case on the rights of women this way:

> Six decades of precedent stating that women could not be included in the term "person" were swept aside by the simple proposition: "The word 'person' may include members of both sexes, and to those who ask why the word should include females, the obvious answer is, why not?"[28]

The authors make another incisive observation that should not be missed. After describing how the women rightly perceived their main battle as a political one directed at Parliament,[29] they continued:

Nevertheless, had the judges favoured the substance of women's claims, had they attached as much force to the concept of a developing democracy [or a growing vision of human rights and social justice] as they did to the idea of an ancient differentiation, they could in good judicial conscience have found for the women. If they had chosen this course, their judgments would have been denounced by some of their contemporaries as contrary to the spirit of the common law and the constitution . . . but hailed by most subsequent commentators as exemplifying the spirit of the common law and the constitution.[30]

Surely the equality and justice women have gained at great personal cost in recent decades, even if yet imperfect, must not be seized or exploited at the cost of even greater injustice to those tiny persons conceived but not yet born. To do so would be seriously to undermine the progress women have made thus far — to transform what might otherwise be rightly considered "progressive social justice" into a highly selective social justice: a sinister elitism of the strong and powerful over the weak and helpless. And that is a long, long way from progressive, or liberal.

YOU MUST BE "BORN ALIVE"

A basic principle of the civil law to which the Court in *Daigle* adverted but then ignored is the principle that "an unborn child shall be deemed to be born whenever its interests require it." This principle was resoundingly affirmed in *Montreal Tramways*,[31] a 1933 decision of the Supreme Court of Canada, but dismissed peremptorily by the Court in *Daigle*.

In *Montreal Tramways*, the Court held that under the civil law an unborn child is deemed to be born whenever it is to its advantage to do so. When subsequently born alive, therefore, the child who was deemed to be born at the time of injury was already clothed with all the rights of action it would have had if actually in existence at the time of injury.[32] In other words, the unborn child was deemed to be born and to possess all these rights while still *in utero*; the rights became *enforceable* upon the child's being "born alive."

This is not how the Court in *Daigle* handled *Montreal Tramways*. It began by quoting the following extract from the judgment of Justice Lamont which the respondent had offered in support of his position:

> To the Company's contention that an unborn child being merely part of its mother had no separate existence and, therefore, could not maintain an action under article 1053 C.C., the answer, in my opinion, is that, although the child was not actually born at the time . . . yet, under the civil law, it is deemed to be so for its advantage. Therefore, when it was subsequently born alive and viable it was clothed with all the rights of action which it would have had if actually in existence at the date of the accident.[33]

The Court concluded, however, that far from supporting the respondent's case, the quotation actually supported the appellant's: " . . . it would not have been necessary for Lamont J. to say that a fetus is 'deemed' to have civil rights if a fetus actually enjoyed such rights."[34] But that is not what Justice Lamont said. The Court in *Daigle* got it backwards. According to Justice Lamont, the fetus is "deemed to be born"; he is not "deemed" to have civil rights — a very different thing. It is precisely because he is deemed to be born before his actual birth that the unborn child is clothed with all the rights he would have had if he existed independently, and the unborn child carries these rights with him into his birth.

The point is made again with crystal clarity by the Court in *Montreal Tramways* in another passage only two pages later, which the Court in *Daigle* conveniently omitted:

> For these reasons, I am of the opinion that the fiction of the civil law must be held to be a general application. *The child will therefore be deemed to have been born at the time of the accident to the mother. Being an existing person in the eyes of the law it comes within the meaning of another in art. 1053 . . .* [35]

This hardly appears to support the *Daigle* court's conclusion that a fetus is treated as a person only where it is necessary to protect its "future interests."[36] On the contrary, it is treated as an *existing person* with existing rights which become enforceable only if the child is born alive.

THE "BORN ALIVE" RULE: AN OUTMODED LEGAL FICTION

The Court sought support for its conclusions in the common law. Yet, it was content merely to cite a few recent cases which held that an unborn child must be born alive to become "a person with full and independent rights."[37]

Where the Court went wrong was in neglecting to undertake a "full and independent" analysis of its own. Had it done so, had the Court fully and independently enquired into the common law origin and meaning of the "born alive" rule in a serious and dispassionate way, it would have discovered that recent scholarship has entirely discredited the rule as an outmoded legal fiction, a legal anachronism that is now obsolete and primitive.[38]

At common law, the "born alive" rule was a rule of medical jurisprudence, an *evidentiary standard* required by the limitations of medical knowledge and technology in the sixteenth and seventeenth centuries. Given the primitive knowledge of life in the womb, live birth was required as an evidentiary standard to prove that the unborn child was alive when the criminal or tortious acts were committed. Otherwise, it could not be established, either as a matter of medicine or as a matter of law, that the unborn child was alive *in utero* at the time of the defendant's acts. The rule, in its origins, was never intended to constitute part of the substantive definition of "person" or "human being,"[39] and recent advances in medical science have rendered the rule obsolete. Yet, as Clark Forsythe observes in his important study, "most modern courts still hold to the rule with a tenacity that is unwarranted in light of their unlearned examination of the rule."[40]

Oliver Wendell Holmes, the great American jurist, once re-marked:

> It is revolting to have no better reason for a rule of law than that it was laid down in the time of Henry IV. It is still more revolting if the grounds upon which it was laid down have vanished long since, and the rule simply persists from blind imitation of the past.[41]

The Supreme Court of Canada in *Daigle* had no better reason for holding to the rule but that "the courts have consistently reached the conclusion that to enjoy rights, a fetus must be born alive."[42] It made no attempt to justify the rule it adopted either as a matter of principle or on grounds of public policy. What is more, the grounds upon which the rule was laid down (namely, the inadequacy of medical science in the sixteenth and seventeenth centuries) have long since disappeared.

So, what is the effect of all this legal hocus-pocus? Among other things, it puts the law in the anomalous position of protecting the legal rights of one who is considered to have no legal right to live. An unborn child may, for example, have certain property rights such as the right of inheritance and other civil rights such as the right to sue for prenatal injuries, but it can't protect those rights before birth. In other words, it is legally wrong for a woman to misappropriate the estate of her unborn child, but not for her to kill the child. Similarly, it is wrong for a negligent driver or other wrongdoer to injure an unborn child, but not to kill it. From a legal point of view, it is therefore to a person's advantage to be sure he has killed, and not merely injured, an unborn child. What nonsense! Surely there is some-thing fundamentally wrong in a legal culture that would pro-duce such anomalous results.

BEYOND *DAIGLE*: THE LIMITS OF CHOICE

What is it about abortion that makes it so divisive, so consum-ing? At bottom, it is a battle about fundamental values. On the one side are the questions of human dignity, bodily integrity, security of the person, liberty, autonomy and equality — all values that imbue life with meaning. On the other side is life itself: the *sine qua non* of these and all other values; the logically prior condition to the enjoyment of anything and everything else. Or as the Law Reform Commission put it: "each person's life is all that person has — snuff that out and you obliterate (for him or her) a universe."[43]

Those who seek to protect the life of the unborn proceed from the basic premise that human life is sacred. Or put another way, that the sanctity of life is non-negotiable. The pivotal question surrounding abortion, therefore, is whether the fetus is a human life. If it is, abortion is wrong: every decision to abort, whatever the "legal rights" or motives, is a decision to kill a human being.[44] All other concerns, as pressing as they may be, are not as fundamental as the concern for the life of an individual human being.

Those who favor wide access to abortion proceed from very different premises: The right to liberty is a constitutional right that is fundamental to human dignity and guarantees personal autonomy over important decisions affecting our private lives. The decision of a woman to "terminate her pregnancy" is one of those. It is a decision that deeply reflects the way she thinks about herself and her relationship to others and society. Thus Chantal Daigle: "I was very, very angry and nobody was going to stop me getting my way."[45]

It is true that there is nothing more precious to Canada's way of life, which better defines who we are as a nation, than the freedoms we have and hold dear. It is one of the deepest of all human intuitions: the longing to choose what we will do and what we will be. Freedom of choice, after all, is the essence of liberty.

Yet liberty, without life, is meaningless. Rights and freedoms, no matter how cherished, can never be absolute in any civilized society. There must always be limits to safeguard and protect, among other things, the rights and freedoms of others. It is intellectually dishonest piously to assert the virtues of equality and the guarantees of a constitutional charter while at the same time insisting that an unborn child does not, or cannot, enjoy legal rights or constitutional protection. It can and, indeed, to a great extent, already does. The real question is whether our vision of human rights and social justice is generous and enlightened enough to accommodate both the legitimate rights and needs of women and those of their unborn children.

CONCLUSION

Daigle was more than just another legal decision to go into the long dusty rows of forgotten court cases. It was a reflection of the failure of modern liberalism's moral credentials and the intellectual duplicity of pro-abortion feminism.[46]

It is tragic that a decision like that in *Daigle*, which required so much, received so little. But then, *Daigle* was a *political* decision: a mere pretext for the Court to deny the fetus any legal or constitutional standing. What weight the Court will place upon the decision when it comes to any further application for constitutional protection of fetal rights remains to be seen. For now, the question of legal protection of the unborn is once again with Parliament, and the abortion debate rages on.

JANET AJZENSTAT

JUSTIFYING DESTRUCTION: PARLIAMENT AND THE COURT

THE CASE OF *Morgentaler et al.* v. *the Queen* provided one of the clearest examples yet of the Canadian Supreme Court's power to limit parliamentary sovereignty under the Charter of Rights and Freedoms. It is true that the justices all entertained the idea of allowing at least some form of legislation to protect the fetus. All argued that it was not unreasonable to consider limiting free choice on abortion under section 1 of the Charter, or under the "fundamental justice" clause of section 7. In this way, they challenged the shallow claim of many members of the pro-choice movement that to allow free access to abortion is to accommodate all reasonable arguments on abortion.

Nevertheless, it remains that the five justices of the majority leaned towards allowing free choice in the majority of cases. They appeared to be recommending, at the least, abolition of restrictions in the first trimester of pregnancy, and it is during the first trimester that close to 90 percent of abortions are now performed in this country. Moreover, since one of their purposes in abolishing restrictions early in pregnancy is to allow more women to obtain early abortions, it seems likely that they had in mind restricting women's choice on abortion in perhaps only 5 or 6 percent of cases. Parliament must now work with and around the Supreme Court's decision that a policy of relatively easy access to abortion is appropriate for this country.

In what follows, I will discuss some ramifications of the majority decisions in *Morgentaler*. Judges, unlike politicians, are under no obligation to make themselves understood to the populace. Although *Morgentaler* has affected the lives of Canadians in an unprecedented fashion, reading it is not easy. Indeed, as I shall show, the logic of their arguments confounds even the judges themselves on occasion.

Both Justices Dickson and Beetz base their arguments upon "security of the person" guaranteed under the Charter. The difficulty with their decisions is that they go such a long way towards opening the door to free choice without confronting the issue of choice squarely. The Justices show little understanding of the seriousness, one could even say dignity, of the pro-choice argument. As a result, they make little sense of the issues that will be raised by facilitating wide access to abortion.

Madam Justice Wilson's decision, in contrast, centers on the issue of choice. She shows us, as Dickson and Beetz do not, how drastically the Court's majority decision would reposition the "invisible fence" (her term) separating the area of individual freedom from the area of community concerns, expanding the one and contracting the other. What complicates Wilson's argument is her acceptance of the view that the entity in the womb, the fetus, is one and the same from the moment of conception to delivery. She goes a long way towards accepting a pro-life premise while attempting to derive from it an argument to justify women's choice on abortion in most cases. It is not surprising that her attempt fails. Nevertheless, both attempt and failure are illuminating exactly because Wilson is so lucid about the ground of individual and political freedoms in our society.

DICKSON AND BEETZ ON THE SECURITY OF THE PERSON

The arguments of Justices Dickson and Beetz turn on the discussion of medical necessities. They maintain that delay in obtaining an abortion to remedy the threat to life or health associated with pregnancy may inflict damaging psychological stress on the woman. Further, they suggest that undergoing a late abortion is only marginally safer than going on with a dangerous pregnancy. "Since the pregnant woman knows her life or health is in danger," argues Beetz, " . . . delay . . . may result in additional psychological trauma" (p. 29).[1] "In the context of abortion," says Dickson, "any unnecessary delay can have profound consequences on the woman's physical and emotional well-being" (p. 16). He notes that the effect of a late abortion can be "serious and, occasionally, fatal" (p. 19). The Justices conclude that, insofar as this stress and danger result from conditions imposed by law, the woman's Charter right to security of the person has been breached. "A pregnant woman's person cannot be said to be secure," says Beetz, "if, when her life or health is in danger, she is faced with a rule of criminal law which precludes her from obtaining effective and timely medical treatment" (p. 13).

The Justices' emphasis on the woman's life and health may appear appropriate given that the statute, section 251 of the Criminal Code, made consideration of the woman's health the condition for legal abortion. Moreover, it is undeniable that delay in obtaining an abortion was sometimes imposed by the operation of the statute and, as the recent Ontario Government Powell Report shows, late abortions are indeed traumatic. But the picture of women steering between the dangers of pregnancy and the dangers of abortion seems, all in all, far removed from reality.[2] Certainly neither the pro-choice nor pro-life movement would accept this picture. The pro-choice movement argues that abortion, even in the second trimester, is not so dangerous that it must be curtailed by law. The pro-life movement argues that pregnancy is seldom so dangerous that abortion is required. Indeed the Justices' depiction of great numbers of women suffering from ills associated with their wombs has a curious aura of misogyny, rivaling the absurd medical pronouncements of the nineteenth century.

In 1985, Statistics Canada reported a total of 60,956 abortions performed in Canadian hospitals, with several thousand unreported abortions performed in illegal abortion facilities. Seventy-eight percent of abortion patients were unmarried; 20.4 percent had had one or more previous induced abortions; 68 percent were between twenty and thirty-four years of age.

The high percentage of women who have abortions in their optimum childbearing years would suggest that danger to biological life and health are not the prime motivation for abortion. As a recent brief from Alliance for Life and Campaign Life Coalition on federal funding of induced abortion commented: "The sheer numbers of abortions performed annually in Canada are evidence that abortion cannot be considered a medical necessity. It is difficult to believe that unmarried women are beset by more health problems requiring abortion than married women; that repeated abortion is a therapeutic solution for 20 percent of abortion patients; or that women in the optimum childbearing years (20-34) are in fact more endangered by pregnancy than older women."[3]

The figures suggest that although the Therapeutic Abortion Committees, in conformity with the requirements of section 251, always declared the woman's health as the ground for granting an abortion, in fact "health" was given such a loose interpretation that almost any qualm the pregnant woman expressed about her personal life was held to count as ill health or a threat to health. Indeed, it has been suggested that, in some areas of the country, "health" had so little real meaning that abortion was available virtually on demand.[4]

Justices Dickson and Beetz accepted without question the supposition that the women of Canada find pregnancy so threatening that more than 80,000 must seek the abortion remedy every year.[5] They did not ask whether abortion indeed improves health or prevents ill health. They dwelt at length on the horrors of second-term abortion but did not ask whether the procedure has adverse physical or pychological consequences in the first term.[6] They did not ask why, if the *mother's* health was the issue under section 251, abortions were so often performed because the *fetus* was deemed unhealthy.

It might be argued that these matters were not strictly relevant to their examination of the statute. The fact remains that even the proponents of choice with respect to abortion do not say that women often apply for abortion because of the dangers of pregnancy. What is at issue in the abortion debate in our society is not whether abortion should be made more easily available in order to protect women's health, but whether it should be made available to facilitate women's free choice. Justices Dickson and Beetz were looking at a paper statute; they had their backs to the real world. The result is that their decision seems likely to have consequences for individuals and Canadian society out of all proportion to the right they sought to protect and the arguments they advanced.

That Chief Justice Dickson had an inkling of the importance of the isssue of choice in the abortion debate is suggested by his attempt to find scope for women's "aspirations and priorities" on abortion. He writes: "Forcing a woman, by threat of criminal sanction, to carry a foetus to term unless she meets certain standards unrelated to her own priorities and aspirations is a profound interference with a woman's body" (p. 16). But the idea that women should act to realize their aspirations cannot be made to fit with the Chief Justice's picture of them as constrained by medical necessities. His mention of women's aspirations merely serves to remind us how far his attempt to secure women from state-imposed threats to health would go to bring in abortion on demand.

WILSON ON FREEDOM

Madam Justice Wilson's consideration of the issue of choice as it relates to abortion begins from classic liberal assumptions. She argues that freedom to choose one's own objectives in life is a great good, essential to human dignity. What makes a liberal polity praiseworthy, she suggests, is exactly that it guarantees citizens an area of choice on important matters, beyond the reach of law. Freedom of choice may sometimes be curtailed by law, she argues, again in classic liberal fashion, but only where it can be shown that others, or the state, have an overwhelming interest. The central question for her, then, is whether the decision to abort the fetus should be regarded as falling into this area of individual freedom. Does the state have an interest in the fetus that can override free choice on abortion? She concludes that the woman's right to liberty takes precedence over the state's interest in the fetus in the earlier stages of fetal development but that the state's interest in the fetus becomes more important from some later point.[7]

If Wilson is bolder than Dickson and Beetz on choice, she is also bolder in confronting what pro-lifers call the facts of life. For millions of pro-lifers the decisions of Dickson and Beetz were perplexing — indeed, for some, the decisions generated considerable distrust of the Court. This is because the Justices simply passed over what the pro-life movement regards as the fundamental (but not the only) civil liberties question of the abortion issue: the right to life of the child before birth. Wilson's decision did something to remedy that deficiency. Although she does not consider the "right to life" clause of the Charter's section 7, she does address the question of the status of the fetus and arrives at something like a pro-life position. "The undeveloped foetus starts out as a newly fertilized ovum; the fully developed foetus emerges ultimately as an infant" (p. 27). It is true that Wilson does not describe the early fetus as "a life," or as a human being. She calls it "potential life." Yet, the fact is that in accepting the idea of the continuum from conception, she commits herself to the view that the fetus is an individual human life, the offspring of human parents, alive and developing. This is the view that prevails in the scientific community today, and is accepted by most people now, at least on some level of awareness.

It is probable that Wilson's position — her coupling of recognition of the living character of the fetus with acceptance of the woman's freedom to destroy it — would not have been possible fifteen, even ten, years ago. When the drive for abortion rights began two decades ago, it was accepted by the public that what was vacuumed out of the womb in an abortion was merely tissue or unorganized cells. But during the years when the argument for free abortion access was gaining ground, remarkable developments in photography began to show us, first still, and then moving, pictures of the fetus from the earliest stages of development. Millions of women have now seen the fetus in their own bodies on the ultrasound screen in the first trimester, moving and kicking. Almost everyone in our civilization now has an image of the very young fetus, with its skinny arms and legs, large head, little hands up before its face.

Until recently, members of the pro-life movement assumed that as the image became known more people would feel repugnance for abortion. But the momentum of the abortion rights drive proved very strong and what has happened is that the public has come to accept the idea of destroying what almost everyone now recognizes to be a living, and remarkably baby-like, small being. It is still the case that the baby-like character of the fetus is seldom admitted in public debate.[8] When speaking in public, spokesmen for the pro-choice movement hedge on the question of when life begins. Madam Justice Wilson's outright acceptance of the mother's right to end the fetus's life is therefore a landmark, especially since she occupies a position of prestige and great influence in our nation.

Wilson supports her claim that life in the womb is a continuum by citing Madam Justice O'Connor of the U.S. Supreme Court (in *City of Akron* v. *Akron Center for Reproductive Health*). What she does not cite or note is the conclusion that, in O'Connor's opinion, must follow from this premise: that the state has an interest in protecting the fetus *throughout* a pregnancy. While Dickson and Beetz suggest the possibility of a distinction between earlier and later abortion only in the course of arguing about the effects of abortion on women, Wilson does so in the context of remarks about the protection of the fetus. It is almost enough to suggest the curious character of her argument here to note that abortion has the same consequence for the fetus at any stage in the pregnancy. But it is important to spell out Wilson's case fully. Her conclusions stand or fall with her argument for a distinction between earlier and later abortions.

Madam Justice Wilson sets herself the task of justifying the destruction of the fetus at one point in its development and its protection by law later. The state's interest in the fetus, she argues, may be measured by the degree of sorrow accompanying the loss of fetal life. The fact that most or many people feel less sorrow at the loss of a fetus in the early stage of pregnancy, she takes as reason to say that the state has less interest in the younger fetus, and this, in her opinion, justifies withdrawal of state protection in the first trimester. "It is a fact of human experience that a miscarriage or spontaneous abortion at six months is attended by far greater sorrow and sense of loss than a miscarriage or spontaneous abortion at six days or even six weeks" (p.27).

The problem is that to say that lives should be protected under law only when and because they are generally seen as valuable runs counter to the bedrock, civil liberties belief that law and human rights codes must, above all, protect those who are vulnerable because they are not valued by the majority, or by social groups or individuals. Although Wilson argues for a law to restrict women's choices to some degree, and although the ground she advances for the protection of the older fetus is that society or many people value it (not that one woman values it), her point, nevertheless, calls to mind the slogan of the pro-choice movement: "every child a wanted child." Both Wilson and the pro-choice movement go a long way towards suggesting that only those who are loved deserve to live.

Wilson's acceptance of the scientific view of the fetus shows courage. But she pays a price. She goes on record as arguing that individuals should be allowed the freedom to choose the destruction of what she herself describes as the developing being who later emerges from the womb as an infant. At the same time, given the grounds she offers for the protection of the developing human being, she implicitly, if unwittingly, suggests that state protection of human life may be held to depend on popular feelings about the lives involved. Whereas the arguments of Justices Dickson and Beetz were disappointing because they were largely irrelevant to the problem of abortion legislation in a liberal society, Wilson's argument is disappointing because it promises to address exactly this problem but appears hopelessly illiberal in so many ways.

Even on her strongest ground, defending liberal rights, Wilson runs into trouble. In her introductory remarks, she describes abortion rights as the latest expression of the struggle for individual freedoms which began in the eighteenth century. She relates the freedom to abort a fetus to the freedom to choose one's religion (or to be areligious), the freedom to choose one's occupation, and marriage partner, and the freedom to bring up children in accordance with family traditions (pp. 7-15). But it is far from obvious that the freedom to abort a fetus is like the other freedoms she describes. Marrying, pursuing one's chosen work, bearing and educating children, reflecting on the meaning of life and worshipping one's deity are usually seen as holding out the possibility of great satisfaction, even joy. Even committed pro-choicers do not see abortion in this way. Pro-choicers champion easy access to abortion, but they do not glorify the procedure. They usually describe abortion as unpleasant, something that a woman may regard as the condition of avoiding greater pain and getting on with the life of real satisfactions. By inviting comparison of abortion with marriage, childrearing, career, Wilson comes close to suggesting that abortion is good in itself, in the way that marriage, childrearing and so on are good. Why?

What she says in this passage on the history of rights shows the influence of a trend of thought common in some feminist circles and sometimes referred to as "post-liberalism."[9] Post-liberalism shares with liberalism a belief in the importance of individual freedom and so is bound to appeal at one level to all those who respect the foundations of our liberal polity. Post-liberalism goes far beyond liberalism, however, insofar as it elevates the idea of individual freedom to the point where not only existing laws but the very idea of law itself is called into question. If a law binds or curtails an individual in her attempt to realize her own moral objectives it is held suspect — the more suspect, some feminists would argue, because law has historically been the product of male thought and so, by definition, inimical to women.

I do not say that Madam Justice Wilson subscribes wholly to this new philosophy. Quite the contrary; she is for the most part a staunch defender of law both as enabling political freedom and as allowing individual freedoms. Nevertheless, a strong hint of post-liberalism is present in her suggestion that abortion is good. Since, as the argument goes, no objectively established code should force an idea of what is good on the individual, "good" can be only what each chooses according to her conscience and her perception of community needs. According to this line of thinking, abortion is good insofar as, and because, it is freely chosen.[10] Wilson's references to the "subjective elements of the female psyche" at the heart of the abortion dilemma and her suggestion that a man cannot respond to such a dilemma even imaginatively, again reflect aspects of post-liberal thought (pp. 14, 15). It is very much part of this way of thinking to suppose that women and men may exist in different moral universes. I suggest that in her attempt to patch up a liberal argument for choice with respect to abortion, Wilson has been led to espouse ideas that reflect a philosophy seriously at odds with liberalism, a philosophy that challenges the very foundations of law and liberal society.

Her difficulties do not entitle us to say that by accepting the scientific view of the nature of the fetus the liberal must necessarily reject abortion. Wilson does not entertain all possible arguments to justify the kind of compromise on abortion that she appears to favor. And I have not been able to raise all possible counterarguments. But the fact that she encounters difficulties is suggestive. Her position would certainly be more consistent were she able to argue that abortion does not end a life. But to say that would be to fly in the face of science and commonsense, something no liberal can accept with ease.

PARLIAMENT'S ROLE

The marathon debate on the government's abortion resolution in July, 1988, was a triumph for Parliament. News commentators argued that the debate was a failure since the members were not able to agree on either motion or amendments.[11] But the wealth of arguments and facts revealed in the debate as well as the sense most members conveyed of sensitivity to public opinion and to the views of their constituents (they reported the results of "householder" polls, read letters from constituents, recounted interviews with interest groups and with individuals) did much to convince viewers that Parliament is the best forum for determining policy on issues like abortion.

According to the usual perception of the abortion debate, the pro-life movement is associated with fetal rights and the pro-choice movement with women's rights. Justices Dickson, Beetz and Wilson all see the issue as pitting women against fetuses. But it is far from clear that the procedure that destroys the fetus leaves a woman unscathed and even less clear that easy access to abortion benefits women as a group.[12] At the outset, a major goal of the women's movement was to involve men in parenting and especially to encourage men to enjoy taking care of very young children. In campaigning for abortion rights, however, the movement insists that only a woman has the right to decide whether the child shall have life or death ("It's a matter for a woman and her doctor") and this has surely strengthened the idea that children are the responsibility of women alone. Is it any wonder then that women are now more often left alone to raise their children? The problem of the very young woman left alone with her child, sometimes in conditions of poverty, has mushroomed over the last twenty years, the years of relatively free access to abortion.

The specific aim of the abortion rights drive two decades ago was to facilitate women's participation in the world of careers. Today, willingness to avoid "inconvenient" pregnancies — sometimes through abortion — has become an implicit condition of that participation. The absence of legislation protecting the fetus may certainly also operate to penalize women whose choice would otherwise have been to carry a child to term.

Since 1969, we have made abortion part of the Canadian way of life for women. Yet, in all this time, there has been surprisingly little public debate on the rights and wrongs of abortion (the media reports slogans, attendance at rallies, confrontations, but seldom arguments) and there has been even less debate about the social consequences. Surely it is time to think in more depth about the issue and about what easy access has meant for women as well as the unborn and for families, young men, siblings, the medical profession, the handicapped.[13] Would it be surprising to find that in the area of abortion law, as elsewhere, the Charter's emphasis on individual freedoms was insufficient to guarantee the rights of communal institutions — specifically to guarantee the survival of laws and customs meant to protect women?

It has become increasingly evident that the courts and Parliament play different roles in protecting the rights and freedoms of Canadians. The courts must think primarily in terms of individual rights, while parliament is the forum in which communal interests, the common good and social policy are determined. The Justices in *Morgentaler* sought to extend women's rights to easy access to abortion. It may be that, from Parliament, we can hope for full consideration of the social and economic consequences of easy abortion access for society and for women.

NOTES

IAN GENTLES
Introduction
1. *Globe and Mail*, September 20, 1976 and September 23, 1976.

GEORGE GRANT
The Triumph of the Will
1. I do not intend to show in this writing that the fetus is a developing individual of our species from conception. This was shown beyond doubt in the testimony of the famous French geneticist, Jerome Lejeune, before a committee of the American Senate. See also the essay by Heather Morris in this volume.
2. For an account of the process which led to this conclusion and which led a great expert in in-vitro fertilization away from certain researches, see *L'Oeuf Transparent* by J. Tesford (Paris: Flammarion, 1986).
3. The more contemporary judges quote philosophy or religious tradition, the less they appear to understand what they are dealing with. (Another long article would be required to spell out the influences in legal and general education that have led to this jurisprudential shallowness. As much as abortion, this question goes to the very roots of modernity.)

IAIN T. BENSON
What's Wrong with "Choice"
1. It would seem necessary, in any meaningful attempt to discuss the

"competition" of interests in abortion, to delineate the two "rights" that are in conflict. The fetus's right is to the continuance of its developing life; this "interest" begins at conception. Any argument that suggests that a "competition" or "balancing" between fetal and maternal rights begins at some other point, must explain what the fetal interest is, since the "developing life right" is not being considered *at all* for some period; there is not, therefore, any "competition of interests" or "balancing" in such approaches. As far as I am aware, no satisfactory answer to this problem with the trimesteral or gestational approaches (such as allowing abortions until the fetus is viable) exists; they must, therefore, be seen as incompatible with notions of a "competition" or "balancing" of interests.

2. For a review of the various approaches, see, for example, L. W. Sumner, *Abortion and Moral Theory* (Princeton: Princeton University Press, 1981). See also Oliver O'Donovan *Begotten or Made?* (Oxford: Clarendon Press, 1984) p. 57ff. Another approach that should be considered is the one discussed by the Spanish Constitutional Court in its recent abortion decision. R. Stith states that in this approach: " . . . the Spanish court considers the fetus neither a person possessing rights, as U.S. pro-life people argue, nor subject to a person possessing rights, as pro-choicers argue. *Instead, unborn life is treated as a distinct constitutionally protected legal good.* (R. Stith, "New Constitutional and Penal Theory in Spanish Abortion Law." *American Journal of Comparative Law* 35 (1987): 514.)

3. This is the phrase employed by the Law Reform Commission of Canada in its paper addressing the issue of euthanasia in Canada. (Law Reform Commission of Canada, *Euthanasia, Aiding Suicide and Cessation of Treatment*, Working Paper no. 28, 1982.) Clearly, debates surrounding the practices of abortion and euthanasia are concerned with the same issue: the circumstances under which it is permissible to end the life of a human being who cannot speak for him/herself.

4. Any approach to the issue of abortion that purports to be moral must perceive and attempt to provide solutions for the very real difficulties faced by women with unwanted pregnancies. The principles upon which a "pro-life" position ought to be based are well set out by S. Callahan in *Abortion: Understanding Differences* (New York: Plenum, 1984), p. 329 and by Diane Marshall and Martha Crean in "The Human Face of a Woman's Agony" in this volume.

5. Sumner (see note 3 above) observes that "in feminist treatments of abortion few meaningful steps have been taken toward clarifying the status of the fetus, locating the threshold of moral standing, developing a general criterion, or deploying a theory that can support such a criterion. By and large the fetus has simply been ignored or forgotten." (p. 57).

6. The law relating to the status of the unborn is in disarray. It would appear that the existing legislative framework in the provincial jurisdictions could be amended so as to provide considerable protection to the unborn. In *Re. "Baby R"*, unreported decision, B.C. Prov. Ct. No.

876215 (Davis J.) Sept. 3, 1987, for example, the Court recognized an interest in a fetus by making it a ward of Court when its mother refused to have a caesarean section in circumstances in which both the mother and child were in peril. On appeal to the British Columbia Supreme Court, the Judge, found that the definition of "child" in the Act, to protect the unborn, must be specific: Re "Baby R" (1988) 30 B.C.L.R. (2d) 237. The decision was not appealed further.

In R v. Sullivan and Lemay, [1988] 31 B.C.L.R. 145, the Court of Appeal of British Columbia found that the offence of criminal negligence causing death of a person was not properly found against two midwives convicted of negligence by the B.C. Supreme Court. The Court of Appeal found that the full-term infant (with its head already delivered outside of the birth canal) was not "a person" within the meaning of the Criminal Code but that the midwives' conviction for criminal negligence could be upheld because the child, while still in the birth canal remains part of the mother. This unusual case is under appeal and will be heard shortly by the Supreme Court of Canada where, presumably, the midwives will argue that the fetus is *neither* a person nor part of the mother. It remains to be seen whether the interesting argument that the full-term child (the Court of Appeal used the word "child") is, in fact, a legal non-entity will find favour with the court.

In D. v. Berkshire C.C., [1987] 1 All E.R. 20., the British House of Lords, in a unanimous decision, ruled that when considering the need to make a care order in respect of a baby girl born with drug withdrawal symptoms, the juvenile court had quite properly considered events occurring and circumstances existing prior to the child's birth. Both sets of reasons in the decision of the Lords stated that the justices should be entitled to have regard to events which occurred before the child was born and that broad and liberal construction must be given to the language of the Children and Young Persons Act, 1969, lest its purpose be thwarted. That Act defined a "child" as " . . . a person under the age of fourteen . . ." See Jane E. S. Fortin's "Legal Protection for the Unborn Child" (1988) 51 Mod. L. Rev. 54.

7. The approaches taken by the Constitutional Courts of West Germany and Spain provide a different manner of evaluating the abortion issue. Both should be considered more fully by Canadian Courts in the future. For the West German approach, see the Decision of 25 February 1975, (1975) 39 BVerfGE 1. Translated into English by Jonas and Gorby, "West German Abortion Decision: A Contrast to Roe v. Wade — with Commentaries," 9 John Marshall J. of Prac. and Proc. 551 (1976).

For the Spanish approach (and useful comments on the West German decision), see R. Stith, "New Constitutional and Penal Theory in Spanish Abortion Law," American Journal of Comparative Law 35 (1987): 513. This latter article points out, for example, that the Spanish Court, in evaluating the constitutional word "everyone," specifically held that the term " . . . includes 'everyone living' and that no distinction can be made, with regard to the right to life, between unborn and born life" (p. 527).

8. One must say *"formerly* accepted" because the recent decision of the United States Supreme Court in *Webster et al.* v. *Reproductive Health Services et al.*, July 3, 1989, suggests that *Roe* v. *Wade*, [1973] 410 U.S. 113 has been, if not expressly overruled, at least significantly narrowed. The majority in *Webster* described the "trimesteral framework" in *Roe* as "unworkable in practice and unsound in principle."

9. Jane E. S. Fortin, "Legal Protection for the Unborn Child," *Mod. L. Rev.* 54 (1988): 59.

10. Ibid., (emphasis added).

11. A review of the language of the abortion and euthanasia debates and how terminology is manipulated in questionable ways is found in two essays by George and Sheila Grant, "Abortion and Rights" and "The Language of Euthanasia," in George Grant, *Technology and Justice*, (Toronto: Anansi, 1986), pp. 103, 117. Given the way in which use of the term "person" has been used historically to deny the rights of women and blacks, we should be skeptical about denials of fetal rights based on a lack of "personhood" in the fetus. On use of the term "person" in the abortion debate, see Oliver O'Donovan, "And Who Is a Person?" in *Begotten or Made?*, pp. 49-66; and "Again: Who Is a Person" in J. H. Channer, ed., *Abortion and the Sanctity of Human Life* (Exeter: Paternoster Press, 1985), pp. 125-37. Finally, a quotation from J. Glover is apposite here: "There is often an immense resistance to killing [which must be overcome] by attempts to make the enemy seem less than human." *Causing Death and Saving Lives* (London: Penguin, 1977), p. 115.

12. There have been recent attempts to suggest that, historically, other reasons for prohibiting abortions were more important than concern for the fetus. (The arguments were inaccurate but they exerted influence on the U.S. Supreme Court in the *Roe* v. *Wade* decision.) For a critique of the methodology of historical reviews in the area of abortion and, particularly, to discover how many discussions of the history of abortion laws have failed to consider the impact of technology on law, see Joseph Dellapenna's "The History of Abortion: Technology, Morality, and Law," *University of Pittsburgh Law Review* 40 (1979): 359-428.

13. I thank Bernard Dickens of Toronto for bringing to my attention the fact that the WHO statement of health was used by therapeutic abortion committees largely by "default" because Canada had no working definition of "health" to use. It scarcely needs stating that it is high time a sound, workable definition of "health" were available for the guidance of physicians in Canada, particularly since the Canadian Medical Association, as early as 1978, petitioned the federal government about " . . . the need for a definition of the term 'health' as used in the Criminal Code relative to the legal grounds for therapeutic abortion" ("The Canadian Medical Association and Abortion," July, 1978).

14. Daniel Callahan, "The WHO Definition of Health," *Hastings Center Studies* 1 (1973): 90-95.

15. Law Reform Commission of Canada, Working Paper no. 26, "Medical Treatment and Criminal Law," 1980, p. 7 (emphasis added). I am indebted to lawyer Colleen M. Kovacs, of Victoria, B.C., for bringing this to my attention. Her unpublished essay, "A Response to *Options for Abortion Policy Reform: A Consultation Document*," April, 1987, contains many perceptive criticisms of the federal Law Reform Commission's consultation document, which, itself, contains no definition of "health."

16. "Psychiatric Aspects of Therapeutic Abortion," *Canadian Medical Association Journal* 125 (September 1981): 427-31.

17. Carlos Del Campo, "Abortion Denied: Outcome of Mothers and Babies," *Canadian Medical Association Journal* 139 (February, 1984): 361-62 (emphasis added).

18. Michael Polanyi, *Science, Faith and Society* (Chicago: University of Chicago Press, 1966), p. 76.

19. C. S. Lewis, *The Abolition of Man* (New York: MacMillan, 1947). (First published in 1944 by Oxford University Press, London.)

20. Ibid., pp. 12, 46.

21. Ibid., pp. 30-31 (emphasis added). For another particularly useful examination of natural law set out in a manner that may be readily grasped by those educated in the liberal tradition and therefore likely ignorant of it, see George Grant, *Philosophy in the Mass Age* (Toronto: Copp Clark, 1966); and for a perceptive diagnosis of the weaknesses and question begging of the social contract theories, with particular reference to the work of John Rawls, see Grant's *English-Speaking Justice* (Toronto: Anansi, 1985).

22. Alasdair MacIntyre, *After Virtue* (London: Duckworth, 1981).

23. Grant, *English-Speaking Justice*, p. 86.

24. Cicero once said, "Only a madman could maintain that the distinction between honourable and dishonourable, between virtue and vice, is only a matter of opinion" (quoted in George Grant, *Philosophy in the Mass Age*, pp. 35-36 — see note 21 above). In a book which splendidly describes the slide into value-begging subjectivism, Allan Bloom has written: "True openness is the accompaniment of the desire to know, hence of the awareness of ignorance. To deny the possibility of knowing good and bad is to suppress true openness." (*The Closing of the American Mind* (New York: Simon and Schuster, 1987), p. 40.)

25. See George Grant's comment on the Canadian judiciary in "The Triumph of the Will," in this volume.

26. This evidence is unlikely to be forthcoming. In what is likely the most broadly represented coalition ever to have appeared before the Supreme Court of Canada as an intervenor, a group calling itself the "Inter-Faith Coalition" recently appeared before the Court, in the case of *Borowski* v. *R.*, to argue for the recognition of the "sanctity of life" and the protection of the unborn from conception. The coalition included the following: the Anishinabe Elders of the Ojibway Cultural Foundation, the Canadian National Council of Hindus, the Council

of Muslim Communities of Canada, the Greek Orthodox Diocese of Toronto, the Council of Christian Reformed Churches in Canada, The Pentecostal Assemblies of Canada, The Baptist Federation of Canada, the Evangelical Fellowship of Canada (representing more than forty Protestant denominations), Rabbi Immanuel Schochet of the Kailcer Congregation of Toronto (a member of the executive of the Rabbinical Alliance of America), and the Canadian Conference of Catholic Bishops.

27. For historical reviews of the laws governing abortion, see Dellapenna note 12; Bernard Dickens *Abortion and the Law* (Bristol: MacGibbon and Kee, 1966); J. D. Butler and D. F. Walbert, eds., *Abortion, Medicine and the Law* (New York: Facts on File, 1986). On the religious and ethical history of abortion, see G. Grisez, *Abortion: The Myths, the Realities and the Arguments* (New York: World Publishing, 1970) and D. Granfield, *The Abortion Decision* (New York: Doubleday, 1969).

28. It is intriguing that in her part of the *Morgentaler* judgement, Madam Justice Wilson attempted to formulate a "compromise" position in a way that contradicted a statement about compromise she made herself in another recent decision. In *Edwards Books and Art v. R.* [1986] 35 D.L.R. (4th) 1, she cited with approval the method of analysis used by the American legal scholar Ronald Dworkin, stating, "When a government legislates on an issue on which people hold widely divergent views, it must do so on the basis of *principle*. Dworkin states . . . : 'If there must be compromise because people are divided about justice, then the compromise must be external, not internal; *it must be compromise about which scheme of justice to adopt rather than a compromised scheme of justice*' (p. 61, emphasis added). In her judgement in *Morgentaler* (with which no other judge agreed), Madam Justice Wilson suggests that a future law ought to allow abortion without restriction for the first three months of pregnancy. Such an approach gives no value at all to the fetus during those three months and is, therefore, just the kind of "compromised scheme of justice" she disagreed with in *Edwards Books*.

29. See, for example, A. and A. T. McLaren, *The Bedroom and the State* (Toronto: McClelland and Stewart, 1986).

30. This gender-based, selective "morality" is actually another form of sexism but a more detailed discussion of this is beyond the scope of this essay.

31. *When Freedoms Collide*, (Toronto: Lester & Orpen Dennys, 1988), p. 255.

32. Borovoy, *When Freedoms Collide*, p. 256. He ignores the manipulation of the jury selection procedure in the Morgentaler trial. See Ian Hunter, "Trial by Jury: *R. v. Morgentaler*," in this volume.

33. Borovoy, *When Freedoms Collide*, p. 258.

34. Not all civil libertarians, however, have abandoned their duty to examine critically the morality of abortion. It was from within the civil liberties sections (provincial and national) that the only resolution came which dealt with the abortion issue at the Canadian Bar

Association's 1989 Annual Meeting held in Vancouver. That resolution urged the "Federal, Provincial and Territorial governments to enact legislation to protect human life *at all stages of its development . . .*" (Resolution no. 13, "Legislative Protection of Human Life," Canadian Bar Association *Resolutions*, Annual Meeting, Vancouver, B.C., August 20-23, 1989, p. 41; emphasis added). In the end, because the majority of provinces wanted more time to consider it, this resolution was withdrawn prior to debate.

35. Borovoy, *When Freedoms Collide*, p. 256.

36. Ibid., p. 390.

37. Baruch Brody, *Abortion and the Sanctity of Human Life: A Philosophical View* (Cambridge: M.I.T. Press, Cambridge, 1975). The relevant chapter of this book can also be found in *The Human Life Review* 1 (Fall, 1975): 42-45.

38. See "New Guidelines Control Research on Human Embryos," *Globe and Mail*, March 5, 1988, p. A3. In England, the Warnock Committee decided that the period beyond which embryo research should not extend ought to be fourteen days. The difference between the two recommendations supports suggestions that such a period is arbitrary and not based on any sound philosophical approach. Whatever the reasons, a point made by Fortin (see note 6 above) is equally applicable to the Canadian setting. Discussing the fourteen-day period chosen by the Warnock Committee, Fortin notes: "The Report implied that since it had a greater potential, [a more developed fetus] had a greater right to protection than a younger one, but ironically, the form of protection envisaged is the embryo's destruction" (p. 60).

39. One might risk being called flippant if one were to suggest that if the fetus is not "human," it is at least worthy of the tears currently being shed so liberally for rabbits, dogs, chickens, mice, etc., that are the subjects of vivisection, testing or other forms of experimentation. Is it not a measure of the extent of current moral confusion that eye irritation (or the blindness) of rabbits warrants the raiding of laboratories, yet the destruction of unborn human life receives no mention from "animal rights" activists? The statistics show, in fact, that thousands of abortions occur in the third trimester in the United States (and hundreds in Canada) and the procedure is certainly not too dissimilar to that condemned as uncivilized when it is performed on animals, except, of course, that it is often more brutal.

SAMUEL AJZENSTAT

The Liberal Crisis: Feminists on Abortion

1. John Locke, *Second Treatise of Government*, various editions, Ch. 6, "Of Paternal Power." See also Thomas Hobbes, *Leviathan*, various editions, Ch. 20.

2. See John T. Noonan, Jr., *A Private Choice: Abortion in America in the Seventies* (New York: The Free Press, 1979), Inquiry 16, "On the Language of the Liberty."

3. Judith Jarvis Thomson, "A Defense of Abortion," *Philosophy and Public Affairs*, vol. 1 (1971): 47-66.

4. Christine Overall, *Ethics and Human Reproduction* (Boston: Allen and Unwin, 1987). See especially chapters 3 and 4.

5. She argues, for example, that many discussions of reproductive ethics depend on the oppression of women and the silencing of their voices.

6. Cf., for example, Margaret A. Somerville, "Reflections on Canadian Abortion Law: Evacuation and Destruction — Two Separate Issues," *University of Toronto Law Journal*, vol. 31, no. 1 (1981).

7. It is also worth noting that though in discussing abortion Overall freely cites such technological developments as *in vitro* fertilization to make it seem implausible to grant the fetus a right of occupancy, elsewhere in the book she is suspicious of the acceptability of these technologies, especially for their effects on women. It may be, then, that a conflict between these technologies and the rights of fetuses should be taken to cast doubt on the former rather than on the latter.

8. See Lorraine Code, Sheila Mullett, Christine Overall, eds., "Editors' Introduction," *Feminist Perspectives: Philosophical Essays on Method and Morals* (Toronto: University of Toronto Press, 1988), p. 6.

9. See the discussion of double effect in Baruch Brody, *Abortion and the Sanctity of Human Life* (Cambridge: The MIT Press, 1975), pp. 14-15.

10. Carol Gilligan, *In a Different Voice* (Cambridge: Harvard University Press, 1982).

11. For an indication of how widespread this way of talking about abortion has become, see the speech by Barbara McDougall in the abortion debate in the House of Commons at the end of July 1988.

12. Quoted in Emil L. Fackenheim, *To Mend the World: Foundations of Future Jewish Thought* (New York: Schocken Books, 1982), pp. 185-86. On the abortion issue see also pp. 216-17.

13. This is not to say that any critic of liberalism along these lines is necessarily pro-choice. But I incline to argue that the fetus (and women as well) are better served by a defence of liberal concepts like individuality and rights than by a critique of them and a search for a more communitarian society.

14. One other aspect perhaps deserves mention. Since the argument based on ethical principles for abortion seems to me strained, I have to ask what besides such argument, may account for the popularity of decriminalization of abortion over the last twenty years. Is it irrelevant that government-financed abortion is the cheapest solution to pressing demands for more social services for poor, single mothers? May support for easy access to abortion be a way to throw a bone to women whose real need is for help coping with their pregnancies and not help in "terminating" them? Have many women taken up the cause of abortion simply as a hard-headed and desperate response to the expectation that abortion was the only help anyone was going to give them? In this light it seems unreal, to say the least, to affirm the right to an empty womb as if this were very high up on the list of requirements for the good life. For a different suggestion on the appeal of

decriminalization for many men, see also Robert M. Campbell and Leslie A. Pal, *The Real Worlds of Canadian Politics: Cases in Process and Policy* (Peterborough, Ontario: Broadview, 1989), pp. 205-6.

HEATHER MORRIS
The Patient before Birth

1. Williams' *Obstetrics*, 18th ed. (1989), Chap. 15, p. 277.
2. American College of Obstetrics and Gynecology, "Ultrasound in Pregnancy," *Technical Bulletin* 116, (May 1988), pp. 328-44.
3. R. J. Wapner and L. Jackson, "Chorionic Villus Sampling," *Clinical Obstetrics and Gynaecology* 31, no. 2 (June 1988).
4. A. L. Medearis and J. R. Shields, "Normal Fetal and Pelvic Anatomy," *Clinical Obstetrics and Gynaecology* 27, no. 2 (June 1984), pp. 276-85.
5. F. A. Manning et al., "Treatment of the Fetus in Utero: Evolving Concepts," *Clinical Obstetrics and Gynaecology* 27, no. 2 (June 1984), pp. 380-85.
6. Ibid., pp. 386-88.
7. A. W. Liley, "Intrauterine Transfusion of the Foetus in Haemolytic Disease", *British Medical Journal*, no. 2 (1963): 1107.
8. A. Ludomirski et al., "Percutaneous Umbilical Blood Sampling: A New Technique for Perinatal Diagnosis," *Journal of Reproductive Medicine* 32 (1987): 276.
9. J. M. Johnson and S. Elias, "Prenatal Treatment: Medical and Gene Therapy in the Fetus," *Clinical Obstetrics and Gynaecology* 31, no. 2 (June 1988).
10. I. Lange et al., "Congenital Anomalies: Present Strategies for Diagnosis," *Journal of the Society of Obstetricians and Gynaecologists Canada* 11, no. 1 (January/February 1989), pp. 11-14.
11. F. A. Manning et al., "Fetal Assessment Based on Fetal Biophysical Profile Scoring," *American Journal of Obstetrics and Gynaecology* 151 (1985): 343.

HEATHER MORRIS, LORRAINE WILLIAMS
Physical Complications of Abortion

1. Margaret and Arthur Wynn, *Some Consequences of Induced Abortion to Children Born Subsequently* (London: Foundation for Education and Research in Childbearing, 1972).
2. Susan Harlap and A. Michael Davies, "Late Sequelae of Induced Abortion: Complications and Outcome of Pregnancy and Labor," *American Journal of Epidemiology* 102 (1975): 217-24.
3. P. I. Frank, C. R. Kay, T. L. T. Lewis and S. Parish, "Outcome of Pregnancy Following Induced Abortion" (Joint Study of the Royal College of General Practitioners and the Royal College of Obstetricians and Gynaecologists), *British Journal of Obstetrics and Gynaecology* 92 (April, 1985): 308-16.

4. I. T. Cameron, A. F. Michie and D. T. Baird, "Therapeutic Abortion in Early Pregnancy with Antiprogestogen R.U. 486 Alone or in Combination with Prostaglandin Analogue (Gemeprost)" *Contraception* 34 (November 1986): 459-68.

5. Beatrice Couzinet, Nelly Le Strat, André Ullman, Etienne Emile Baulieu and Gilbert Shaison, "Termination of Early Pregnancy by the Progesterone Antagonist R.U. 486 (Mifepristone)," *New England Journal of Medicine* 315 (December 18, 1986): 1565-70.

6. I. T. Cameron and D. T. Baird, "Early Pregnancy Termination: A Comparison between Vacuum Aspiration and Medical Abortion Using Prostaglandin (16,16 demethyl trans Δ_2 P.GE$_1$ methylester) or the Antiprogestogen R.U. 486," *British Journal of Obstetrics and Gynaecology* 95 (March, 1988): 271-74.

7. P. I. Frank, C. R. Kay, S. J. Wingrave, T. L. T. Lewis, J. Osborne and C. Newell, "Induced Abortion Operations and Their Early Sequelae" (Joint Study of the Royal College of General Practitioners and the Royal College of Obstetricians and Gynaecologists), *Journal of the Royal College of General Practitioners* 35, no. 273 (April, 1985): 175-80.

8. J. Buehler, K. Schulz, D. Grimes and C. Hogue, "The Risk of Serious Complications from Induced Abortion: Do Personal Characteristics Make a Difference?" *American Journal of Obstetrics and Gynecology* 153, no. 1 (September 1, 1986): 14-20.

9. M. Freedman, D. Jillson, R. Coffin and L. Novick, "Comparison of Complication Rates in First Trimester Abortions Performed by Physician Assistants and Physicians," *American Journal of Public Health* 76, no. 5 (May, 1986): 550-53.

10. J. Bueler et al., "The Risk of Serious Complications": 18. (See note 8 above.)

11. Frank et al., "Induced Abortion Operations and Their Early Sequelae": 314. (See note 3 above.)

12. C. S. Chung, P. Steinhoff and R. G. Smith, *Effects of Induced Abortion on Subsequent Reproductive Function and Pregnancy Outcome* (Honolulu: University of Hawaii Press, 1981).

13. A Levin, S. Schoenbaum, P. Stubblefield, S. Zimicki, R. Monson and K. Ryan, "Ectopic Pregnancy and Prior Induced Abortion," *American Journal of Public Health* 72 (1982): 253.

14. "Annual Ectopic Totals Rose Steadily in 1970's but Mortality Rates Fell," *Family Planning Perspectives* 15 (1983): 85.

15. J. Daling, W. Chow, N. Weiss, B. Metch and R. Soderstrom, "Ectopic Pregnancy in Relation to Previous Induced Abortion," *Journal of the American Medical Association* 253, no. 7 (February 15, 1985): 1005-8.

16. D. Dicker, D. Feldberg, N. Samuel and J. Goldman, "Etiology of Cervical Pregnancy," *Journal of Reproductive Medicine* 30, no. 1 (January, 1985): 25-7.

17. Lars Heisterberg, Søren Hebjørn, Lars F. Andersen and Helle Petersen, "Sequelae of Induced First-Trimester Abortion: A Prospective Study Assessing the Role of Poastabortal Pelvic Inflammatory Disease and

Prophylactic Antibiotics," *American Journal of Obstetrics and Gynecology* 155 (July 1986): 76-80.

18. Carol Hogue, W. Cates, Jr., and C. Tietze, "Impact of Vacuum Aspiration Abortion on Future Childbearing: A Review," *Family Planning Perspectives* 15, no. 3 (May/June, 1983): 119-126.

19. B. G. Wren, "Cervical Incompetence — Aetiology and Management," *Medical Journal of Australia* 60 (December 29, 1973): 1146.

20. K. Schulz, D. Grimes and W. Cates, Jr., "Measures to Prevent Cervical Injury during Suction Curettage Abortion," *The Lancet* (May 28, 1983): 1182-84.

21. Ibid.

22. Ruth M. Pickering and John F. Forbes, "Risks of Preterm Delivery and Small-for-gestational Age Infants Following Abortion: A Population Study," *British Journal of Obstetrics and Gynaecology* 92 (November, 1985): 1106-12.

23. Frank et al., "Induced Abortion Operations and Their Early Sequelae": 308-16. (See note 3 above.)

24. S. Wadhera, "Legal Abortions among Teens, 1974-1978," *Canadian Medical Association Journal* 122 (June, 1980): 1386-89.

25. W. Cates, Jr., "Risks Associated with Teenage Abortions," *New England Journal of Medicine* 309, no. 11 (June, 1980): 621-24.

26. N. Binkin, J. Gold and W. Cates, Jr., "Illegal Abortion Deaths in the U. S.: Why Are They Still Occurring?" *Family Planning Perspectives* 14, no. 3 (May/June, 1982): 163-67.

27. D. Grimes, "Fatal Hemorrhage from Legal Abortion in the United States," *Surgery, Gynecology and Obstetrics* 157, no. 5 (November, 1983): 461-66.

28. Robert G. Castadot, "Pregnancy Termination: Techniques, Risks, and Complications and Their Management," *Fertility and Sterility* 45, no. 1 (January, 1986): 8.

29. W. Cates, Jr., D. Grimes, R. Habar and C. Tyler, Jr., "Abortions Deaths Associated with the Prostaglandin F2a," *American Journal of Obstetrics and Gynecology* 127, no. 3 (February, 1977): 219-22.

30. D. Grimes, "Second Trimester Abortions in the United States," *Family Planning Perspectives* 16, no. 6 (November/December, 1984): 260-65.

31. Castadot, "Pregnancy Termination": 6. (See note 28 above.)

32. Grimes, "Fatal Hemorrhage from Legal Abortion": 461-66. (See note 27 above.)

33. Suneeta Mital and Sneh Lata Misra, "Uterine Perforation Following Medical Termination of Pregnancy by Vacuum Aspiration," *International Journal of Obstetrics and Gynaecology* 23 (1985): 45-50.

34. G. Woodward, "Estimate of Blood Loss in the Second Trimester D and E Abortion," *Obstetrics and Gynaecology* 63, no. 2 (1984): 230-32.

35. Cates, "Risks Associated with Teenage Abortions": 621-624 (See note 25 above.)

36. Buehler et al., "The Risk of Serious Complications": 14-20. (See note 8 above.)
37. L. Roht, H. Aoyama and E. Fonner, "Increased Reporting of Menstrual Symptoms among Women Who Used Induced Abortion," *American Journal of Obstetrics and Gynecology* 127, no. 4 (February 15, 1977): 356-62.
38. L. Brenton, R. Hoover and J. Fraumeni, Jr., "Reproductive Factors in the Aetiology of Breast Cancer," *British Journal of Cancer* 47, no. 6 (1983): 757-62.
39. Hogue et al., "Impact of Vacuum Aspiration Abortion": 119. (See note 18 above).
40. Freedman et al., "Comparison of Complication Rates": 550-53. (See note 9 above.)
41. W. Fielding, "Continued Pregnancy after Failed First Trimester Abortions," *Obstetrics and Gynecology* 63, no. 3 (March, 1984): 421-24.
42. A. Kaunitz, E. Rovira, D. Grimes and K. Schulz, "Abortions That Fail," *Obstetrics and Gynecology* 66 (1985): 533-37.
43. Harlap and Davies, "Late Sequelae of Induced Abortion": 222. (See note 2 above.)
44. Castadot, "Pregnancy Termination": 8. (See note 28 above.)

L. L. De Veber, Mary Parthun, Dorothy Chisholm, Anne Kiss
Abortion and Bereavement

1. Statistics Canada reported 63,508 hospital abortions in 1986. However, statistics obtained under the Freedom of Information Act indicate that over 80,000 induced abortions were performed in 1988. (*Vitality*, Oct. 1989.) This figure does not include abortions disguised by hospitals as D and C's.
2. See Elizabeth O'Brien, "Women Who Mourn the Anniversary of Abortion" in Denyse O'Leary, ed., No Easy Answers (Burlington, Ont.: Welch, 1988), pp. 76-82.
3. See American Psychiatric Association, *Diagnostic and Statistical Manual of Mental Disorders*, 3rd ed. (Washington: Psychiatric Press, 1987).
4. H. P. David, N. Rasmussen and E. Holst, "Postpartum and Postabortion Psychiatric Reactions," *Family Planning Perspectives* 13 (1981): 88-92.
5. J. Rogers, J. Nelson and J. Phifer, "Validity of Existing Controlled Studies Examining the Psychological Effects of Abortion," *Perspectives on Science and Christian Faith* 29 (1987): 20-29.
6. C. Brewer, "Incidence of Post-Abortion Psychosis: A Prospective Study," *British Medical Journal* 1 (1977): 476-77.
7. M. Sim, "Abortion and Psychiatry" in T. W. Hilgers, D. J. Horan and D. Mall, eds., New Perspectives on Human Abortion (Frederick, Maryland: University Publications of America, 1974), pp. 151-63.
8. D. Gold, C. Berger and D. Andres, *The Abortion Choice: Psychological Determinants and Consequences* (Montreal: Concordia University Department of Psychology, 1984), pp. 80, 84.

9. Ibid., pp. 142-43.
10. R. F. Badgley, D. F. Caron and M. G. Powell, *Report of the Committee on the Abortion Law* (Ottawa: Minister of Supply and Services, 1977), pp. 313-19.
11. Ibid., pp. 319-21.
12. C. Everet Koop, letter to President Reagan, 9 January 1989. The letter was distributed to the press and interested groups. Copies are available from the Surgeon General's Office, Washington, D.C.
13. See Rogers, et al, note 5 above.
14. See the comments by David R. Evans in M. Parthun and A. Kiss, *Abortion's Aftermath: Psychological Effects of Induced Abortion*, 2nd ed. (Toronto: Human Life Research Institute, 1987), p. 14.
15. See, for example, M. Gibbons, "Psychiatric Sequelae of Induced Abortion," *Journal of the Royal College of General Practitioners* 34 (1984): 146-50.
16. See A. Lazarus and R. Stern, "Psychiatric Aspects of Pregnancy Termination," *Clinics in Obstetrics and Gynaecology* 13 (1986): 125-34.
17. I. Kent and W. Nicholls, "Bereavement in Postabortion Women," *World Journal of Psychosynthesis* 13 (1981): 14-17.
18. M. Gibbons, "Psychiatric Sequelae of Induced Abortion," *Journal of the Royal College of General Practioners* 34 (1984): 146-50.
19. I. Kent, R. C. Greenwood, J. Loeken and W. Nicholls, "Emotional Sequelae of Elective Abortion," *British Columbia Medical Journal* 20 (1978): 118-19.
20. W. J. Warden, *Grief Counselling and Grief Therapy: A Handbook for Mental Health Practitioners* (New York: Spring Publishing, 1982), pp. 91-92.
21. See S. S. Joy, "Abortion: An Issue to Grieve?" *Journal of Counselling and Development* 63 (1985): 375-76; and N. H. Horowitz, "Adolescent Mourning Reactions to Infant and Fetal Loss," *Social Casework* 59 (1978): 551-59.
22. J. O. Cavenar, A. A. Maltbie and J. L. Sullivan, "Psychological Sequelae of Therapeutic Abortions," *North Carolina Medical Journal* 39 (1978): 103.
23. Parthun and Kiss, *Abortion's Aftermath*, pp. 5-6. A good example of such a study is the 1987 *Report on Therapeutic Abortion Services in Ontario: A Study Commissioned by the Ontario Ministry of Health*. The author, Marion Powell, consulted only the personnel of abortion hospitals and clinics, public health units which refer women to abortion hospitals and Planned Parenthood groups, which are also involved in abortion referrals. Not surprisingly, she found nothing to suggest that free access to abortion is less than an unmitigated benefit to women.
24. A. Speckhard, *The Psycho-Social Aspects of Stress Following Abortion* (Kansas City: Sheed and Ward, 1987), p. 42.
25. See Note 12 above.
26. For example, see M. K. Zimmerman, *Passage through Abortion: The Personal and Social Reality of Women's Experience* (New York: Praeger Special Studies, 1987).

27. J. O. Cavenar, A. A. Maltbie and J. L. Sullivan, "Aftermath of Abortion: Anniversary Depression and Abdominal Pain," *Bulletin of the Menninger Clinic* 42 (1978): 433-38. See also J. S. Wallerstein, P. Kurtz and M. Bar-Din, "Psychosocial Sequelae of Therapeutic Abortion in Young Unmarried Women," *Archives of General Psychiatry* 27 (1972): 828-32.

28. Speckhard, *The Psycho-Social Aspects of Stress Following Abortion.* (Kansas City: Sheed & Ward, 1987): 62.

29. M. K. Zimmerman, "Psychosocial and Emotional Consequences of Elective Abortion: A Literature Review" in P. Sachev, ed., *Abortion: Readings and Research* (Toronto: Butterworth, 1981), pp. 65-75.

30. "Psychological Sequelae of Therapeutic Abortion," *British Medical Journal*, no. 1 (1976): 1239. See also: D. S. Heath, "Psychiatry and Abortion," *Canadian Psychiatric Association Journal* 16 (1971): 55-63; M. Sim and R. Neisser, "Post-Abortive Psychoses: A Report from Two Centers" in D. Mall and W. F. Watts, eds., *The Psychosocial Aspects of Abortion* (Washington: University Publications of America, 1979), pp. 1-13; A. B. Sclare and B. P. Geraghty, "Therapeutic Abortion: A Follow-up Study," *Scottish Medical Journal* 16 (1971): 438-42.

31. *Report of Scientific Group on Spontaneous and Induced Abortion* (Geneva: World Health Organization, 1970), pp. 41-42.

32. C. M. B. Pare and H. Raven, "Follow-up of Patients Referred for Termination of Pregnancy," *The Lancet*, no. 1 (1970): 635-38; L. L. de Veber, "Children, Cancer and Death" in I. Gentles, ed., *Care for the Dying and the Bereaved* (Toronto: Anglican Book Centre, 1982), pp. 111-14; K. Stern, *The Flight from Woman* (New York: Farrar, Strauss and Giroux, 1965), pp. 21-23; C. I. Tishler, "Abortion and Suicide," *Pediatrics* 68 (1981): 670-71.

33. J. R. Ashton, "The Psychosocial Outcome of Induced Abortion," *British Journal of Obstetrics and Gynaecology* 87 (1980): 1115-22.

34. B. D. Blumberg, M. S. Golbus and K. H. Hanson, "The Psychological Sequelae of Abortions Performed for Genetic Indication," *American Journal of Obstetrics and Gynecology* 122 (1975): 799-808.

35. S. Borg and J. Lasker, *When Pregnancy Fails: Families Coping with Miscarriage, Stillbirth and Infant Death* (Boston: Beacon Press, 1981), pp. 41-50.

36. W. Rayburn and J. J. Laferla, "Mid-gestational Abortion for Medical or Genetic Indications," *Clinics in Obstetrics and Gynaecology* 13 (1986): 71-82.

37. J. Lloyd and K. M. Lawrence, "Sequelae and Support after Termination of Pregnancy for Fetal Malformation," *British Medical Journal* 290 (1985): 907-09.

38. See note 27.

39. A. J. Margolis, L. A. Davison, K. H. Hanson, S. A. Loos and C. M. Mikkelsen, "Therapeutic Abortion Follow-up Study," *American Journal of Obstetrics and Gynaecology* 110 (1971): 243-49.

40. M. G. Perez-Reyes and R. Falk, "Followup after Therapeutic Abortion in Early Adolescents," *Archives of General Psychiatry* 28 (1973): 120-26.

41. David, Rasmussen and Holst, "Postpartum and Psychiatric Reactions," *Family Planning Perspectives* 13 (1981): 89-91.

42. David et al. report 22.2 admissions per 10,000 for the first group; 13.4 per 10,000 for the second.

43. See Gold et al. (note 8), pp. 80, 84.

44. E. R. Greenglass, "A Canadian Study of Psychological Adjustment after Abortion" in R. Sachev, ed., *Abortion: Readings and Research* (see note 29), pp. 76-90.

45. A. Lazarus, "Psychiatric Sequelae of Legalised Elective First Trimester Abortion," *Journal of Psychosomatic Obstetrics and Gynaecology* 4 (1985): 141-50.

46. C. M. Friedman, R. Greenspan and F. Mittleman, "The Decision-making Process and the Outcome of Therapeutic Abortion," *American Journal of Psychiatry* 131 (1974): 1332-37; E. Senay, "Therapeutic Abortion: Clinical Aspects," *Archives of General Psychiatry* 23 (1970): 409-15.

47. For another extensive review of the literature evaluating distress following abortion, see Philip G. Ney and Adele Rose Wickett, "Mental Health and Abortion: Review and Analysis," *Psychiatric Journal of the University of Ottawa* 14, 4 (November 1989), pp. 506-16. Basically Ney and Wickett confirm our findings.

48. See the accounts in D. C. Reardon, *Aborted Women: Silent No More* (Westchester, Illinois: Crossway, 1987).

49. N. Buckles, "Abortion: A Technique for Working through Grief," *Journal of the American College of Health Association* 30 (1982): 181-82; E. Jones, "A Psychiatrist's Experience with Legal Abortion in Canada" in E. J. Kremer and E. A. Synan, eds., *Death before Birth*, (Toronto: Griffin House, 1974), pp. 177-86.

50. See Note 3 above. See also R. Stirtzinger and G. E. Robinson, "The Psychological Effects of Spontaneous Abortion," *Canadian Medical Association Journal* 140 (1989): 799-801. Stirtzinger and Robinson detail the psychological problems and deficiencies in health care of women suffering spontaneous abortion. Many of these are common to women who have had induced abortions.

51. V. M. Rue, "Post-Abortion Syndrome," a paper presented at the first National Conference on Post-Abortion Counselling, University of Notre Dame, South Bend, Indiana, August 1986.

CHRIS BAGLEY

Social Service and Abortion Policy

1. In the whole of Canada, there were more than 80,000 legal terminations in 1988 (see p. 116, note 23), and 1.5 million in the U.S.A. (S. Henshaw, "Abortion in the United States, 1978-1979," *Family Planning Perspectives* 13 (1981): 6-18). A statement by the Alan Guttmacher Institute in February 1982 indicated that about one-quarter of all pregnancies in the United States end in abortion. The official figures on abortion in Canada do not include data from private clinics; see the *Globe and Mail* (Toronto), November 24, 1982. In Britain the

number of abortions continues to rise by about 7 percent *per annum*. In 1980, 160,903 legal abortions were performed in England and Wales, by 1988 the figure had reached 183,798; see *Abortion Statistics 1980: England and Wales*, (London: H.M.S.O., 1982) and *Abortion Statistics 1988: England and Wales*, (London H.M.S.O., 1989). In many urban centres, including Toronto, the number of abortions exceeds the number of live births. See also B. MacKenzie "Therapeutic abortion in Canada," *Canadian Social Trends* 8 (Spring 1988): 2-5. Further data on Canada and U.K. are in C. Tietze, *Induced Abortion* (Washington: Guttmacher Institute, 1986).

2. Registrar General, *Supplement on Abortion* (London: General Register Office, 1973); *Globe and Mail* (Toronto), December 7, 1983.

3. See *Globe and Mail* reference, note 4, above.

4. For a discussion of these findings, see the essay by Ian Gentles and Denyse O'Leary, "Abortion, Law and Human Behavior," pp. 107-133 in this volume.

5. "Our Thalidomide Children: Three Years On, the Gloom Lifts," *Sunday Times* (London), November 16, 1975, p. 5.

6. S. Rose-Ackerman, "Mental Retardation and Society: The Ethics and Politics of Normalization," *Ethics* 93 (1982): 81-101.

7. H. Eckstein, G. Hatcher and E. Slater, "New Horizons in Medical Ethics: Severely Malformed Children," *British Medical Journal* 1 (1973): 284-88.

8. "Campaign to Guard Spina Bifida Babies," *Times* (London) December 29, 1977.

9. D. Campbell, "Sanctity of Life," *Times* (London), January 5, 1982.

10. A. Ferriman, "Alexandra in Foster Home," *Times* (London), September 2, 1981. Independent adoption agencies specializing in placing handicapped children have been more vigorous in their efforts to save the lives of these infants, both born and unborn. See P. Sawbridge, "Life of a Child," *Times* (London), August 25, 1981.

11. D. Nicholson-Lord, "Care of the Handicapped: Babies' Rights to Live Backed," *Times* (London), March 26, 1982.

12. For justification of the Kantian position see, T. Hill, "Humanity as an End in Itself," *Ethics* 91 (1980): 84-99.

13. N. St. John-Stevas, *The Right to Life* (London: Hodder, 1963).

14. P. Ney, "The Relationship Between Abortion and Child Abuse," *Canadian Journal of Psychiatry* 24 (1979): 610. There is also a link between abortion and child murder by depressed parents. See M. Rodenburg, "Child Murder by Depressed Parents," *Canadian Psychiatric Association Journal* 16 (1971): 41-48.

15. See note 12, above,

16. K. Popper, *The Poverty of Historicism* (London: Routledge, 1957).

17. C. Bagley, "On the Sociology and Social Ethics of Abortion", *Ethics, Science and Medicine* 2 (1975): 1-11.

18. One effect of this "baby shortage" has been to increase the number of adoptions by Americans and Europeans from Third World countries.

See C. Bagley and L. Young, "The Long-term Adjustment and Identity of a Sample of Inter-country Adopted Children," *International Social Work* 23 (1980): 16-22.

19. C. Bagley, "Adjustment, Achievement and Social Circumstances of Adopted Children in a National Survey," *Adoption and Fostering* 102 (1980): 47-49.

20. M. Bohman, *Adopted Children and Their Families* (Stockholm: Proprius, 1970).

21. A leading British obstetrician has commented on what he terms "the half-caste child." R. Gardner, *Abortion: The Personal Dilemma* (London: Patemoster Press, 1972).

22. D. Tunnadine and R. Green, *Unwanted Pregnancy: Accident or Illness?* (London: Oxford University Press, 1970).

23. A. Liley and B. Day, *Modern Motherhood* (New York: Random House, 1969) and A. Liley, "The Fetus as a Personality," *Delta* 21 (1977): 3-10. For further references on fetal life, see C. Bagley, "On the Sociology and Social Ethics of Abortion," (note 19) above and A. DeCasper and W. Fifer, *Science*, June 6, 1980, p. 1174.

24. A popular account of such research is presented by T. Verny and J. Kelly in *The Secret Life of the Unborn Child* (Toronto: Collins, 1981). Recent research reported by Dr. Norman Krasnegor of the National Institute of Child Health and Human Development indicates that a young baby has a pleasant memory (as indicated by sucking reflex) of stories which mothers had read to the child *in utero*, when he or she was in a "waking state." The infants showed a clear preference for these stories over other stories read by the mother (Newhouse News Service, Washington D.C., May 24, 1984). This research suggests that fetuses do have an intelligent discrimination and memory for stimuli.

25. R. Schmidt, "The Experience of Abortion," *New Society*, February 2, 1978, pp. 242-43.

26. See *Evening Argus*, June 14, 1971 for a report of the child's birth and early survival. See the *Globe and Mail*, June 18, 1982, for report of child surviving from birth weight of 476 grams.

27. *The Use of Fetuses and Their Material for Research* (London: Her Majesty's Stationery Office, 1972).

28. "Hospital Denies 'Live Baby' Abortion," *Guardian* (London), March 26, 1979, p. 2.

29. R. Butt, "This Awful Silence Hanging Over Abortion on Demand," *Times* (London), January 23, 1975, p. 12.

30. *Times* (London), July 16, 1983.

31. J. Masters, "Prenatal Child Abuse," *Maclean's*, January 30, 1982.

32. "Abortion Doctor Cleared by JPs," *Times* (London), September 16, 1983.

33. Report on surrogate parenting by Dr. Philip Parker, Wayne State University, April 1983. See, too, A. Lovell, "Some Questions of Identity, Late Miscarriage, Still-birth and Perinatal Loss," *Social Science and*

Medicine 17 (1983): 755-61.

34. "The Exploitation of Human Fetuses," *International Child Welfare Review* 56 (1983): 41-43; and 57: 45-48; 49: 45-47.

35. "Foetuses 'Used in Cosmetic Research,'" *Times* (London), December 16, 1983.

36. "Protest Against the Use of Fetuses Extracted Alive From their Mothers' Wombs," *International Child Welfare Review* 59 (1984): 45-47. The Committee on Research and Technology of the EEC recommended in 1983 to the European Economic Commission that the marketing and use of living fetuses should be prohibited. This recommendation has not yet been acted on.

37. G. Chamberlain, "An Artificial Placenta: The Development of an Extra Corporeal System for Maintenance of Immature Infants with Respiratory Problems," *American Journal of Obstetrics* 100 (1968): 624. Ironically, the "ethical" justification for this research was that it would enable premature infants to be kept alive.

38. P. Phillips and F. Rozendal, "Giving Birth to Child or Idea: The Feminine Dilemma," *Social Behaviour and Personality* 11 (1983): 59-64.

39. Reuter News Agency, July 23, 1982. It is interesting to compare this practice with earlier practices in India. See L. Panigrahi, *British Social Policy and Female Infanticide in India* (New Delhi: Monshiram Manoharlal, 1972); and K. Gangrede, *Sex Discrimination: A Critique* (University of Delhi: Office of the Pro-Vice Chancellor, 1988).

40. G. Greer, *Sex and Destiny: The Politics of Human Fertility* (Toronto: Stoddart, 1984). See also A. Dworkin, *Intercourse* (New York: Free Press, 1988); and G. Brown, *The New Celibacy* (Toronto: McGraw-Hill, 1981).

IAN GENTLES, DENYSE O'LEARY
Abortion, Law and Human Behavior

1. Eleanor Pelrine, *Abortion in Canada* (Toronto: New Press, 1971), p. 56 (emphasis added).

2. See for instance, Leslie Aldridge Westoff and Charles F. Westoff in *From Now to Zero: Fertility, Contraception and Abortion in America* (Boston: Little, Brown, 1971), p. 117; Mary S. Calderone, ed., *Abortion in the United States: A Conference Sponsored by the Planned Parenthood Federation of America, Inc.*, at Arden House and the New York Academy of Medicine (New York: Hoeber-Harper, 1958), p. 180.

3. See, for example, Dorothy G. Wiehl, "A Summary of Data on Reported Incidence of Abortion," *Millbank Memorial Fund Quarterly* 16 (1938): 80-88. This paper summarized data available from a number of studies and concluded that only 4 to 5 percent of married women had sought induced abortions.

4. Albert Kinsey was the American pioneer of the study of human sexuality. Paul H. Gebhard, Wardell B. Pomeroy, Clyde E. Martin and Cornelia V. Christenson, *Pregnancy, Birth and Abortion* (New York: Harper, 1958), p. 14. Among young women in particular the difference

was fairly substantial. In the twenty to twenty-four age group, the number of live births per female in the Kinsey study was 0:19. A comparative estimate for white urban females adjusted to the Kinsey sample by level of education and marital status was three times as high, at 0.56. Similarly, in the twenty to twenty-four age group, 77.9 percent of the Kinsey women were unmarried (i.e., single and never married) compared with 62.7 percent of urban white females in 1945 (based on census data of 1940 and 1950, adjusted by level of education). In the twenty-five to twenty-nine age group, the margin narrowed slightly: 39.4 percent of the women in the Kinsey sample compared to 29 percent of urban white females. In the forty-five to forty-nine age group, there was a marked difference in the incidence of divorce, separation or widowhood: 41.4 percent of the Kinsey women were "never separated, divorced or widowed" in comparison with 23.6 percent of the control sample.

5. Germain Grisez, *Abortion: The Myths, the Realities and the Arguments*, (New York: World Publishing, 1970), pp. 41, 14.

6. Ibid., p. 36. "What indicates almost unbelievable sloppiness . . . is that Bates and Zawadski, simply by adjusting for the intervening population increase, apparently projected Taussig's total figure of 681,600 abortions annually, which was intended to include 35-40 percent non-criminal abortions, into 'about one million criminal abortions.'"

7. Ibid., p. 38. Thirteen abortions in New York City in a two-month period in 1893 were used as the basis for projecting 80,000 annually, on the assumption that "one in a thousand" is reported.

8. Bernard Nathanson, *Aborting America* (New York: Doubleday, 1979), p. 193.

9. Cited in Thomas W. Hilgers, *Induced Abortion: A Documented Report* (Owatonna, Minnesota: Minnesota Citizens Concerned for Life, Inc., 1973), p. ii. The conference was sponsored by the Harvard Divinity School and the Kennedy Foundation. See also Daniel Callahan, *Abortion: Law, Choice and Morality* (New York: Macmillan, 1972), p. 134.

10. *Basic Facts on Therapeutic Abortions, Canada* (Ottawa: Statistics Canada, 1983); Alan Guttmacher Institute, research agency for Planned Parenthood Federation of America, "Abortion Services in the U.S.: Each State and Metropolitan Area 1979-80." For live births: Guttmacher Institute "Live Births by Age of Mother and Race from Standard Metropolitan Statistical Areas of the United States, 1980." For the total number of abortions estimated in the United States, see the Guttmacher Institute's survey of abortion providers across the United States, published by Stanley K. Henshaw, *Family Planning Perspectives* 14, no. 1 (January/February, 1982): 5.

11. Glanville Williams, *The Sanctity of Life and the Criminal Law* (New York: Knopf, 1957), p. 210; Bernard M. Dickens, *Abortion and the Law* (Bristol: MacGibbon and Kee, 1966), p. 83.

12. "Report of the Council of the Royal College of Obstetricians and Gynaecologists, Legalised Abortion," *British Medical Journal*, 2 April,

1966. They assumed that not more than one in every five of 72,400 abortion cases treated in 1962 was induced or self-induced rather than spontaneous.

13. C. B. Goodhart, "On the Incidence of Illegal Abortion," *Population Studies* 27 (1973): 208.

14. Ibid., p. 213. The Royal College also notes in the report cited in note 12 above (p. 851) that if estimates of 100,000 per year are accepted, one is forced to the rather embarrassing conclusion that, based on mortality rates from induced abortions, "the results of criminal abortionists and of women interfering with themselves are better than those which can be produced by specialist gynaecologists terminating early pregnancies in the best hospital conditions."

15. Ibid., p. 214. This figure includes all spontaneous and threatened abortions and also counts separately each hospitalization of the same mother.

16. Ibid., p. 218. So few women claimed to have had an abortion that the inclusion of a single mistaken "yes" answer would result in a misleading extrapolation of thousands of additional induced abortions.

17. E. Lewis-Faning, "Report on an Enquiry into Family Limitation and Its Influence on Human Fertility during the Past Fifty Years," *Papers of the Royal Commission on Population*, vol. 1 (London: H.M.S.O., 1949).

18. Office of Population Censuses and Surveys, *Abortion Statistics 1983*, series AB, no. 10 (London: H.M.S.O., 1985), p. 2; Abortion Statistics 1988, Series AB, no. 15 (London: H.M.S.O., 1989).

19. Pelrine, *Abortion in Canada*, p. 56.

20. Robin F. Badgley et al., *Report of the Committee on the Operation of the Abortion Law* (Ottawa: Supply and Services Canada, 1977), p. 66.

21. Ibid., p. 71.

22. Ibid., p. 72.

23. This figure was totalled from provincial and territorial statistics obtained under the Freedom of Information Act and reported in *Vitality* (October, 1989). It does not include the substantial number of abortions camouflaged by hospitals under the heading "D and Cs."

24. Department of Health Services and Hospital Insurance, *Vital Statistics of the Province of British Columbia*, Maternal Mortality Tables, 1955-68 (Victoria, B.C.: various years); W. D. S. Thomas, "Abortion Deaths in British Columbia, 1955-1968," *British Columbia Medical Journal* 12 (May, 1970): 112. In another article, A. and A. T. McLaren distort the significance of these figures by confining themselves to the five-year period 1955-59 when the official figures did not exceed those of doctors' reports. Their purpose is to show that government statistics drastically underestimated mortality from illegal abortion. See "Discoveries and Dissimulations: The Impact of Abortion Deaths on Maternal Mortality in British Columbia," *B.C. Studies*, no. 64 (Winter 1984-85): 3-26.

25. H. Forssman and I. Thuwe, "One Hundred and Twenty Children Born

after Application for Therapeutic Abortion Refused," *Acta Psychiatria Scandinavica* 42 (1966): 71-88.

26. K. Hook, "Refused Abortion: A Follow-up Study of 249 Women Whose Applications Were Refused by the National Board of Health in Sweden," *Acta Psychiatria Scandinavica*, Supplement 168 (1963): 58, 61.

27. V. Schuller et al., "The Unwanted Child in the Family," *Mental Health Research Newsletter* 14, no. 3 (Fall, 1972): 2,6; Z. Dytrych et al., "Children Born to Women Denied Abortion," *Family Planning Perspectives* 7 (1975): 165-71; Z. Matejcek et al., "Children from Unwanted Pregnancies," *Acta Psychiatria Scandinavica* 57 (1978): 70, 76-86; Henry P. David et al., *Born Unwanted: Developmental Effects of Denied Abortion* (New York: Springer, 1988), p. 85.

28. Badgley et al., *Report*, p. 167.

29. Carlos Del Campo, "Abortion Denied — Outcome of Mothers and Babies," *Canadian Medical Association Journal* 130 (February 15, 1984): 361.

30. In some studies it has been a practice to list as maternal deaths all deaths to mothers during pregnancy or within three months thereafter, however caused. We are here concerned only with deaths relating directly to the fact of being pregnant.

31. Cited in *Time*, November 27, 1978.

32. At the time of writing, the constitutionality of this law has been challenged.

33. I. Gentles, "Abortion, Law and Human Behavior," *Human Life Review* 13, no. 2 (1987): 75-8.

34. Los Angeles *Times*, February 11, 1988.

35. The Professional Insurance Management Company is based in Jacksonville, Florida. This information was supplied by Dr. Matthew Bulfin, an obstetrician-gynecologist practicing in Fort-Lauderdale-by-the-Sea.

36. In an article in *Family Planning Perspectives* 7, no. 3 (May/June, 1975), "The Effect of Legalization of Abortion on Population Growth and Public Health," Christopher Tietze stated that maternal deaths from illegal abortions had decreased in the United States in recent years. The statement is questionable, however, since improved medical care has led to a decrease in deaths from all causes during pregnancy during the past several decades, and since permissive laws do not seem to control actual abortion practices very effectively, it is difficult to see why they should be credited with the decline in maternal deaths.

37. Office of Population Censuses and Surveys, *Mortality Statistics, Childhood and Maternity, 1978*, series DH3, no. 5 (London: H.M.S.O., 1980). Note: Table 18, "Maternal Deaths," was discontinued after 1978.

38. *Criminal Statistics for England and Wales 1977* (London: H.M.S.O., 1978). In 1978 a new category was created: "unspecified abortion," which included all those not classified as spontaneous, legally induced or illegally induced. It is likely that this category concealed a consid-

erable number of illegal abortions. The Summary Tables for 1979-82 in a Department of Health and Social Security document entitled *Hospital In-Patient Enquiry* (London: H.M.S.O., 1980-84) show the categories, and indicate the following hospital patient admissions for "unspecified abortion": 1979 — 37,160; 1980 — 35,470; 1981 — 35,660; and 1982 — 34,490.

39. "Report of the Council of the Royal College of Obstetricians and Gynaecologists, Legalised Abortion," *British Medical Journal* (April 2, 1966).

40. Paul Cavadino, "Illegal Abortions and the Abortion Act 1967," *British Journal of Criminology*, 16, no. 1 (January, 1976): 67. See also A. Howard John and Brian Hackman, "Effects of Legal Abortion on Gynaecology," *British Medical Journal* (July 8, 1972): 99-102, which shows a rise in criminal abortions in Bristol since the passage of the Act.

41. *Report of the (Lane) Committee on the Workings of the Abortion Act* (London: H.M.S.O., 1974), vol. 1, section Q, para. 509. In this report, the observation that illegal abortionists were using antibiotics in increasing measure was given as a reason for difficulty in establishing figures for illegal abortions.

42. Alphonse de Valk, *Morality and the Law in Canadian Politics* (Dorval: Palm Publishing, 1974), p. 12, note to p. 13; pp. 23-28.

43. Ibid., p. 45 (emphasis added).

44. House of Commons, Standing Committee on Health and Welfare, *Proceedings — Abortion*, no. 24, March 13, 1968, pp. 24/3, 24/4.

45. World Health Organization, *Basic Documents*, 32nd edition, (Geneva: WHO, 1983), p. 1.

46. See W. J. Harris and L. S. Tupper, "A Study of Therapeutic Abortion Committees in British Columbia," *University of British Columbia Law Review* 11 (1981): 101.

47. *Globe and Mail*, March 21, 1984; May 4, 7, 8, 1985.

48. The WHO definition does not mention the fetus, nor does it refer to pregnancy. Nor is it actually a "definition" of health in any medical or biological sense, but a statement about it in the ideal sense, one of the nine principles stated in the preamble of the WHO constitution to be basic to happiness, harmony and security. In their *Working Paper on Medical Treatment and Criminal Law* (Ottawa: Supply and Services, 1980), the Law Reform Commission of Canada pointed out that, "the concept of 'social well-being' far exceeds the meaning presently contemplated in Canadian criminal law for it includes political injustice, economic scarcity, food shortages and unfavourable physical environments. All human misfortunes and disorders are not forms of illness from which one must be saved under the rubric of health in the criminal law . . . " (p. 7).

49. *Toronto Star*, April 3, 1984.

50. S. Wadhera, "Early Complications of Legal Abortions, Canada, 1975-80," *Canadian Journal of Public Health* (November/December, 1982): 396-401.

51. In their decision, no. 24-75-0001.

52. H. Morgentaler, "Report on 5641 Outpatient Abortions by Vacuum Suction Curettage," *Canadian Medical Association Journal* 109, no. 12 (December 15, 1973): 202-5.

53. Montreal *Gazette*, December 24, 1974.

54. *Globe and Mail*, January 14, 1985.

55. Toronto *Star*, February 29, 1980.

56. See note 29 above.

57. Statistics Canada, *Vital Statistics*, no. 84-204 (Births and Deaths) (Ottawa: Supply and Services, 1988, March 30, 1990).

58. Thomas Frejka, "Induced Abortion and Fertility: A Quarter Century of Experience in Eastern Europe," *Population and Development Review* 9, no. 3 (1983): 517.

59. However, if pregnancies increase and induced abortions decrease, there would normally be an increase in reported spontaneous abortions in any case. Ibid.; pp. 511, 517.

60. Ibid., p. 500.

61. B. Berelson, "Romania's 1966 Anti-Abortion Decree: The Demographic Experience of the First Decade," *Population Studies* 33, no. 2 (1979): 219. Berelson lists a sixfold increase. Using a slightly different timespan, Frejka ("Induced Abortion and Fertility": p. 511) shows a sevenfold increase.

62. New Zealand's abortion figures are published annually by the Abortion Supervisory Committee. Birth figures are tabulated by the Department of Statistics at Wellington, which publishes an Official Yearbook with a separate Population Extract.

63. For instance, on a New Zealand TV One Programme on March 11, 1983, abortion consultants opined that a mother was entitled to an abortion if "distressed" by pregnancy. This is not in accordance with New Zealand law.

Diane Marshall, Martha Crean

The Human Face of a Woman's Agony

1. Sexuality should be affirmed as a gift designed for *mutual* consent and pleasure. We can no longer ignore the fact that women often have sex involuntarily.

2. James Burtchaell, *Rachel Weeping* (New York: Harper and Row, 1982).

3. *Hospital News*, September, 1989.

Ian Gentles

The Unborn Child in Civil and Criminal Law

1. I refer to the unborn child as "she" and "her" in this essay, as a reminder that half the victims of abortion are female.

2. James B. Pritchard, *Ancient Near Eastern Texts Relating to the Old Testament*, 2nd ed. (Princeton: Princeton University Press, 1955), pp. 175,

184ff., 190.

3. Translated by Ludwig Edelstein, *Ancient Medicine*, (Baltimore: Johns Hopkins Press, 1967), p. 6.

4. Dennis J. Horan et al., "The Legal Case for the Unborn Child," in T. W. Hilgers and D. J. Horan, eds., *Abortion and Social Justice* (New York: Sheed and Ward, 1972), pp. 122-24.

5. *Blackstone's Commentaries*, vol. 1, 15th ed., (London: A. Strahan, 1809), p. 129.

6. Edward Synan, "Law and the Sin of the Mothers," in E. A. Synan and E. J. Kremer, eds., *Death before Birth: Canadian Essays on Abortion* (Toronto: Griffin Press, 1974), pp. 146ff.

7. 43 George III, c. 58 (1803).

8. *Thellusson* v. *Woodward* (1798-1799), *English Reports*, vol. 3, p. 163.

9. *Western Weekly Reports* (1919), vol. 1, p. 163.

10. *Giddings* v. *Canadian Northern Railway Company, Dominion Law Reports* (1920), vol. 53.

11. *Supreme Court Reports* (1933), p. 456.

12. *Ontario Reports* (1972), vol. 2.

13. *Victoria Reports* (Australia), 1972, p. 353.

14. *Revised Statutes of Ontario* (1980) C.230, s. 28(1), pp. 127-28.

15. William L. Prosser, *Handbook of the Law of Torts*, 4th ed. (St. Paul: West, 1974), pp. 335-36. The other eminent authority on tort law, the Australian John G. Fleming, agrees that courts in Britain and the Commonwealth are now willing to entertain suits for prenatal injuries. *The Law of Torts*, 5th ed. (Sydney: Law Book Company, 1977), p. 159 (emphasis added).

16. Prosser, *Law of Torts*, p. 338. See also the essay by Robert Nadeau below, pp. 186-200.

17. Horan et al., "The Legal Case for the Unborn Child," p. 113 (see note 4, above).

18. Ibid., p. 115.

19. *Globe and Mail*, November 16, 1981.

20. *Globe and Mail*, November 3, 1979.

21. *Globe and Mail*, November 8, 1979. In 1988, however, the B.C. court of appeal ruled that a full-term infant with its head emerging from the birth canal could still not be considered a person within the meaning of the Criminal Code. See. *R.* v. *Sullivan* and Lemay (1988) 31 B.C.L.R. 145. The decision is presently under appeal to the Supreme Court of Canada. See also above, p. 28 n. 6.

22. *In Re the Matter of Judicial Review of a Decision of Judge P. d'A. Collings Respecting Female Infant Born Dec. 11th, 1981*, Supreme Court of British Columbia, April 13, 1982 (emphasis added).

23. David M. Steinberg, *Family Law in Family Courts*, (Toronto: Carswell, 1981), 2nd ed., vol. 1, p. 112.

24. *Globe and Mail*, April 2, 1982.

25. E-H. W. Kluge, "The Right to Life of Potential Persons," *Dalhousie Law Journal* 2 (1977): 846-47.

26. See, for example, a standard textbook, Leslie B. Arey, *Developmental Anatomy*, 7th ed. (Philadelphia: Saunders, 1974), p. 54.

27. See "Abortion, Law and Human Behavior," above, pp. 107-133.

28. See *Report on the Operation of the Abortion Law* (The Badgley Report) (Ottawa: Supply and Services, Canada, 1977), pp. 70-71, and C. B. Goodhart, "On the Incidence of Illegal Abortion," *Population Studies* 27 (1973): 207-33.

29. See above, pp. 118-122.

IAN HUNTER
Trial by Jury: *R. v. Morgentaler*

1. The trial took sixty-three days on motions to quash the indictment or stay proceedings prior to plea, and nineteen days after plea.

2. *R. v. Morgentaler, Smoling and Scott*, [1985] 19C.C.C. (3d) 573, 44 C.R. (3d) 189 (Ont. C.A.). Chief Justice Howland's decision to refuse intervenant status to pro-life groups may usefully be compared to his decision ten months later to allow intervenant status to the women's Legal Education and Action Fund; *R. v. Seaboyer and Gayme*, [1986] 50 C.R. (3d) 395 (Ont. C.A.).

3. *R. v. Morgentaler Smoling and Scott*, [1985], 22 C.C.C. (3d)353, 48 C.R. (3d)1,22 D.L.R. (4th)641 (Ont. C.A.), discussed below.

4. The development of juries is traced by Sir Patrick Devlin in *Trial by Jury*, (London: Stevens & Son, 1956).

5. Quoted in Devlin, *Trial by Jury*, p. 4. (See note 4.)

6. *R. v. Makow*, [1974] 20 C.C.C. (2d)513, p. 518; 28 C.R.N.S. 87, p. 94; [1975] W.W.R. 299 (B.C.C.A.).

7. *R. v. Hubbert*, [1975] 29 C.C.C. (2d)279, p. 291; 31 C.R.N.S. 27, p. 39; 11 O.R. (2d)464 (C.A.).

8. "Selection of Jury Slowed Down Again at the Morgentaler Trial," Toronto *Star*, October 17, 1984.

9. [1973] 1 All E.R. 240.

10. [1985] 81 Cr. App. R. 217.

11. Ibid., p. 219.

12. *R. v. Hubbert*, p. 290 C.C.C., p. 38 C.R.N.S. (See note 7.)

13. "Religion Called Key in Selecting Jurors," Toronto *Star*, November 9, 1984.

14. *R. v. Hubbert*, pp. 289-90 C.C.C., p. 37 C.R.N.S. (See note 7.)

15. "Religion Called Key," Toronto *Star*. (See note 13.)

16. "Morgentaler's Lawyer Defends Jury Selection," Toronto *Star*, December 15, 1984.

17. *R. v. Morgentaler, Smoling and Scott*, pp. 432-34 C.C.C., pp. 88-90 C.R. (See note 3.)

F. L. MORTON

The Meaning of *Morgentaler* : A Political Analysis

1. Supreme Court of Canada, January 28, 1988.
2. 410 U.S. 113 [1973].
3. The primary agents of the reform that came to fruition in 1969 were the Canadian Medical Association and the Canadian Bar Association and the minister of justice of the time, Pierre Elliott Trudeau. See Alphonse de Valk, *Morality and the Law in Canadian Politics: The Abortion Controversy* (Montreal: Palm Publishing, 1974).
4. See R. Knopff and F. L. Morton, "Nation Building and the Canadian Charter of Rights and Freedoms," in Allan Cairns and C. Williams, eds., *Constitutionalism, Citizenship and Society in Canada* (Toronto: University of Toronto Press, 1986), pp. 133-82. Also see Sandra Burt, "Women's Issues and the Women's Movement in Canada since 1970," in Allan Cairns and C. Williams, eds., *The Politics of Gender, Ethnicity and Language in Canada* (Toronto: University of Toronto Press, 1986), pp. 111-70.
5. Former section 12(1)(b) of the Indian Act stripped Indian women who married non-Indians of their official Indian status. No similar disability applied to Indian men who married white women. In 1972 the Supreme Court rejected a sex discrimination challenge to this section in *A.-G. Canada* v. *Lavell and Bedard*, [1974] S.C.R. 1349.
6. In the 1976 case of *Bliss* v. *A.-G. Canada*, [1979] 1 S.C.R. 183, the Supreme Court had upheld the denial of regular unemployment insurance benefits to women who could not qualify for the more restricted maternity leave benefits. See Leslie A. Pal and F. L. Morton, *Bliss* v. *Attorney-General of Canada*: From Legal Defeat to Political Victory," in *Osgoode Hall Law Journal* 24, no. 1 (Spring, 1986): 141-60.
7. This was how the Supreme Court disposed of the Alberta Social Credit government's "Accurate News and Information Act" in the *Alberta Press Reference*, [1938] S.C.R. 100. Rather than strike down the statute as a violation of freedom of the press, the majority of the Court disposed of it on federalist grounds — that it was legislation in relation to criminal law and thus fell under federal not provincial jurisdiction. See Carl Baar's insightful discussion of this case, "Using Process Theory to Explain Judicial Decision Making," *Canadian Journal of Law and Society* 1 (1986): 57-79.
8. I have developed this argument more fully in another essay: "The Politics of Rights: What Canadians Should Know about the American Bill of Rights," *The Windsor Review of Legal and Social Issues* 1 (1989): 61-96.
9. Stuart Scheingold, *The Politics of Rights: Lawyers, Public Policy and Political Change* (New Haven: Yale University Press, 1974), p. 83.
10. According to Sankey the constitution is like "a living tree capable of growth and expansion [and that judges should not] cut down the provisions of the Act by a narrow and technical construction, but rather [should] give it a large and liberal interpretation." [1930] A.C. 124.

11. Ibid., pp. 6-7.

12. *Reference: re Alberta Public Service Employee Relations Act*, [1987] 1 S.C.R. 424.

13. F.L. Morton, Peter H. Russell and M.J. Whitney, "The Supreme Court's First One Hundred Charter Decisions: A Statistical Analysis," paper delivered to the Canadian Political Science Association, annual meeting, May 27-29, 1990, Victoria, B.C.

14. The "Bork Affair" refers to President Ronald Reagan's nomination of Judge Robert Bork to the U.S. Supreme Court. Bork was an outspoken critic of the judicial activism characteristic of the liberal Warren Court. His appointment would have created a majority of five conservative judges, a group that might well have overturned a number of liberal precedents, including the 1973 *Roe* v. *Wade* abortion decision. Liberals in the Senate organized to defeat the Bork nomination. For a more detailed discussion, see F. L. Morton, "The Politics of Rights: What Canadians Should Know about the American Bill of Rights" (see note 8).

15. V. O. Key, *Politics, Parties and Pressure Groups* (New York: Thomas Y. Crowell, 1958), p. 154.

16. "Public to Demand Say in Court Appointments?" *Lawyers Weekly*, February 12, 1988, p. 1.

17. "Reduced Role for Politicians Urged in Naming of Judges," *Globe and Mail*, May 16, 1988, p. 1.

18. David Taras makes and documents the same criticism of the media's coverage of the Meech Lake Accord. See Taras, "Television and Public Policy: The CBC's Coverage of the Meech Lake Accord." *Canadian Public Policy*, 15:3 (1989), 322-334.

19. Taras, "Television and Public Policy," p. 322.

20. See J. L. Lennards, "The Canadian Professoriate," unpublished paper, York University, 1986.

21. The advocacy character of much charter scholarship has been noted and criticized by Allan C. Cairns in his 1989 Timlin Lecture, "Ritual, Taboo and Bias in Constitutional Controversies in Canada," Nov. 13, 1989, University of Saskatoon.

22. The "legitimating function" of judicial review was first developed by Charles Black, *The People and the Court: Judicial Review in a Democracy* (New York: Macmillan, 1960), ch. 3. For a more recent analysis, see F. L. Morton, "Judicial Review in France: A Comparative Analysis," *The American Journal of American Law* 36, no. 1 (Winter, 1988), p. 101.

23. At the time of writing, Parliamentary hearings have been scheduled for the government's proposed legislation (Bill C 43), originally introduced in November 1989.

ROBERT D. NADEAU

The Anatomy of Evasion: A Critique of *Daigle*

1. Richard John Neuhaus, *The Religion and Society Report* 4, no. 10 (Octo-

ber 1987): 1. Of course, there is no recognized constitutional "right of privacy" in Canadian law (and serious controversy abounds whether such a right actually exists in the U.S. Constitution). But the present notion of a right of privacy in U.S. constitutional law is roughly equivalent to the Canadian constitutional concepts of "liberty" and "security of the person."

2. Bill C 43 tabled in the House of Commons on November 3, 1989. At time of writing, the bill is in committee for public hearings and further study. It has yet to be reported for third reading.

3. *Daigle* v. *Tremblay* (1990) 102 N.R. 81 (S.C.C.) Supreme Court of Canada, November 16, 1989. The actual decision of the Court was reached the day the appeal was heard (August 8, 1989). The Reasons for Judgement were delivered three months later on November 16.

4. Intervenors in the *Daigle* case included the Attorneys General of Canada and Quebec, the Canadian Abortion Rights Action League (CARAL), the Women's Legal Education and Action Fund (LEAF), the Canadian Civil Liberties Association, Campaign Life Coalition, Canadian Physicians for Life and REAL Women of Canada.

5. *Borowski* v. *A.G. of Canada* (1989) 92 N.R. 110 (S.C.C.).

6. Ibid., p. 123 (per Sopinka, J.).

7. Kirk Makin, "Swift abortion verdict expected," *Globe and Mail*, July 28, 1989, p. A1.

8. Ibid., p. A4.

9. Ibid.

10. This is not to say that the question of fetal rights will not wind its way up to the Supreme Court again, someday. After all, the *Daigle* case dealt with the "right to life" under provincial human rights legislation and the civil law (although the Court also considered the treatment of prenatal rights in the common law). But the Court refused to consider the question of fetal rights under the federal Charter of Rights and Freedoms citing the "private" nature of the dispute between the parties and leaving the door open to further constitutional challenge.

11. *Daigle* v. *Tremblay*, p. 29.

12. Ibid., p. 16. There were actually three main issues in the case, though the Court chose to rest its decision on the first: (1) whether the substantive rights asserted by the father and the pro-life interveners to support the injunction actually existed; (2) regardless of what the Court's answer might be to the first of these issues, whether an injunction was an appropriate remedy in this case (the argument being that an *interlocutory* injunction is meant to preserve the status quo — something that was impossible in this case); and (3) whether the injunction amounted to an improper encroachment of provincial law into the federal power over criminal power (the so-called division of powers argument). Because the Court chose to proceed as it did, it was unnecessary for it to consider questions (2) and (3).

13. It is true that the *Daigle* case did not deal with the Canadian Charter of Rights and Freedoms. But the Court was plainly aware that any

recognition of a right to life in the unborn, either in the Quebec Charter or the common law, would constitute a right in the nature of a *fundamental* right with far-reaching constitutional implications. To allow a fetus legal protection as a "human being" in the civil or common law but to deny it constitutional protection in section 7 of the federal Charter would almost surely be seen by an increasingly skeptical public as arbitrary and whimsical. The Court did the only thing it could do if it wished to preserve intact the freedom to kill prenatal life.

14. *Daigle* v. *Tremblay*, p. 16 (emphasis added).

15. Ibid.

16. Ibid.

17. The uncontradicted evidence of prenatal life and humanity was overwhelmingly established at trial in *Borowski* and remains the most damning indictment yet of the "pro-choice" liberalism that has enchanted the Court and the power centres of Canadian society. Yet, far from being progressive, it is intensely reactionary in its dogmatic refusal even to consider alternative claims to "truth" or the nascent claims to life of the weakest and most vulnerable of the human family: *Borowski* v. *A.G. of Canada* (1984) 8 C.C.C. (3d) 392; (1984) 4 D.L.R. (4th) 112 (Sask. Q.B.). See also M. Shumiatcher, "I Set Before You Life and Death," *Univ. of Western Ont. L. Rev.* 24, no. 2 (1986): 1.

18. *Daigle* v. *Tremblay*, p. 19.

19. *Daigle* v. *Tremblay*, p. 21.

20. *Edwards* v. *A.G. of Canada* (1928) S.C.R. 276; rev'd. (1930) A.C. 124 (P.C.).

21. J. G. Snell and F. Vaughan, *The Supreme Court of Canada: History of the Institution*, (Toronto: University of Toronto Press, 1985), pp. 141-42. The authors continue: "Their reasons indicate a desire to reaffirm the status quo; it was for the legislature to initiate change . . . nevertheless, in the context of the late 1920's, as the *Ottawa Evening Journal* pointed out, the decision made not only the law but the Supreme Court appear an ass."

22. *Edwards* v. *A.G. of Canada* (1930) A.C. 124 (P.C.). Appeals to the Privy Council were abolished by an Act of Parliament in 1949. The Court was supreme at last. But the abolition of appeals to the Privy Council did not come easy. Public opinion was ambivalent. And the constitutional authority of Parliament to transform the Supreme Court of Canada into the final and ultimate court of appeal in the Dominion had to be settled by the Judicial Committee of the Privy Council itself. For an absorbing account of the legal and political evolution of the Court to full legal "personhood," see Snell and Vaughan, *The Supreme Court of Canada: History of the Institution*, pp. 171-95.

23. *Edwards* v. *A.G. of Canada*, p. 128. This critique of blind allegiance to the past will be particularly germane to my analysis, later in this essay, of the doubtful lingering validity of the "born alive" rule in modern times.

24. Ibid., p. 138.
25. See, for example, the decision of the Massachusetts Supreme Judicial Court in *Commonwealth* v. *Cass*, 392 Mass. 799, 467 N.E. 2d. 1324 (1984), in which Chief Justice Hennessy, writing for the Court in a case involving the question whether a state homicide statute encompasses an unborn child, noted that "giving terms their ordinary meaning, the word 'person' is synonymous with the term 'human being.'" He continued: "An offspring of human parents cannot reasonably be considered to be other than a *human being*, and therefore a *person*, first within, and then in the normal course outside, the womb;" 392 Mass. 799, at 801; 467 N.E. 2d 1324, p. 1325. See also the uncontradicted and irrefutable evidence of prenatal human life marshalled in *Borowski*, note 17.
26. *Winnipeg School Division* v. *Craton*, [1985] 6 W.W.R. 166 (S.C.C.), per McIntyre, J.
27. Professor Gibson, commenting on human rights legislation and common law principles of interpretation, notes that quite apart from interpretation statutes, the common law already includes two presumptions: the first of these is that "legislation is to be construed for the benefit of the subject — penal laws narrowly, and remedial laws liberally." Dale Gibson, *The Law of the Charter: General Principles*, (Toronto: Carswell Co., 1986), p. 16. For a forceful critique of the expansiveness of human rights legislation and the insidious tendency of equality rights to diminish and destroy liberty, see I. Hunter, "When Human Rights Become Wrongs," *Univ. of Western Ont. L. Rev.* 23 (1985): 197.
28. Albie Sachs and Joan Hoff Wilson, *Sexism and the Law: A Study of Male Beliefs and Legal Bias in Britain and the United States*, (London: Martin Robertson & Co., 1978), p. 41.
29. Cf. the debate in the press and in Parliament over Bill C 43, tabled in the House of Commons on November 3, 1989.
30. Sachs and Wilson, p. 50.
31. *Montreal Tramways Co.* v. *Léveillé*, [1933] S.C.R. 456. Although a civil law decision, the Supreme Court in *Montreal Tramways* drew on the underlying principles of both the civil law and common law to break new ground in the field of prenatal rights. The decision was incorporated into the common law in *Duval* v. *Séguin*, [1972] 2 O.R. 686 (per Fraser, J.); affd. (1974) 1 O.R. (2d) 482. For more on the history and evolution of the cause of action in tort for prenatal injuries, see Ian Gentles, "The Unborn Child in Civil and Criminal Law," pp. 147-158 in this volume.
32. *Duval* v. *Séguin*, p. 482.
33. *Montreal Tramways*, p. 463, quoted in *Daigle* v. *Tremblay*, pp. 27-28.
34. *Daigle* v. *Tremblay*, p. 28.
35. *Montreal Tramways*, p. 465 (emphasis added).
36. *Daigle* v. *Tremblay*, pp. 26, 29.

37. See, for example *Dehler* v. *Ottawa Civic Hospital,* (1979), 101 D.L.R. (3d) 686 (Ont. H.C.); affd. (1980) 117 D.L.R. (3d) 512 (Ont. C.A.). Also, *Medhurst* v. *Medhurst,* (1984), 9 D.L.R. (4th) 252 (Ont. H.C.).

38. See, for example, Clarke D. Forsythe, "Homicide of the Unborn Child: The Born Alive Rule and Other Legal Anachronisms," *Val. Univ. L. Rev.* 21 (1987): 563-629; also J. Bopp, Jr., B.A. Bostrom and D.A. McKinney, "The 'Rights' and 'Wrongs' of Wrongful birth and Wrongful Life: A Jurisprudential Analysis of Birth-Related Torts," *Duquesne Law Rev.* 27 (1989): 479-82. This analysis was recently adopted by the Massachusetts Supreme Judicial Court in *Commonwealth v. Cass,* see above note 25.

39. Forsythe, notes 216-30 and accompanying text.

40. Ibid., p. 565. Bopp, Bostrom and McKinney echo Forsythe and add, in the context of property rights, that "the unborn child's property rights are conditional on live birth merely because the benefits of those rights cannot be enjoyed until birth. Rather than a substantive value judgment, live birth is merely a procedural requirement, similar to venue or standing, which must be met to enforce the intrinsic right." Bopp et. al., p. 481.

41. O. W. Holmes, "The Path of the Law," *Harv. L. Rev.* 10 (1897): 457-69. The common law is not a fixed or immutable body of rules or principles that cannot be changed, enlarged or abandoned as required over time. It is a body of precedents, developed by judges. As such, it is inherently adaptable. In any case involving the application of common law principles, the "right" decision is one that emerges out of settled law but deals justly with the conditions of the times and the unique facts of the case. That is both the beauty and the strength of the common law.

42. *Daigle* v. *Tremblay,* p. 33.

43. Law Reform Commission of Canada, *Crimes Against The Foetus,* Working Paper 58 (Ottawa: LRCC, 1989), p. 38.

44. This is not to say that there are no cases where abortion may be necessary. Such cases, however, fall under the right of self-defence as when a mother's life is endangered by the continuation of her pregnancy.

45. For an incisive critique of modern liberalism, see George Grant, *English Speaking Justice* (Toronto: Anansi and University of Notre Dame Press, 1985). See Samuel Ajzenstat's "The Liberal Crisis: Feminists on Abortion" in this volume for a discussion of the anti-liberal consequences of pro-abortion feminism.

46. "Had abortion to protect baby from boyfriend, Daigle says," *Globe and Mail,* August 14, 1989, p. A5. In her recent book, Daigle describes how she was urged in a dream to have the abortion by the fetus that presumably no longer wished to live. ("Asked by fetus to get abortion, Daigle reveals in her new book," *Globe and Mail,* March 8, 1990, p. A1.)

JANET AJZENSTAT

Justifying Destruction: Parliament and the Court

1. *Morgentaler, Smoling and Scott* v. *The Queen* (1988). Page references to *Morgentaler* appear in brackets in the text.

2. Given their description of the threat to women from delay and late abortion, it is perhaps surprising that Justices Dickson and Beetz did not entertain the idea of banning second trimester abortions outright. But it is their contention that facilitating access to early abortion would enable women to rid themselves of dangerous pregnancies, while more often avoiding late abortion.

3. Alliance for Life and Campaign Life Coalition, *A Brief to the Hon. Jake Epp, Federal Minister of Health, and Provincial Ministers of Health, Concerning Medicare Funding of Induced Abortion*, February, 1988.

4. That the medical profession itself was concerned about the vagueness of the interpretation is suggested in a *Globe and Mail* story indicating that the Canadian Medical Association had made regular requests to the federal government over the years for definitions of "health." *Globe and Mail*, July 28, 1988, p. 11.

5. The total number of legally induced abortions was 80,435 in 1987 (see p. 116).

6. For a review of the literature on the physical and psychological consequences of abortion, see essays in this volume: by de Veber, Parthun, Chisolm and Kiss, "The Psychological Effects of Induced Abortion" and Morris and Williams, "The Physical Consequences of Abortion." The literature suggests that the pyschological effects of first-term abortions may be serious, and that very young women and emotionally disturbed women — two groups often considered suitable candidates for abortion — are more likely to suffer adverse consequences than women in their twenties and women with no history of emotional disturbance.

7. With Madam Justice Wilson's treatment of the security of the person, on the other hand, we appear to stumble into a dimension of unreality. She argues that it was a consequence of section 251 that a "woman's capacity to reproduce is not to be subject to her own control"; a woman, she says, "may not choose whether to exercise her existing capacity." The decision is made by others whether the woman's "body is to be used to nurture new life." She appears to be saying, in short, that women were sometimes forced to have abortions against their will. Pro-lifers have sometimes speculated that counsellors in abortion hospitals on occasion bully women into abortions, but they are usually unwilling to make the charge outright. Wilson's argument on this is entirely unsupported and certainly sits oddly with the overall thrust of her decision which is that section 251 was at fault not for forcing women into abortion but for denying them abortion.

8. Philosophers took on the task of thinking through the consequences of accepting the prevailing scientific view on the fetus years before the problem came to public attention. Judith Jarvis Thompson's "A De-

fense of Abortion," *Philosophy and Public Affairs*, vol. 1 (1971) is well-known in this connection. Another author who takes this tack is L. W. Sumner, an important source for Madam Justice Wilson, in *Abortion and Moral Theory* (Princeton, New Jersey: Princeton University Press, 1981).

9. For a recent collection of essays, some representing and some discussing the post-liberal perspective, see Lorraine Code, Sheila Mullett and Christine Overall, eds., *Feminist Perspectives: Philosophical Essays on Method and Morals* (Toronto: University of Toronto Press, 1988).

10. For a criticism of this perspective in connection with abortion, see George Grant, "The Triumph of the Will," in this volume. By way of contrast, see also the essays by pro-life feminists Diane Marshall and Martha Crean in this volume.

11. See for example, Jeffrey Simpson, "Lesson in Chaos," *Globe and Mail*, July 29, 1988, p. A6.

12. It is worth noting that polls regularly show more women than men opposing abortion on demand. A *Globe and Mail* poll of June, 1985, showed 9 percent more men favoring easy abortion access. Forty percent of some 200 physicians who signed a pro-life advertisement in the Winnipeg *Free Press* in April, 1988, were women. *Vital Signs* (the Canadian Physicians for Life newsletter), August, 1988.

13. References to studies in some of these areas can be found in "The Association of Pro-life Groups of Southwestern Ontario, Response to Report on Therapeutic Abortion Services in Ontario, A Study Commissioned by the Minister of Health, by Dr. Marion Powell (The Powell Report), February 9, 1987." Pro-life groups distributed this document in the Ontario Legislature in early March, 1987.

CONTRIBUTORS

JANET AJZENSTAT is a visiting assistant professor of political science at the University of Calgary.

SAMUEL AJZENSTAT is associate professor of philosophy at McMaster University.

CHRISTOPHER BAGLEY is professor of social welfare at the University of Calgary.

IAIN T. BENSON, a Vancouver lawyer, is chairman of the civil-liberties section of the Canadian Bar Association in British Columbia.

DOROTHY CHISHOLM is a Toronto writer.

MARTHA CREAN is a teacher of English as a second language in Toronto, and a founder of Women for a Just Life.

L.L. DE VEBER, M.D., F.R.C.P.(C), is professor of pediatrics at the University of Western Ontario, and president of the Human Life Research Institute, Toronto.

IAN GENTLES is associate professor of history at Glendon College, York University, and research director of the Human Life Research Institute, Toronto.

The late GEORGE GRANT was professor of political science at Dalhousie University, and a member of the Order of Canada.

IAN HUNTER is professor of law at the University of Western Ontario.

ANNE KISS is a former lecturer in nursing at Concordia University.

DIANE MARSHALL is a marriage and family therapist at the Institute of Family Living in Toronto.

HEATHER MORRIS, M.B., F.R.C.O.G.(C) is assistant professor of obstetrics in the faculty of medicine, University of Toronto.

F.L. MORTON is associate professor of political science at the University of Calgary.

ROBERT NADEAU is an Ottawa lawyer.

DENYSE O'LEARY is a Toronto writer and editor.

MARY PARTHUN was for many years a social worker with Catholic Family Services in Toronto. She completed her Ph.D. in social work at the University of Toronto shortly before her death in 1988.

SUZANNE SCORSONE is director of the Office of Catholic Family Life of the Archdiocese of Toronto, and a member of the Royal Commission on Reproductive Technology.

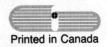

Printed in Canada